The Hussar

The Hussar
A German Cavalryman in
British Service Throughout
the Napoleonic Wars

Norbert Landsheit
& G. R. Gleig

*The Hussar: a German Cavalryman in British Service
Throughout the Napoleonic Wars*
by Norbert Landsheit & G. R. Gleig

Published by Leonaur Ltd

Text in this form copyright © 2008 Leonaur Ltd

ISBN: 978-1-84677-504-8 (hardcover)
ISBN: 978-1-84677-503-1 (softcover)

http://www.leonaur.com

Publisher's Notes

The opinions expressed in this book are those of the author and are not necessarily those of the publisher.

Contents

Introduction	7
My Early Life & Adventures	11
The Soldier & His Duty	20
I See Other Lands	30
I See Some Service	38
I Return to England	49
Disbanded	62
I Join the 20th Light Dragoons	71
Service at the Cape	81
I Strike a Few Blows	94
The War & My Own Adventures	104
Good Luck & Bad	116
I Go to Portugal	126
The Battle of Vimiero	136
Adventures in Portugal & Sicily	145
More Adventures in Sicily	155
To Minorca & Spain	163
A Skirmish With the Enemy	172
The Campaign Opens	180
Some Adventures	190
We Lay Siege to Tarragona	202
New Leaders & New Operations	208
Amusements in War	218
The Consummation	229
We Take the Field Again	238
Adventures at the Outposts	249
Hostilities Come to an End	258
My Changes of Fortune	266

Introduction

The following pages contain a simple and unadorned relation of the principal occurrences in the life of the individual whose memoirs they proved to be. The subject of them—one of the most respectable of the many respectable inmates of the Chelsea Hospital—is still alive to vouch for the accuracy of the statement, being in every respect competent to satisfy the most distrusting that no liberties whatever have been taken with historical truth in the management of his story. I do not know how far I may be expected to account for the publication of the narrative at all; but the circumstances which led to it, as they involve no mystery, so they are certainly not worth concealing.

My acquaintance with the habits of the brave men with whom I am now professionally associated, soon made me aware that, in Sergeant Landsheit, Chelsea Hospital could boast of an inmate possessed of more than ordinary intelligence. I accordingly begged of him to relate to me some of his personal adventures while actively employed in the army, with the design of adding his story to other "Traditions" of the place. I found, however, as we went on, that the narrative grew, not only in bulk, but in interest; so I determined to send it forth as a separate work. I am willing to believe that the public will not blame me for this proceeding: because numerous as such narratives have now become, I, at least do not know where one is to be found containing a greater variety of curious and interesting matter.

It will be seen that I have confined myself in writing to the use of the first person. This, indeed, I was in some sort compelled to do;—for our practice was, that my friend Landsheit came to me every morning, and told his tale till one or two o'clock in the day; after which I wrote—being sometimes unable to keep pace with him, even though I repeatedly encroached far upon the short hours of the night. And, to insure the correctness of the story, he has listened to each proof-sheet as it went through the press. *The Hussar*, therefore, is no work of fiction,—but just as much the *Memoirs of Norbert Landsheit*, as Captain Carlton's delightful volume is a memoir of himself.

If it be asked, why was this man left in the ,—,— of a non-commissioned officer?—why was he never promoted? I answer, that I, too, put the question to himself; and the reader will judge of the character of the man by the sort of answer which he made to me.

"I will reply to you, sir," said he, in his slightly-broken English, "by reminding you of a passage in the *Life of Frederic the Great*. There was a poor curate, somewhere near Potsdam, who, after many years' faithful service in the diocese, applied to the bishop for a living. The bishop assured him that he was alive to his merits, and that he might depend upon being one day or another provided for. Encouraged by this assurance, the curate kept quiet, till he ascertained that a certain living was vacant; upon which he repaired again to the bishop, and entreated that he might be inducted to it

"'Ah!' replied the bishop, 'so you knew that living was vacant, did you? Well, I am very sorry. I cannot give you that, for I have promised it to one of my nephews; but you shall have the next that falls.'

"The curate returned home scarcely disappointed, for he thought that the bishop's reason was a fair one; and he counted surely on succeeding to the very next benefice that should become vacant One did fall soon after; and he flew on the wings of hope to the palace.

"'It is very provoking, my dear sir,' said the prelate; 'but I cannot give you this. I have promised it to my sister's son; but you shall have the next.'

"The curate was disappointed this time, but he said little; neither was he much surprised when, on repairing a third time to the episcopal residence, a similar result attended his application. And so it continued to be, over and over again. There was always a brother, or a nephew, or a cousin, between him and the realization of his day-dreams—till his patience became at length exhausted, and he began to consider what was best to be done. He was a sharp-witted man, and his meditations brought him to a happy issue.

"It chanced, once upon a time, that Frederic the Great, who always rose early, and was accustomed to walk before breakfast in the palace-garden, looked out from his window, and, to his infinite surprise, saw an ecclesiastic, with a lantern in his hand, stooping and poking close to the ground, as if in search of something. The sun was up, yet the man's lantern contained a lighted candle; and he seemed to depend in his search entirely upon that, and not upon the sun's rays. Frederic's curiosity was roused. He desired his attendant to order the man up, and bid him wait in the anteroom till the King should be dressed. When he was dressed, the King went forth; and lo! the stranger, instead of meeting him like a reasonable person, continued still to keep his lantern close to the floor, and to peer about him.

"'What are you looking for, sir?' demanded the King.

"'I am looking for a cousin, please your Majesty,' was the reply.

"'A cousin, you fool!' said Frederic; 'what do you mean by that?'

"'Because I have none,' answered the man; 'and I can't do without one.'

"These strange answers only whetted the King's curiosity, who went on questioning the ecclesiastic, till the whole truth came out.

"'Oh! that's it,' exclaimed Frederic, laughing. 'You could not get a living, because you had no cousin among the bishops. Never mind—I will be your cousin, if you deserve one—and then we will see what can be done.'

"The King made his inquiries—found that the curate was

a deserving person—made him fix upon the best living in the bishop's gift which was then vacant—and desired the bishop to make out the presentation in his favour. The bishop demurred a little, spoke of a cousin to whom he had promised it, and assured the King that his protegé should have the very next that fell.

"'That won't do,' replied Frederic; 'your curate is my cousin for this time—so you must give him the living.'

"The curate got the living. But I had no cousin, Sir; so I got no living."

I was much struck with Landsheit's story. But if he got no living, he has at least earned for himself the reputation of a good soldier in his youth, and a good man in his old age.

CHAPTER 1

My Early Life & Adventures

My name is Norbertos Landsheit, my Christian name being familiarly pronounced in my own country, Norbert I was born on the 4th of November, 1775, at a place called St Dennis, a village in the Bishopric of Cologne, not far from Crefeldt My origin was at least respectable, and my prospects were at one time good; for my father was an officer of gendarmes, in the service of Maximilian the Second, and my mother, a native of Prussian Silesia, came from an honourable stock. But the profession of a soldier is not very lucrative anywhere, and least of all in the Bishopric of Cologne. Wherefore my father was prevailed upon soon after my birth to quit the army, and to establish himself as a distiller, and the keeper of a creditable hotel in the village where I first saw the light

His business proving, on the whole, a profitable one, and I being his only son, my father determined to make of me a Lutheran clergyman, and in order to qualify me for the office, he bestowed upon me as good an education as the state of the country and his own circumstances would permit from him and from my mother I learned to read and write as well as to repeat my catechism, and to know something of scripture history; while the curate of the parish taught me the rudiments of Latin, and encouraged me to aspire after still higher attainments. But long before I had made any proficiency in scholastic lore, a calamity overtook both my mother and myself, which was to her the beginning of many sorrows, and to me proved irremediable. I was barely seven years old when my father died, leaving his son and his twofold occupation, to be managed as she best could, by his widow.

My father and mother had been sincerely attached to one another, and her grief at his loss was in consequence excessive; yet being a strong-minded woman, she did not permit it to interfere with the steady discharge of the duties which she owed to herself and her family. She continued to carry on both the distillery and the hotel, as had been done during his lifetime, and my education was not for a moment interrupted. On the contrary, finding that St Dennis could not supply such tuition as I came by this time to require, she sent me to Kempen, where, till I attained to my seventeenth year, I resided as a pupil, in a respectable academy.

Such was my condition when those extraordinary events befell, which produced throughout Europe other and more violent revolutions than the conversion of a parson in embryo into a hussar. The French people, victorious at home over religion, law, order, and humanity, but, like a river that has broken down its banks, across their own frontier, and carried, wherever they appeared, desolation and misery into the districts which they came avowedly to set free. One of their armies, under the command of General Coustine, after driving the Austrians back upon the Rhine, advanced, in the summer of 1792, into our province, where they pursued the system which was acted upon everywhere else, in reference as well to the persons as to the property of the inhabitants. Not content to live at free quarters, to levy contributions of money, grain, horses, and either material, they brought the conscription into active play among the young man of the country; compelling all between the ages of sixteen and forty to take up arms and serve under the republican banner. Now, my mother had no particular fancy that I should become a soldier under any circumstances, and least of all, that I should serve France, She therefore took time by the fore-lock, and while the invaders were yet at a distance, packed me off to one of her brothers, who resided in Dusseldorf.

I arrived in Dusseldorf some time in June, and was kindly received by my uncle. He put me to school, and treated me in every respect as if I had been his own— indeed I should have been perfectly happy under his care, bat for the strange desire which, in common with other lads of my standing, I experienced to see something of the French. For we were told from day to day of their inroads; we saw the Bavarian garrison march out and an Austrian arrive in its room; and not knowing what war was, we longed to be eye-witnesses of scenes, concerning which we had read, and heard others speak with the deepest interest. Not that I harboured at that time the smallest wish to wield a sword or wear a uniform. Mine was a mere boyish curiosity, which was perhaps the more whetted in consequence of the rebukes which it drew forth from older and wiser men. But this is not worth dwelling upon, so I will pass it by.

At the period to which I am now referring, Dusseldorf was crowded with French emigrants. Multitudes of all ranks, from the Duke de Broglie down to the meanest artisan, had taken refuge there, and as each brought with him a certain supply of cash, money was, for a while, abundant in the city, and all fared well. By degrees, however, the resources of the less wealthy began to foil, sad then might be seen the devoted generosity with which their richer neighbours—men of family and high name— stepped forward to the relief of their necessities. The Duke de Broglie in particular seemed to regard himself as nothing more than a trustee for his suffering countrymen—for whose benefit he hired a large hotel, with all its accompaniments of cooks, waiters, and other attendants, and caused a dinner to be daily provided there at his own expense for not fewer than four hundred persons. Such munificence could not of course be displayed without utterly draining, in a very short time, the resources of him who indulged in it. The Duke de Broglie became in a few months almost penniless, and was forced to seek a supply by despatching his son in disguise through the enemy's lines into the heart of France. The young man's first expedition proved to be eminently successful. His father's tenants paid their rents cheerfully, and he returned with the proceeds unobserved to Dusseldorf— but the supply thus procured went as other moneys had gone, and a second expedition was decided upon. But it was a rash act, however dictated by the noblest feelings —and led to results the most disastrous. The young Duke being discovered, was put to death; and his untimely fate was mourned in every house in Dusseldorf, with as much sincerity as if each had lost a relative.

I have said, that not long after my arrival the Bavarian garrison marched out, and a body of Austrians, both horse and foot, reached Dusseldorf. Now, as the Bavarians had taken neither side in the strife, and the Austrians were principals in opposing the French, this movement naturally convinced us that the period could not in all probability be distant, when we should see something of the invaders. Each new day, moreover, brought intelligence of their successes, which more and more prepared us to receive a visit The Austrians were falling back; they had crossed the Rhine, and it was very doubtful whether, even with that obstacle in their front, the enemy would be arrested. October—it was announced that the French were approaching. In common with others, I hurried to the ramparts, and saw, sure enough, with a glass, three or four heavy columns in movement on the opposite side of the river—of which a portion established themselves in rear of some houses that crowned the bank, within less than half cannon-shot of the town.

It was not, however among us civilians alone that a visit from General Coustine's army had for some time been anticipated. The military authorities had caused the flying bridge, which connects the two banks of the Rhine, to be hauled in. Far and near, above and below the town, every vessel and boat was secured, while posts were established here and there, in order to provide against the possibility of some sudden dash, such as might give to the enemy a moment's command of the river. Moreover, as soon as the French columns showed themselves in rear of the houses opposite, there went forth an order to rip up all the pavements, a strict observance of which converted a clean and well-regulated town, in the course of four-and-twenty hours, into one huge puddle. For no sooner were the stones removed than straw, mud, horse-dung, and every other filthy substance was accumulated in the streets, with the view, as I afterwards found, of rendering the shells which were expected to fall among us, comparatively innocuous. Unfortunately, however, there were weak points in Dusseldorf, which no providence, on the part of the governor, could defend. In the heart of the town stood a Mews—a large stable-yard—accessible by one gate only, and surrounded by buildings capable of containing a brigade of horse, with the forage necessary for their maintenance. That enormous pile was, at this juncture, full of combustibles, and a regiment of Austrian dragoons had established in it their quarters. It was found impossible to protect the Mews from shot, while numerous storehouses, wharfs, and other places of commerce, were likewise exposed. Still the distance between us and the enemy's position was considerable, and something it was assumed might be trusted to their ignorance of our localities,—while ten or twelve of our own guns, which looked towards the houses on the opposite bank, would, it was hoped, when the proper time came, keep their fire under.

There had been no discharge from the other side, though the guns from the city had ruined the houses opposite; when on the sixth of October I retired to my bedroom as usual, about ten o'clock at night. My curiosity was more awakened than ever, so that I made it a constant practice to look out the last thing before I stepped into bed; and tonight I had been not less careful than on former occasions, though just to as little purpose, in my endeavours to see anything that might please by its novelty. My astonishment was therefore very great, when, having heard the report of a cannon a long way off I saw hissing over my head, in the declivity of a half-circle, some substance loaded, with a fiery tail. Presently another, and then another, shone in the sky, which so delighted me that I ran downstairs, and communicated my discovery to my uncle. I was yet speaking when the mystery, for such it was to me, received its solution. The French had opened a mortar battery, and were bombarding the place; and such was the precision with which they threw their shells, that scarcely one fell short of its mark. The Mews was soon in a blaze. Then followed store-houses and market-places without end; while an incessant shower of red-hot balls rendered it utterly impossible, either to extinguish the flames already raised, or to hinder them from extending elsewhere. What a night of confusion and dismay was that! The Governor had in the outset refused to give passports to the in-habitants; the emigrants were indeed permitted to withdraw and take shelter in Elberfeld; but the people of the place it was considered more politic to detain in their houses, in order that the feelings both of them and of their relatives might be enlisted on the side of the attacked. But now the clamour was so great that the Austrian commandant could not resist it. He threw open one of the gates, by which crowds of men, women, and children made their escape, and beyond which I, very much to my own annoyance, was hurried. That night, however, I went not beyond the glacis; and the splendour of the scene—the burning town—the ceaseless shower of fiery projectiles—the roar of cannon—the shouts of men—I have no language to describe; though the effect produced by all these I can never forget.

The weather was very cold, and my uncle making a point of our removing to a place of safety, we travelled next day as far as Elberfeld, where, however, it was judged imprudent to detain me long, lest the enemy should prevail, and make a conscript of me after all. As fortune would have it, there was no ground for these apprehensions, inasmuch as the French never forced the passage of the Rhine; but were compelled, by some demonstration made upon their flank, to raise the bombardment of Dusseldorf and march away. But we could not foresee all this, and as my mother had exacted a pledge that my uncle would provide for my security, he determined to remove me from the seat of war, by sending me to his brother in Hanover. I spent the winter, indeed, in Elberfeld, but early in the spring, alone, and but moderately supplied with money, I began my journey towards Ousnabruck. I reached it in the month of April, and again met with the kindest treatment; my uncle being annoyed at nothing except that I should have been left at my years to travel unattended. By this time, however, though still a raw youth, I had learned somewhat to take care of myself, so I only laughed at my good uncle's anxiety, and for several months pursued under his roof the studies which recent events had interrupted.

My opportunities of observation were not such as to authorize my giving any account of the progress of the war. At Ousnabruck we only heard of it at a distance, though even in Ousnabruck the foiling of hostility which then pervaded all Germany in reference to France, was perceptible enough. In particular my uncle began to talk to me frequently of taking up arms against these enemies of the human race, and easily won from me a declaration, that if he joined the army of the Emperor, I would accompany him. Not yet, however, was an opportunity afforded of realizing our day-dreams; for though recruiting parties were out in every direction, my uncle appeared to take no interest in their proceedings: but towards the end of the summer he left me. It was necessary for him, he said, to proceed as far as Celle, whence he would return within the week, and it was not impossible but that when next he visited the place, I might accompany him. There was something in this journey of his, which, I could not tell why, excited in me a deep interest. I watched for his return with the utmost anxiety, and when he came, true to the hour appointed, the hilarity of his manner, instead of allaying the ferment in my mind, only increased it At last, in the latter part of July, he carried me to Celle, and gave me a room in his lodgings; where, for the first time, he presented himself to my wondering gaze, in the uniform of an officer of hussars. The facts of the case were these: Baron Charles de Hompesch had been for some time occupied in raising a regiment of cavalry, in which my uncle, having been very successful in procuring recruits, had obtained a commission; and now, the corps being ordered to assemble on the heath of Schwarm, it was necessary for him to join. I need scarcely add, that the splendour of my uncle's appearance altogether dazzled me. I declared that nothing should prevent my joining the corps as a cadet, a determination to which my uncle was far from opposing himself, though he required that I would take time to deliberate ere I acted; and proposed that I should attend him to the camp in the quality of a friend.

I went with him cheerfully, being willing to humour him so far as might not be inconsistent with the gratification of my own desires, and continued a civilian up to the month of August, 1793. Then, however, I enlisted, and received both from my uncle and the officer commanding his squadron, assurances, that 'provided I behaved well, I should never want a friend, nor find the road to promotion barred against me.'

What a magnificent encampment was that of Schwarm! where were assembled six regiments of cavalry, the weakest upwards of eight hundred strong—besides a corps composed entirely of French gentlemen, whom the success of the Revolution had driven into exile. Hompesch's Hussars, the regiment of the Prince of Salem, Soicelles, Old Ruen and New Ruen,—both made up of emigrants,—and a regiment of Ulans, equipped after the Polish fashion, with square caps and lances, were each very fine. But the most brilliant corps of all was that of Montelambert. It consisted entirely of the flower of the nobility of France, who provided their own uniforms, their own horses,—every thing, in short, except their arms and accoutrements—and, glittering with silver, had their tents in a quarter apart from the rest of us, though on service they did the duty of private soldiers. I have seen many a regiment since, of what might well be accounted the *élite* of the armies of Europe; but such a body as that—so full of fire, so gallant, so gay, so chivalrous—were you to search the world over, you would probably not succeed now in getting together its parallel.

Here then we lay for many months, well fed, well attended, and regularly paid; having for our sole occupation the business of drill, together with frequent field days, under the orders of the English General Lord Cathcart. At last, however, in the spring of 1794, our regiment received orders to march for the Low Countries, in order to reinforce the army which it was intended to oppose to the French General Pichegru. Perhaps fortunately for myself, though at the time I bitterly lamented it, a severe kick from a horse while I led him to water, hindered me from accompanying my uncle on that expedition. My shin-bone was so much injured, that it seemed at one time doubtful whether I should ever again be able to do duty; and I was confined, to my inexpressible chagrin, in the hospital. Yet was the campaign pregnant with nothing but disasters to Hompesch's Hussars. Somehow or another, I know not when, nor under what circumstances, they were attacked at a disadvantage, and almost to a man, either killed or taken prisoners. Among others, my poor uncle paid the debt of nature while employed on that service. He was in the act of lighting his pipe at the pipe of a brother officer, both sitting on horseback in front of their troop, when a cannon-ball from the enemy's lines took off their heads, and deprived me of the only real friend I ever had in the world. Hot and bitter were the tears which I shed, when the sad news reached me; and many a time since have I felt my cheeks moist, when the image of my excellent relative has come back to my memory.

CHAPTER 2

The Soldier & His Duty

The campaign of 1794 ended, as I have said, very much to the disadvantage of Hompesch's Hussars. Out of the twelve hundred men that followed Baron Charles to the field, only a handful returned, on which, as on a nucleus, he began, in the autumn of the same year, to form his regiment anew. Nothing could exceed the success which attended his recruiting. To be sure, we were not particular as to the country or lineage of the individual who offered himself as our companion in arms. So long as he was fit for military service, could ride, or was willing to be taught, no further questions were put to him; by which means we soon brought together into our camp, Germans, Russians, Prussians, Danes, Swedes, Hanoverians, Poles, and even one or two Tartars. But there was a circumstance attending the re-formation of the corps to look back upon which even now gives me pain. Baron Hompesch, though a German himself, entertained so strong a partiality for the French, that out of the whole body of his officers, more than two-thirds were selected from that nation. Now I have nothing to say against the bravery or skill of the French as officers. They are fine fellows certainly; but I do think that the Germans are quite equal to them; and I am certain that the consequence of our having such a preponderance of emigrants in our regiment was, that against all but Frenchmen the avenues to advancement were well-nigh closed.

It was singular enough that this new regiment of Hompesch should have assembled for training on the very same heath which had witnessed the training of the old regiment, and that it should have had as its consorts in the camp and field the identical corps which had manoeuvred so often with the gallant dead. Yet this was not the only, nor the most remarkable circumstance that attended us. I know not whence it came about, but a rumour gained by degrees credit among us, that the whole of the six regiments (for Montelambert's was not included) were designed for transportation to England. Now at the time of which I am speaking, there prevailed throughout all Germany the greatest horror of England, and of the English service. We had been taught to believe that England was never at peace, and that all her soldiers were liable to be sent, and were sent, to act as marines on board of the fleet. Of the sea, however, we had one and all the utmost dread. Born far inland, and knowing nothing of the customs of the coast, we took our opinion on such subjects from the reports of men who, having ventured down to Rotterdam, either on business or pleasure, had there been themselves kidnapped, or witnessed the kidnapping of others. Our consternation, therefore, I am quite incapable of describing, when first the rumour began to spread that our chiefs intended to carry us to England —because we took it for granted that, were we once fairly embarked, we should never see our native land again, nor, indeed, escape from our floating-prisons. Still, with very many, the feeling thus excited and kept alive produced no results that appeared to be dangerous to themselves or others. There were some, on the contrary, who took a different view of this matter, and of the plot into which they entered; and though, at the time, I was profoundly ignorant of it, it will be best if I give here a detailed relation.

The proportion of French to German officers in the regiment of Hompesch was, as I have said, about three to one: in several of the other corps, particularly the Old and New Ruen, and the regiment of Salem, it was still greater. Now there was scarcely one of these Frenchmen whose object in taking up arms had not been to act against the republican oppressors of his own country, and in whom an order to withdraw from the seat of war would not have occasioned the deepest mortification. No sooner were they made aware of the sentiments of the men, than the bolder spirits among them resolved to take advantage of it A conspiracy was entered into, at the head of which a Captain Dalwig, of our regiment, placed himself, to march in a body and join the Prince of Conde, so soon as it should be ascertained, beyond the possibility of doubt, that England was our destination. Nay, I happen to know, that nothing, except the absence of funds, hindered these conspirators, if such they ought to be called, from carrying their device into execution as soon as it was matured. But they were all poor. They did not know where to find money, and they were afraid to move without it At last Captain Dalwig made a bold effort to remove the obstacle, out of which the following results came to pass.

It was late in the autumn, and the rain fell so heavily, that no man, except at the call of duty, or when pressed by urgent business, ever ventured beyond the camp, Twice a day, indeed, the horses were led to water at a large pond or tarn, about five hundred yards beyond the rear-guard; but except when thus employed, or when standing sentry, we seldom emerged from our tents. The officers, to be sure, had the mess-house, a temporary wooden building, where they often spent the day together; and the colonel did his best to amuse and keep the men in good humour, by providing ample supplies of beer and tobacco. But we were not a little flat, when an event befell which put us, for a while at least, a good deal on our mettle. There was in our regiment one Major Tagtunck, with whom Captain Dalwig lived on terms of great intimacy. This gentleman received, during the autumn, a sum of money from home, and his friend Captain Dalwig resolved to gain possession of it He had seen in the major's tent a small box, standing in a corner by itself, in which he naturally concluded that the cash lay hid; and having watched his opportunity, he one morning seized, put it under his cloak, and walked away with it. It was a day of great storms: the wind blew high, and the rain came down in torrents, so that, except the vidette at the colonel's tent-door, nobody was abroad to watch him; and as his cloak was ample in its folds, he had every reason to conclude that the real cause of his wearing it would never come to light.

Well, Captain Dalwig stole the box; but, instead of carrying it home to his own tent, he walked to the rear, passed the guard, made his way to the pond, of which the edges were covered with tall spear grass; and penetrating into the swamp, he sought out a convenient spot, and there thrust his prize into the mud. This done, he returned to the camp, and for a while attracted no attention.

But the absence of his box was not slow in being discovered by the major. He questioned his servant, who had left it safe, and had seen nobody enter the tent by whom it was likely to be removed. He applied to the sentry, who declared that, since he came to his post, only Captain Dalwig had gone and come.

"Had he entered the tent?"

"Yes."

"Did he carry any thing out?"

The man could not say, for the captain was wrapped up in his cloak.

"Whither did he go?"

"To the rear."

Here then was something of a clue, at all events, and the major followed it up with great pertinacity. He examined the rear-guard. They had seen Captain Dalwig go to the pond, and fish, as they supposed, for eels; but the day was so rough that nobody could face it, so he soon returned again.

On to the pond went the major. He saw the print of feet, and being satisfied that he had got on the right scent, he hurried back to the camp. There he summoned to him the adjutant, one or two officers besides, and the man who had stood sentry on the colonel's tent; and he carried the whole body down to the pond, without giving them a hint of the business on which they were about to be employed. But it was now time to speak out. He stated what had befallen, as well as the nature of his own suspicions, and the grounds on which they rested; and passing into the swamp, they discovered the missing box, covered over with weeds, as the delinquent had left it. The consequences to Captain Dalwig could not fail to be serious. He was put in irons, and sentries placed over him, while an express was sent off to the colonel, then residing in Bremen, to make him aware of what had happened. I am sorry that I cannot tell what was the ultimate fate of Captain Dalwig; I only know that, by Baron Hompesch's orders, he was removed from the camp a prisoner, and that we never saw him afterwards.

The incidents which I have just related were known to us all at the moment Of the motives by which Captain Dalwig was swayed, we were not informed till long afterwards. But it appeared that his failure to secure this money, though it cast a temporary damp upon,the spirits of the mutineers, by no means caused them to waver in their determinations. A new leader stood forward in the person of an officer belonging to the regiment of Salem; a fine old soldier, who had served as lieutenant-colonel in the French regiment of the Dauphin's dragoons. This man conducted their correspondence with equal skill and energy, and warned them that the day for action could not be far distant Nor was it far distant One day, in the mouth of December, it came out, through the Colonel's lady, that our destination would certainly be England, where we were to take rank and do duty as Queen Charlotte's body guards. Now, as I have already stated, the ideas of England, and of perpetual imprisonment on board of ship, could not in our minds be separated; and the conspirators, whose plans were all matured, determined not to waste another hour, but to take advantage of the effect of this confirmation of the men's fears at once to accomplish their purposes.

The tents which we occupied were like those issued to the English troops—of a bell or sugar-loaf form, having a pole in the centre, and flaps beneath which our saddles and other horse accoutrements might be kept dry. Each tent was assigned to eight men, who, spreading straw or hay upon the ground, slept at night with their heads towards the pole, and their feet to the walls of the tent. One night I had retired as usual, and, together with three of my comrades, stripped, and was about to lie down, when we observed that the other four not only made no movement to undress, but appeared to be unusually busy. They drew their furniture out of its place—they examined their pistols and carbines, and filled their pouches with ammunition. Now we had no ammunition, neither had any been served out to the brigade. We were, therefore much struck by their proceedings, and demanded the cause of them.

"Oh, there's cause enough," said one of the men, "and you won't be many minutes older ere you know all about it. The best thing you can do is to throw in your lot with us. We are not going to England, and we advise you not to go neither."

This announcement led of course to a communication of the mighty plot, which for months had been carried forward in the camp, and we learned to our amazement, that on the firing of a couple of pistols, multitudes from every regiment, with their arms and horses, would meet and move off in good order. We listened to the tale in breathless wonder, but we positively refused to join the narrators. Betray them, indeed, we could not, had we even desired to do so, for we were naked, and they armed, but neither their arguments nor their jokes prevailed to shake our constancy; and ceasing at last to urge the point further, they addressed themselves once more to their preparations. Nor had these been long completed, when bang went first one pistol in the front, and then bang, another in the rear. As quick as thought our four comrades sprang to their feet. Their saddles, bridles, and other appointments were on their arms in a moment; the next saw them fitted to their horses, and at the third all were mounted and pushing at full speed to the appointed rallying ground in front of the camp. Thither, too, proceeded, from all the other alignments, scores of troopers in the best order, who fell into their places with the regularity of a parade, wheeled into column and set forward. Moreover, the whole thing was managed by those who knew perfectly what they were about. Trumpets. sounded, advanced-guards and rear-guards were equally thrown out, and away they went at a brisk trot, leaving behind them a scene of indescribable alarm and confusion.

The report of the pistol-shots, followed by the braying of trumpets, and the rapid tread of hoofs as the conspirators passed through the lines, soon roused every man and officer in the camp. The bugles began to sound, and in all directions might be seen people hurrying to and fro, some naked, others half dressed, and all demanding from those who met them the cause of the disturbance. At last the retreat of the conspirators was ascertained, and the whole of the remaining force received orders to accoutre, and to pursue with as little delay as possible. For in Germany, where there are so many independent states, which abut one upon another, the escape of deserters, if not immediately intercepted, is inevitable, inasmuch as he who once passes the frontier of a foreign principality is safe from pursuit. Now the heath of Schwarm lies at no great distance from the borders of Brunswick on one side, and of Prussia on the other; it was therefore of the utmost consequence to cut off the conspirators from both these points, otherwise all control over them would be lost. On therefore we went, at the top of our speed, as soon as the regiments were formed, with such a preponderance of numbers as nothing it was imagined could resist. But as we closed upon the fugitives our inferiority in one essential respect was painfully taught us. We had no ammunition, they were well supplied; and their rear-guard, by a continued and well-directed fire of carbines, kept us at a distance. And never have I seen an officer play his part more gallantly than the French colonel did, by whom the conspiracy came in the end to be managed. He took his station with the last of the rear-guard; he changed his positions from time to time, according to the nature of the country through which he passed; and showed himself anxious only to secure for his people a safe retreat. But all the exertions did not prevail. There lay on the frontier an English regiment, the Fifteenth Dragoons, commanded, I believe, by Lord Cathcart in person. An express reached them in time, and the general, throwing himself between the fugitives and their line of retreat, stopped there. Then we closed upon them from the rear, in such force that resistance became hopeless; we surrounded them, and after a fruitless effort to break through, they laid down their arms.

The conspirators were brought back to the heath of Schwarm and thoroughly sifted. The multitude were reasoned with as deluded men, and sent back to their duty, while three, of whom the French colonel was one, were selected as fit, from their rank, and conduct in the business, to be made examples of to the rest They were sent close prisoners to Bremen, tried by a court-martial, and condemned to suffer. Meanwhile Baron Hompesch paraded his regiment, and addressed them in a speech so moving, that it brought tears into my eyes. He assured them, that the misconduct of a portion had not diminished his affection for the whole; that he pitied even the delinquents, whose noble feelings had been imposed upon; and that his only wish was to recover their confidence, which could nowhere be more safely reposed than in him and in the rest of his officers. Let them never listen again to designing men. Wherever the regiment went there should he go also; whatever their fortunes might be, he should share them; his ambition never having extended farther than to be treated by his men as their father. Finally, having told us not to believe every idle rumour that might reach us—for we should certainly pass that winter on the Elbe, he dismissed us, not indeed reconciled to the prospect of transportation to England, but much moved by the force of his eloquence. Nevertheless, it soon became apparent that, on the part of our superiors, very little confidence was reposed on us. The camp was broken up the very next day, and the six regiments were scattered over the face of the country, each pitching its tent in a field by itself, and no two being permitted to keep up the slightest intercourse with one another.

We had occupied our new position but a very few days, when a general parade was ordered, and we heard, as we proceeded towards the place of muster, that the heads of the conspiracy were that morning to be shot. Accordingly the six regiments met on the heath of Schwarm, where they drew up on three sides of a square, the fourth side being vacant. Yet the objects which there met our eyes were striking enough. Three graves had been dug over-night, beside which stood three open coffins; and the country people, who soon began to collect in crowds, made us aware, by-and-by, that those by whom they were to be occupied were approaching. It may be necessary to add, that on our flank stood detachments of artillery, who loaded their guns with canister, and turned their muzzles towards us—while the English regiment kept somewhat apart, as if ready to act should occasion require. Well, we had remained thus about an hour and a half, when the sound of military music, low and plaintive, was heard in our rear. It grew gradually louder, and we could by-and-bye distinguish that a dead march was played, a circumstance which, of itself, would have sufficed to inform us, had the peasantry been silent, that the prisoners were at hand. They came, each attended by a clergyman and all strictly guarded; and two out of the three walked dejectedly, like men who felt their situation. The third, namely, the lieutenant-colonel, kept his head erect, and, instead of attending to his spiritual companion, looked earnestly from time to time towards a large Newfoundland dog. This noble animal had been his companion for some years; and now, as it walked by his side to the place of execution, he ceased not to pat its ample head, and seemed pleased when it answered to his caress, Such was the order in which they came, till having reached our ground, a squadron wheeled back by threes, and they were admitted into the heart of the square. It is customary in like cases to tie up the eyes of the prisoners, in order that they may not shrink when the signal for firing is given; while they themselves, kneeling upon their coffins, await the word in the attitude of prayer. His companions readily acceded to the wishes of the officer by whom the firing party was commanded: but the colonel would do nothing of the sort. No; he had faced death too often to fear him now; he would neither permit himself to be blindfolded, nor bend the knee. In an upright position, and smoking his cigar, he stood to receive the volley; and when he saw the carbines levelled, he held out his breast proudly towards them. There was but one discharge, several balls passed through his head, others riddled his companions in misfortune, and all three, after we had marched round and gazed upon them, were thrust into their coffins, and committed to the dust

I must not forget to say one word relative to the, colonel's dog. When he found himself beside his coffin, the colonel embraced his four-footed companion, and gave him to one of the soldiers on duty, who led him aside by the collar, like one who understood his part, and was prepared to play it out. The dog whined and struggled a little, as if anxious to return to his master—but no time was afforded for such a display. The volley pealed out; the dog bounded on his hind legs, and barked aloud; but his new master held him tight. He was led off the ground, vainly resisting, and I cannot tell what became of him afterwards.

Chapter 3
I See Other Lands

We returned to our camp on the evening of that day, very much down-hearted; for the spectacle which we had witnessed was a melancholy one, and our hopes concerning the future were far from bright. To be sure, Baron Charles was kind and considerate towards us; and his assurance that we should winter on the Elbe had the effect of throwing our fears a good deal into the distance. But the passage of a few days sufficed to renew again, to their utmost pitch, the apprehensions under which we laboured. There came an order, we knew not whence, to inspect the horses, and to cast such as might be unfit for service; and the severity of the weather had of late so affected them, that a considerable proportion out of the whole number were condemned. Immediately a suspicion arose that we were all to be dismounted; and when, in addition to this, we received orders to march for Staden, to a man we concluded that we should thenceforth act as infantry on board the English fleet. Not often has a regiment of German Hussars executed a movement in worse order than that which marked the progress of our journey from the heath of Schwarm to Staden. In spite of a strong rear-guard, and all the vigilance of the officers, many deserted by the way; and many more, when brought into the town, got drunk, and broke out into mutiny. I do not know that any lives were lost, though even that is possible, for swords were drawn and blows struck without regard to consequences. Nevertheless, after a good deal of trouble and confusion, both men and horses were embarked, after which the ships parted from their moorings, and dropping down to an anchorage off the port of Gluckstadt there took their stations.

I had never seen the mighty ocean till now. I had never beheld a fleet, nor witnessed the wonders that are visible to those who occupy their business in great waters; and I acknowledge that the effect produced upon my mind was quite overwhelming. We lay at the very mouth of the Elbe, and though land was on either side of us, in front was the North Sea, rolling its huge waves to and fro in unspeakable magnificence. There was around us, too, a perfect forest of masts; while the music of the different bands, as they played on the ships' decks—the occasional booming of signal-guns—the constant interchange of communications, by flags during the day, by blue lights at night—produced altogether such an effect, as to stupify by reason of its intensity. Nor was it by me alone that the influence of novelty was experienced. The men in general forgot their fears in the contemplation of so many wonders, and for a brief space, being well supplied with provisions of every sort, they appeared reconciled to their destiny. But week after week passed on, and we still continued stationary; and the winter set in with its furious storms and terrible sea-sickness; whatever of enthusiasm might have been excited for a moment soon died away, and we became as anxious as ever to give Baron Hompesch the slip, and to return to our own homes. It was a most unwise policy that which kept us confined in narrow transports during the whole winter; for it taught us to regard our colonel as a deceiver, who, keeping the word of promise to the ear, and breaking it to the sense, was not to be trusted.

Desperate as our situation might well appear to be, there were not wanting among us those who still continued to meditate an escape, and to devise plans for effecting it We were visited daily, particularly from the Danish side, by bum-boats, which brought alongside bread, beer, tobacco, and fruit, and drove with us, to whom pay had been recently issued, a very profitable trade. It was resolved by some of our most determined sea-haters, to seize one of these vessels; and, to the number of about a dozen, they accomplished their purpose. There was a sort of cutter, or large open sail-boat, which came every day to the ship's side, about noon, and was in the habit of staying one, or two, or three hours, according to the facility with which the owner might dispose of his wares. Her crew consisted of only two men, and these my comrades made up their minds to overpower. Accordingly, one day, when all hands were below watering their horses, and the officers had withdrawn into the cabin to lunch, the conspirators, having armed themselves with swords and pistols, rushed upon deck—seized the two boatmen, who had just come on board—thrust them down into the hold—shut the hatches upon them, with threats of doing more—and passed, in a shorter space of time than I have taken to describe it, into the bum-boat. In an instant it was up sail and away. They waved their caps to us, gave us a hearty cheer, and, having the wind in their favour, we saw them skim through the deep like a water-fowl, when some enemy has scared her, and she is too much alarmed to fly. It was to no purpose that the officers, taking the alarm, shouted to them to return—or that a signal-gun being fired, the man-of-war's launches all hastened in pursuit The fugitives got so near to the Danish shore, that they ran the boat aground, and then leaped, up to their necks, into the water. Moreover, Baron Hompesch, who chanced at the time to be sojourning in the town of Gluckstadt, vainly offered them a free pardon if they would return. They had made up their minds to dare the worst; and as the authorities of the place could not refuse them passports, they set out next day on their progress homewards. What became of them eventually I do not know; but it is probable that they either returned to their homes, or took service with some other of the corps which were then collecting recruits for continental service every where throughout Germany.

The escape of these twelve had the natural effect of increasing the vigilance of those whose business it was to hinder so mischievous a precedent from being followed. Great precautions were taken to keep the rest of us where we were, and they succeeded; for after a cheerless winter, about eleven hundred men, with perhaps half as many horses, still answered to the name of Hompesch's Hussars; and in spite of our reluctance to cross the sea, it was felt by most of us as a relief, when on the 7th of April, 1795, the signal for sailing was hoisted. Our voyage, to be sure, was a rough one, for we had scarce lost sight of land, when a storm arose, during the continuance of which we were battened under batches. Yet we got through it at last; and but for the circumstance that one of our men's wives brought a little one into the world during the height of its violence, I do not know that I should have paused to remark upon it. Poor things, they were as well taken care of in the trying hour as circumstances would allow; and they survived it, only to be committed a few months subsequently to the deep.

We had been just a week at sea, the latter portion of which was fine, when the shores of England became visible, and we gazed upon them from the vessel's side full of admiration and wonder. We steered for Portsmouth, between which and the Isle of Wight we cast anchor; our berth being in the middle of such a fleet as might have struck with awe the oldest sailor that ever ploughed the deep. Ships of war of every size and class were there without number. Merchantmen, transports, victuallers, crowded round them, while to and fro boats were continually passing, as if all the maritime affairs of the whole world had been under discussion. Nobody from our vessel, however, was permitted to go on shore. On the contrary, after laying in a slight stock of fresh provisions, we again hoisted sail, and made for the mouth of the Southampton river, where, at a place called Hythe, on a neck of land jutting into the sea, we were finally disembarked, and marched into quarters.

We had every reason to be satisfied with the pains which the English government must have taken to render us comfortable. Hut barracks, composed of wood, were prepared for us, and commodious stables for our horses; while our bedding, provisions, pay, and general allowances, were all on the most liberal scale. Neither did any great while elapse ere a thorough remount was provided for us; so that in the course of a week or two we felt as soldiers ought to do, who respect themselves, and are taught from experience to feel, that they are in the service of a just and liberal government It seemed, too, as if the English were determined to load us with honours, and by so doing, to remove whatever of disinclination to the new service might linger in our minds. We had been less than a month in the country when his Royal Highness the Duke of York, the Prince of Wales, and the whole of the headquarter-staff, came down to review us. I knew that we went through the manoeuvres of the day in a very creditable manner, and that our appearance, bearing, and general state of discipline deserved approbation; but I fancy, now, that the encomiums bestowed upon us were exaggerated. Not content to feast us, after the review was over, upon roasted sheep and hogsheads of ale, the Prince of Wales caused it to be announced that he had adopted us as his own regiment; and taking away our old buttons, gave us new richly plated, and stamped with the ostrich feathers and the motto of the principality. After this there was not a man among us that doubted that our next remove would be to London, and our next duty ever Queen Charlotte; and when in the month of June there came an order to embark, we concluded that the only means of reaching the English capital was by water.

We went on board of ship as quietly as possible, and congratulated one another on our good fortune, wondering, indeed, how long the voyage would last, but never doubting as to its purpose. Thus it was, when, on the morning of the third day some staff-officers went round the ships, and read from an orderly-book the commander-in-chief's direction, that we should proceed without loss of time to St. Domingo. There was not a soul among us who knew where St Domingo lay, or what we should do when we arrived there, till the colonel, who followed the *cortègo*, explained that it was a place where gold and silver abounded; and that the King of England sent us to that favoured spot, in order that we might return, each man, with a fortune. He spoke with great animation, and seemed to expect that we should cheer him when his speech ended; but we had not forgotten the harangue on Schwarm Heath, and continued silent. Neither were we left long in ignorance as to the real nature of the country towards which it was the will of our new masters that we should proceed. The sailors soon informed us that our destination was the West Indies, and it is but justice to add, that we heard their declaration without surprise. Yet we were surprised when it came to be bruited about, that Baron Hompesch was not to accompany us. "It is only of a piece with the rest of his behaviour," said we; "let him stay—who cares? his successor, Colonel Hellemer, is as good a soldier as he, and we will follow him cheerfully, for he will never forfeit his word."

Our voyage to the West Indies occupied the space of seven weeks; for we quitted Southampton about the middle of June, and beheld the lovely shores of Barbados loom above the waters, some time in the beginning of August We did not land here, though we lay at anchor some time in the roadstead, and were liberally supplied by the Governor with fruit at the public expense, and with fresh provisions at our own. Neither had there occurred during the passage anything worthy of mention, except that the woman and child, to whom I have already alluded, both died, and were both committed to the deep. In like manner, though we formed part of the force which, under Sir Ralph Abercrombie, reduced the island of St Lucie, I cannot say that in the glories of that enterprise we had any right to share. It is true that an *aide-de-camp* came on board with an order that we should leave our horses, and disembark as light infantry to aid in the assault of the fort. But this our gallant colonel positively refused to do. "My regiment," said he "is a cavalry regiment: we are quite ready to serve anywhere as such, but we know nothing of the duties of infantry soldiers, and must refuse to undertake them." The consequence of this remonstrance was, that we remained quietly in our ships, whence we beheld with the liveliest interest the progress of the assault; which, as it was carried on chiefly by night, presented to us a spectacle such as soldiers love to gaze upon, and civilians to read about. Three days' fighting sufficed to reduce the fort, which stood upon the top of a conical hill, and was gallantly defended; after which the whole island submitted, and the troops employed being left free to proceed to their respective destinations, we, as a matter of course, steered for St. Domingo.

It is no business of mine to state what the circumstances might be which carried an armed hostile force in the year 1794, from England to St Domingo. I knew at the time too little of the English language to inquire into that matter; and had the contrary been the case, I should have scarcely thought with my notions of a soldier's duty and the habits of a soldier's life of instituting such inquiry. All, therefore, that I am now required to say is, that our regiment landed at a place called Cape Nicholas Mole, where we found an encampment already formed, and whence, after some time given to repose and refreshment, we passed forward to the chief harbour on that coast, the city of Port au Prince. There we disembarked, carrying with us our horses, baggage, and all other things necessary for service; being nothing loath to escape from the imprisonment of a ship, and mightily pleased both with the scenery and the excellent living that was afforded. For all the necessaries, and most of the luxuries of life were abundant; and our arrears of pay being punctually accounted for, we had funds at our disposal amply sufficient for the gratification of our most extravagant wishes. Yet there occurred an incident here which had well-nigh led to serious consequences.

We were marched to a sort of bazaar or public market surrounded on all sides by long ranges of buildings, the egress to which was through a single gate, at which of course a guard was mounted. There, together with some English infantry, quarters were assigned to us, which in themselves were far from being commodious, and which were rendered the less so by reason of their lying at some distance from the stables where our horses were accommodated. Now, it so happened that an order had been issued to hinder the English soldiers from passing into the town without leave—whereas we were free to go and come when we liked, so long as we came back at the usual hour of roll-call, nine o'clock at night I don't know by what motive the English soldiers were actuated, but they took it into their heads to refuse a passage to us, and the officer commanding the guard, instead of reproving them for the act, openly joined in it We were not inclined to endure such treatment as this. We knew not one word of their language—we were quite ignorant of their customs—we only felt assured that nothing had been said to us which could be construed into an order of restraint, and we determined to resist Accordingly, about a hundred of us in number came forth, sword in hand, knocked down the sentry, burst through the gate, and called upon our comrades to follow. In a moment the officer on duty turned out his guard and made the men prime and load. Information was sent off to the general commanding, and some six-pounders galloping down, were turned towards the barracks. Meanwhile the hussars within complained to their officers, and demanded either that they would see their wrongs redressed; or give them leave to vindicate their own honour with their own hands. And truly, it was well for all parties that Colonel Hellemer arrived in time to repress the fury of a thousand angry men, all of them armed; for we felt that we were more than a match for the English infantry, and as to the guns, these we could have carried at a rush. Bat the colonel having assured us that he would see into the matter, we became quiet, while he hurried away to head-quarters and gave his version of the story. The result was, that in a quarter of an hour the cannon were withdrawn. An order came out that no one belonging to our corps should be interrupted, and we spent a fortnight or three weeks agreeably enough; enjoying full liberty of egress and ingress, and subject only to the accustomed restraints to which all soldiers are liable.

CHAPTER 4

I See Some Service

Our sojourn in Port au Prince, after the date of this adventure, was not very protracted. It was judged expedient to reinforce the army in advance, and we were marched, in consequence, some miles towards the mountains, where we occupied the plantations of Jemecour, Cheitre, Bershlaw, &c., as far as St. Mary, in the district of St. Marc. There we remained for some months, in the presence, as we were told, of our enemy, and engaged, according to the language of the day, in the business of real war; but for my part, I could not avoid remarking to those with whom I associated, that if this were indeed war, we had no cause to wish, at any moment, for the return of peace. Our commissariat, be it observed, was supplied, not only with regularity, but in abundance. We had no fighting, or next to none, nor did any troops show themselves for whom we should have been justified in entertaining sentiments even of respect. Numbers of brigands endeavoured, it is true, to penetrate from time to time within our outposts; and under cover of night they occasionally succeeded in stealing a horse or two, or committing some other petty theft But as to military operations, properly so called, there were none; our most perilous duties never going beyond a patrol, or at the most, an escort of scores of provisions to head-quarters. It may not be amiss, however, if I describe what befell on a certain occasion, when I chanced to be one of a party whose business it was to bring up corn, money, and a stock of medicines, from Port au Prince to Cheitre, the head-quarters of the regiment

In the warfare which they carried on in the Isle of St. Domingo, the English were opposed by two parties, by the French republicans, including the whole of the regular army, on the one hand; and by swarms of runaway negroes, headed by their own chiefs, on the other. These latter were not only very active, but very orderly and intelligent. They acted chiefly by night, when moving about among the underwood, in a state of absolute nudity, and encumbered by no load whatever, except their fire locks and accoutrements, they harassed such of our piquets as kept post at a distance, and now and then made their way into the rear. On the day above referred to, a half troop of Hompesch's hussars, consisting of forty men, marched to Port au Prince in the morning, and having received their convoy, set out again for the front, which they hoped to reach long before midnight. They were far on their way, and darkness had set in some time, when being in a narrow road, between two hedges of prickly citrons, they were suddenly attacked by a body of brigands, and thrown into some confusion. The brigands, it afterwards appeared, had discovered, God knows how, that there was money in charge of the troops; and seeing a mule loaded with a large chest, they dashed towards her. They were successful in the attack, and drove her off. But their chagrin may be judged of by the mirth which was excited among us, when it was ascertained that the chest carried off contained only medicines. Neither were they so fortunate by-and-by, though they made a fierce attempt to retrieve their error. We were now on the alert—our rear-guard was strengthened, and having lost a man or two, with a couple of horses, we brought in the rest of our valuable charge safely to headquarters.

Up to this period, and for some time afterwards, our supplies came in regularly, and in abundance. A large portion of them we drew from Merabelle, a town of considerable importance in the interior, of which our allies (for we had allies among the French royalists), aided by a corps of blacks, kept possession. They were attacked, however, by the republicans, and overpowered which threw us, for a while, upon the fleet's stores—and though they rallied, the enemy proved too strong for them, and Merabelle was lost. Our general determined to recover it, and the army received orders to advance for that purpose. We marched in three columns those upon the right and left moved along the common roads of the country—that in the centre, to which our regiment was attached, was compelled to make a way for itself. Nor was the labour of doing so light. The entire face of the country was overspread with forests, the roots of which were closed up with the prickly pear, so close, so formidable, and so impervious, that the pioneers were kept continually at work, to open out for us a passage. The consequence, of course, was, that we rarely compassed more than eight miles in a day; and sometimes fell short of six. Still the march was conducted with perfect regularity, and every night rockets and blue lights were thrown up, so that each of the divided columns might know exactly the point where the others had halted.

We met with no opposition from the enemy; it was impossible indeed that we should; but the nature of the country threw in our way some severe obstacles. For, besides the forests, of which I have just spoken, there were here and there rocky hills to surmount, which, to the cavalry at least, occasioned much trouble and some loss. On one occasion in particular, after we had been toiling all day under a burning sun, we saw before us a precipitous ridge, which our guides informed us we must needs pass, because there was no spring nearer than at its opposite extremity. I must not forget to state that we had suffered that day terribly from the effects of thirst. There was no water to be had along the road, and the little which the men had brought in their canteens was all exhausted. Numbers had, therefore, become so faint, that they could scarcely sit on their horses, and some had even fallen to the ground. In particular, I recollect seeing a poor fellow stretched by the wayside, whom an officer saved from death, by pouring the last drop out of the canteen which he himself carried, into the sufferer's mouth;—-and before two hours were passed, I saw the same officer perish for the lack of that which he had generously given away. However, I cannot linger over scenes like this; for the precipice was before us; and spent and feeble as we were, we faced it, under the expectation of finding relief on the other side. There was no riding up the face of that rock, which here and there opened out into terrible fissures, even to cast the eye down upon which, caused the brain to turn round, for no bottom could be discerned. On, therefore, we went, each man leading his horse, which gathered up its feet like a cat on the edge of the gulf, and sprang over. Yet, all passed not thus. From time to time, a cry from the lookers-on told of man and horse having missed their spring; and the crash among the branches was all that proclaimed their progress to annihilation. Nevertheless, we gained the summit of the ridge at last, and began to descend. But our horror may be conceived when the guides whom we had sent forward reported that the spring was dry. We had no power to complain. Our lips were black, our tongues clave to the roofs of our months; we could only look up to Heaven, as if to seek that support from above which the earth refused to furnish. Nor did we ask it in vain. When our misery was at its height, the sky became all at once black with clouds, and God gave us water from above. Ay, some who have never felt as I did then, may smile when they are told that Providence interfered to save the lives of his creatures; but when the rain came down, and we caught it in our handkerchiefs, and drank from them, or from the long grass at our feet, there were few among us so hardened as not to return thanks to Him from whom alone all blessings flow. Nay, the very horses seemed conscious of the arm that had sustained them. They dashed their noses into the wet grass and satisfied the demands, both of hunger and thirst, at the same moment. With the rain came a furious storm of thunder and lightening, which lasted all night. Every flash as it went forth showed the whole of the surrounding scenery for a moment, and then all was dark; white rock and covert sent back in long and terrible echoes, the peals which in vapid succession followed one another. Not a murmur escaped us, however, conscious as we were, that by such means alone could our lives have been preserved; and when daylight returned, we resumed our march down into the plain, in the highest possible spirits. Again we were compelled to lead our horses, and our progress was slow, while the plain into which we emerged proved quite unfit for the operations of cavalry, inasmuch as the whole of its surface was covered by fragments of rock, hurled down, as it seemed, from the peaks overhead, by some convulsion of nature. Yet this was a day of greater excitement than had occurred to us since first the advance began. The enemy showed in our front a battery of ten pieces, guarding a sort of avenue through a wood, which it was necessary to force; and after a fruitless effort to silence their fire by some discharges from our mountain. guns, the infantry were moved on for the purpose of storming it. Nothing could be executed in better style than this attack. One rush put the assailants in possession of the battery; from which the enemy retreated in disorder, leaving some prisoners behind.

Having cleared the way of this obstacle, we resumed our march, and about two o'clock found ourselves on the bank of a river, beyond which lay a rich and open plain of about six miles in extent, with the town of Merabelle in its centre. So well, too, had the movement been arranged, that in ten minutes after we halted, the heads of the other columns showed themselves, and all crossing the stream simultaneously entered the cultivated country, just out of cannon-shot of the enemy's works. Our general now sent in to summon the place, but the governor refused to surrender; and we made immediate dispositions for the assault. That night, the outworks were carried at the point of the bayonet, and next day saw the town of Merabelle committed to the flames.

This service accomplished, and Merabelle converted into a heap of ruins, so that it should not again be used by the enemy as a post for interrupting our supplies, we began our march back towards the lines in front of Port au Prince; during our progress towards which, an adventure befell me, of which it is necessary that I should make mention. The whole army now proceeded by the regular roads, and we were distributed by regiments and squadrons, as far as circumstances would allow, every night for shelter among the planters' settlements that lay by the wayside. I think it was in the evening of the second day, that the squadron to which I was attached took quarters in a respectable dwelling, that lay in a position of singular beauty, just under the elbow of a lofty mountain. We were well received by the inhabitants, who hastened to kill and dress some sheep for our supper, and who being informed that the morrow would be a halting-day, assured us that we should fare then, just as we did now. I was by this time a sergeant, and being well pleased with the civility of our hosts, was exhorting the men to net generously towards them, when the master of the house came in, and eyed me with great attention. At last he said in German, "I perceive that you are not English; what countryman are you?" I told him. He then demanded the name of my birth-place. It was useless to say St Dennis, for nobody knew where St. Dennis lay—so I replied Dusseldorf. My host grasped my hand, said it was his own native city; insisted upon my accompanying him into his parlour, and being his particular guest while we remained; and I, as may be imagined, felt nothing loath to indulge him. Accordingly I was conducted into a well-furnished room, made to sit down at table, introduced to the lady of the mansion, a *mulatto*, with two good-looking daughters, and treated in every respect as if I had been one of the family. By and by the ladies withdrew, and my new friend proceeded to make me acquainted with his history,

His name, it appeared, was Kiester. He was the son of a labourer upon the quay, and had himself worked when a boy at the crane, but getting tired of this business had joined a barge, which traded between Dusseldorf and Rotterdam. At the latter place he was kidnapped and carried on board a Dutch ship of war, where the treatment afforded him was of the worst kind, and his life became a burden to him. At last, when the vessel touched for water at Port Nicholas de Mole he found an opportunity to desert, and made his way alone and penniless into the interior. After sustaining various changes of fortune, he reached the plantation where I found him, and acted as clerk to the proprietor, a Frenchman from Alsace, who both spoke and understood German, and who behaved to him with the tenderness of a father. This man had one child, a *mulatto*. He gave her to his clerk to wife, and Mr. Kiester became, in consequence, at the decease of his benefactor, one of the wealthiest planters in this part of the colony. "And," continued he, "if you will be guided by me, a similar good fortune shall gild your latter days. I have no family except these two girls—choose which you will for your wife; and I will immediately settle you on another of my estates, and adopt you as my son."

The offer was a very enticing one, but I rejected it. I did not relish the thought of deserting, and with numerous acknowledgements to Mr. Kiester for his generous intentions, I told him so. He laughed at my scruples, and as to what I hinted touching the risk of being taken, that he held in sovereign contempt. "Rest thou satisfied," was his reply, "I will hide thee where they will never be able to penetrate, and by-and-by when they are all driven out of the island, thou wilt be secure. For the English will never became masters of St Domingo, and be assured, the period is not very distant when they will be glad to escape from it." I looked at this moment upon my host's statement as a mere idle boast; and continued inflexible to his entreaties; little imagining that the latter part of his prophecy, at least, would so soon receive its fulfilment Accordingly, having spent the next day in riding with him over his lands, and the evening in the society of his family, I mounted my horse on the following morning, and marched with my troop. it is just to add, that Mr. Kiester pressed upon my acceptance a couple of *doubloons*, and accompanied me to the end of our first day's march, nor did he leave me till he had exacted a promise that I would well weigh his proposal, and inform him should any change occur in my sentiments.

We returned to our old alignment, which, extending from one bay to another, covered the approaches to Port au Prince, St Nicholas de Mole, and St Marc, with other places of note lying between them. For sometime, however, we had, in a military point of view, hardly any employment; for the enemy were aware of our superior strength, and held aloof from us. But if casualties rarely occurred from fire or sword, sickness began by degrees to make fearful havoc in our ranks. Fever burst in amongst us, and our men died by dozens every day. When it came to this, there were established at Cradobuckee two large hospitals—one for those in the first or worst stage of the malady, the other for convalescents—yet though the utmost care was taken of the patients, both by doctors and nurses, the former sent comparatively few tenants to the latter. On the contrary, the mortality became such, that we ceased to bury the dead with any kind of ceremony; but sent a mule or donkey cart twice a day to the hospital, whence the corpses wore borne off, heaped one upon another, and tossed into pits. It was a sad state of things when you missed a comrade from parade today, and on inquiring for him the day after, ascertained that he was in his grave; neither did the evil end here. The enemy were soon informed of our losses, and in exact proportion to our inability to cope with them, they became more bold and more obtrusive.

While things were in this state, one or two incidents took place, which, as illustrating the habits of the brigands, and the nature of the perils to which we were exposed, I may be permitted to describe. The brigands, be it observed, had no taste for fighting. They would exchange long shots with us freely enough, if necessity required; but they never voluntarily brought on a skirmish—their sole object being plunder, particularly of horses and arms. We lay, at this time, by squadrons, in various *estancias*—one of which, called Chetree, contained the head-quarters of the regiment It chanced that I formed part of the head-quarter squadron, which kept its horses within a sort of *kraal* or enclosure, surrounded by long poles driven into the earth, at the distance of, perhaps, six inches from one another. The horses of the officers, again, were lodged in the stables of the plantation, and there was one of these, Captain Mayatt, who being possessed of three beautiful animals, loved them as other people do their children. Captain Mayatt, however, was one of those cautious persons, who never expend a shilling if they can help it; and finding no lock on the stable door, he would not go to the expense of providing one. He was content to give the sentry directions to look sharp after his treasure, and lay down night after night with an easy mind—undisturbed by any other cry than "All's well."

There came on one night, after the fever had terribly reduced us, a furious storm of thunder and rain, amid which, the darkness, except when dispelled for an instant by the lightning, was impenetrable. Throughout the whole of the tempest the sentry kept his guard; and from time to time Captain Mayatt heard him call, with composure, "All's well." But when the morning broke, beheld, all was not well. Some brigands had made their way into the stable, cut the halters by which the Captain's favourites were fastened, and as the prints of their feet demonstrated, had them quietly conveyed to a redoubt upon a hill, which the main body occupied at some distance. When the sun arose, and Captain Mayatt ascertained all this, he was inconsolable. He ordered his troop to mount; he followed the track within gunshot of the redoubt, and was hindered from going farther only by a positive prohibition from the colonel; for the prints of the hoofs were still before him. At last he halted, and lifting up his telescope, applied it to his eye —"Ah! there is Jack," cried he bitterly, "there is Jack sure enough, and Spinster too—Oh! unhappy man that I am; there she stands looking at me, with her own bright eyes, and I cannot come near her." There was no standing this, and we all laughed aloud, very much to the captain's chagrin, who day after day repaired to the same spot, in order that he might feast his eyes upon the dear creatures, and ascertain their condition.

It was not, however, upon the horses of the officers alone, that the brigands made an attack—they would steal along upon their bellies to the fencing of the *kraal* —tear up or cut down some poles, and lead away sometimes as many as six or eight troopers in a night Nay, they went even further than this. There was a picket of a serjeant and twelve, mounted at sunset to protect the *kraal*. Two acted as videttes two more patrolled—and the remainder tying up their horses, were accustomed to sleep round a fire, or otherwise dispose of themselves according to their own humour. One morning when they were about to come off duty, one of those who had slept from twelve till two, observed that his carbine was missing. He knew that he had left it in the boot, fastened to the saddle; but behold, it was gone. This excited the curiosity of another and another, when it appeared that all were in the same predicament. The brigands had stolen upon the horses while the men slept; and being afraid to lead away the animals themselves, they had cut off every carbine, and emptied every holster of its pistol. But all our adventures with these woolly rascals were not so ludicrous.

In rear of the *kraal* stood a pigeon-house—supported upon four legs—of such a height, that during rain, a mounted vidette could place himself beneath, and so obtain some shelter. There had been a storm one night, and the man on duty was supposed to have taken refuge under this strange canopy; but when the hour of relief returned he was nowhere to be found. The horse came back riderless to the *kraal*; but the rider was gone. Well, day after day passed by and still no trace of him, till in the end, a notion became general, that he had deserted; but it was not so. Two of our people having resolved to plunder the pigeon-house, got a ladder and ascended. They were struck by the horrible stench which issued from the place; but they still went forward —and there, with his head cut off, they beheld all that remained of their late comrade, passing rapidly into decay. The fact was this. Some brigands got into the pigeon-house, and casting a lasso over the poor fellow's head, dragged him from his horse by the neck, and hauled him up to their lurking-place. They there put him to death, and plundering him of his arms and accoutrements, escaped unobserved to their fastnesses.

In proportion as hardships increased upon us, the discontent which some had from the outset experienced towards the service, became more settled. Desertions, for the first time, occurred, and the enemy, as if emboldened by this circumstance, closed upon us with increased activity, rendering each patrol a service of danger, and threatening all our communications. Among others, there quitted our ranks a man, of whom I shall have occasion to speak in the sequel, a native of Alsace, and a thorough soldier—sergeant Bliss. He went over to the enemy with his horse and other appointments, and was immediately promoted by them to the rank of a brigadier of cavalry. Well inured to the operations of war (for he had served formerly in the French army), Bliss became from that time our most formidable opponent. He headed all the scouting parties that broke in upon our lines—he led the advance wherever our outposts were to be attacked, and he was particularly active in causing; handbills and printed papers to be thrown about—of which it was the object to entice our men into the adoption of his example. Many a plan was laid for seizing him, but they all failed; for he was an admirable horseman—he was particularly well mounted, and always contrived to keep at such a distance from his old comrades that none ever succeeded in crossing swords with him.

Such was the condition of the army in general, and of the Prince of Wales's Hussars in particular; when even my iron frame, which had hitherto withstood all imaginable attacks, yielded to the violence of the prevailing epidemic, and I became alarmingly ill. I was sent to the hospital at Cradobuckee, whence neither I nor any of my friends expected that I should be removed alive; but my constitution was excellent, and being treated with the greatest care, I weathered the five days, which few before me had seen out, and began slowly to recover. It is but just to state that my recovery I owe, in a very great degree, to the kindness of a negro nurse, who watched over me as tenderly as if I had been her own son; and was not tempted, even by the prospect of gain, to neglect me. For I had saved a pretty large sum of money, which I brought to the hospital in my saddle-bags, and in the simplicity of my heart, showed to her, assuring her, at the same time, that if I died, all should be hers, whereas if I recovered, she should have only a part.

Chapter 5

I Return to England

I have as yet said nothing to illustrate either the manners of the settlers in St. Domingo, or to convey to my reader's mind any idea of the influence which these exerted on the minds of our officers. Like almost all the planters from France or Spain with whom, in the course of a wandering life, it has been my fortune to come in contact, the white people of this island were singularly illiterate. Their great passion seemed to be for gaming, a vice which they carried to such an excess, as to stake upon a card or the turn of a die, not only their ready money, but horses, carriages, slaves—nay, even their very lands. I have seen a French gentleman drive into Port au Prince on one evening (with what was there accounted an elegant equipage), in his carriage, drawn by four mules, and attended by a numerous *cortège* of servants—and return from it the next day on foot, after losing all, in addition to some thousands of dollars, at the faro-table. It was scarcely to be expected that from the influence of this dangerous vice our officers should altogether protect themselves. Several took to the gambling-house as they would to a mercantile occupation; and one, in particular, underwent such curious reverses of fortune, that I may, perhaps, be permitted to allude to them.

Captain Von Beckenhaupt, of our corps, was a very good officer, though somewhat violent in his temper, and very wilful. He was one of the first to visit the faro-table at Port au Prince; and beginning at first with small stakes, he went on from day to day till he became as bold and dexterous a player as the best of them. I remember his returning to his quarters in the advance on several occasions, loaded with money. So weighty, indeed, were the bags of dollars, that he was forced to hire persons to carry them; and once he emptied them out on the floor of his apartment, being too much elated even to count them. Next night he returned in equal triumph; while on the third he brought with him, not money alone, but a carriage, mules, slaves, and various trinkets, all of which he had won from an unfortunate planter. So much good luck could not fail, however, to render an ardent minded man giddy. Captain Von Beckenhaupt grudged even the time that was required for the performance of his ordinary duty; and being ordered to march with his troop to a distant station, he refused to obey. The consequence was, that, rather than be tried by a court-martial, he sent in his resignation, which was accepted. But behold the result! Having removed to Port au Prince, and resigned himself wholly to gaming as to a business, his luck changed, and his winnings went from him; and so reduced was he when we marched in for the purpose of embarkation, that he was forced to solicit the charity of his former companions, in order to hinder him from starving. A subscription was raised for him in the corps, of which he received the amount. But how he used it, or what ultimately became of him, I do not know.

At the period of which I have just spoken as that of our return to the capital of French St. Domingo, the Prince of Wales's Hussars were sadly reduced in point of numbers. When we landed at St. Nicholas de Mole, we could muster very nearly eleven hundred men; we were now about two hundred and twenty fit for duty, and about as many more in hospital. Of the latter, some, who considered themselves convalescent, followed us on board ship, and not a few out of this number were committed, during our homeward passage, to the deep. But the circumstance which gave greatest annoyance to the healthy members of the corps was the wretched condition of the vessel into which we were crowded. A drunken captain, an idiotic mate, with swarms of rats, mosquitoes, cockroaches, and other reptiles, tormented us from morning till night, and put us in continual fear of our lives; so that at one time both officers and men had well-nigh risen in mutiny, and refused to quit the island. But our scruples were finally overcome by the assurance that other vessels were just as miserably provided; and we were preparing to put to sea, when a cutter worked up, having Baron Hompesch himself on board. It was too late for him to address us now, though he did so with tears in his eyes. His expressions of esteem and commiseration produced upon us no effect, for he had deceived us once, and we believed him capable of deceiving us again; so he went away without receiving one mark of respect, and we never saw him afterwards.

Our homeward passage was attended only by those accidents to which all who cross the Atlantic are liable: we had some heavy gales, which dismasted us, and for a considerable time we navigated the seas alone, under a couple of jury-masts. In the Channel, a frigate hove in sight, to which we made signals of distress; and she, taking us in tow, carried us into Plymouth. There we remained for about a fortnight, while the ship was refit. ting, very much refreshed by the supplies which reached us from the shore, and permitted occasionally to stretch our limbs by a walk in the town; after which we again put to sea, and steered for Guernsey. We landed in that island, with our baggage and equipments, and spent a month in St. Helier Barracks, as happily as need be—for Guernsey was then full of life and gaiety. Crowds of privateers filled its harbours, the crews of which circulated prodigious sums of money among the natives; while we, having large arrears of pay and other allowances to receive, felt ourselves quite in a condition to keep pace with them. On the whole, I hardly recollect a month of more incessant festivity than that to which I now refer; nor a more general lamentation when the order at length arrived to take shipping and pass over to the main land.

From Guernsey we removed to Southampton, or rather to the village of Ealing, where, to our great surprise, we found the skeletons of the two regiments of Old and New Rouen, cantoned in the same barracks. They, like ourselves, had served in the West Indies, and were so much reduced, that it was judged inexpedient at the Horse-Guards to keep them up as separate corps. Accordingly we had not long occupied our new quarters, when it was announced to us on parade, that his Royal Highness, the commander-in-chief, would permit any man to volunteer into any of his Britannic Majesty's regiments of horse or foot, and grant a bounty to all who thus transferred their services. It may be necessary to observe, that among continental troops, no man who has begun in the cavalry, and above all in the Hussars, ever dreams of enrolling himself in a regiment of infantry. Such a step would be accounted a degradation, and as hussar regiments in general are dressed with very great magnificence, the individuals belonging to them acquire an *esprit de corps*, such as you will scarcely find in any other armed body. This feeling was particularly evinced at Southampton, when first a party from the Twenty-Fifth English Light Dragoons, and afterwards a similar party from some foot regiment came among us. Our uniform was of the most splendid description. We wore scarlet *shakos*, with white lace—blue jackets richly ornamented, white buckskin pantaloons, and three-quarter boots; while our appointments were a sabre and sabretash—the latter covered with scarlet, edged with white, and suspended by strings of such length as to keep it dangling to our heels. Thus clothed, and accustomed to our sheep-skin saddles, we were, if the truth must be spoken, prodigious dandies; and our appearance, for we were all well-grown men, would have done no discredit to the best household-troops in Europe.

When the proclamation was first read upon parade, there were many among us who experienced no disinclination to act upon it; but the arrival of the party from the Twenty-Fifth Dragoons at once effaced the impressions These men were dressed in dirty gray jackets, leather helmet-caps fearfully heel-balled, white leather breeches, and shoes, and long black gaiters. They wore white feathers thrust into the sides of the helmets, and sabretashes tucked up so as to descend no lower than the hips, On the whole, we never had seen such spectacles; and hence, though the non-commissioned officers exerted themselves with laudable pertinacity in the cause, not one man could they get from us. The infantry were just as unsuccessful, and both retired. Then it was that after an interval of a few weeks, our major announced to us upon parade, that a fresh project had been entertained is reference to some of us. In Guernsey, it appeared that the patrol-duty had hitherto been performed by detachments from the yeomanry cavalry, a species of force, which being composed of the sons of gentlemen and farmers, did not always find it convenient to turn out. The designs of the supreme authorities now pointed to enrol one hundred men from our regiment, under the denomination of Guernsey Hussars, and to employ them permanently in guarding the island from invasion by the French, with which it was continually threatened. The major played his cards very skilfully, and won his game. One hundred of the best men volunteered, and having equipped us in splendid dresses, he put himself at our head, and we again passed over to our old quarters, as Guernsey Hussars.

It is not worth while to describe the order of our duties here, which consisted in furnishing pickets, and passing patrols nightly along the coast. We thought nothing of these things, and very little of our drilling and parades, but we found the major grow daily more and more strict; for every petty irregularity which used in former days to be overlooked, was now rigidly punished. Neither were our punishments of a trifling nature. It is true that we had no cat-o'-nine-tails, but the *bastinado* was at all times freely administered, and that, which constitutes the universal punishment in the armies of Germany, is no trifle. The order of it is this.

We have no such thing as a regimental court-martial among us. Every officer, every sergeant, every corporal, can send a man, either to the guard-house or to the black-hole, according to the nature of his offence, care being taken that the causes of his confinement are stated in the grand report, which is sent in to the commanding officer next morning at relieving time. Besides this, a subaltern may, of his own authority, order a man to receive five-and-twenty lashes, a captain may give fifty, and a commandant as many as a hundred; which are thus inflicted. The culprit is laid across a truss of straw, either stripped to his drawers or not, according to the crime of which he has been guilty, and a corporal stands over him, having in his hand a hazel stick, of a circumference just sufficient to pass freely into a carbine, but no more. With this, on a signal given, he gives two flourishes in the air, and at the third, comes with all his strength across the prisoner's body: taking care to drive the point of his stick into the flesh, and to produce a wound which is sometimes terrible to look upon. Talk of flogging! I tell you the *bastinado* is a thousand times more severe; in fact, I do not believe that any man could take a hundred blows well laid on and live. Still such is the effect of custom, that among us the punishment is little regarded. We will avoid it if we can; for we all dread it very much; but no man fancies that he is disgraced by it, provided he do not suffer for a crime which is in itself disgraceful. And let me add, we have no teasing punishments; such as drill, confinement to barracks, and other things which, without preventing crime, only irritate the criminal. Ours is summary justice, which we all know, and hold in respect

Well, the *bastinado* went with awful rapidity in Guernsey, and what is more, when the bounty came to be distributed, we found, that instead of four pounds each man, the sum originally promised, we received but a dollar, with which to drink the king's health. This was a grievous disappointment to us; but as we were all flush of cash, we could have easily got the better of it, but for the tyranny to which we were subjugated. Now we had not reckoned upon this, and having been heretofore little accustomed to it, a spirit of insubordination, bordering upon mutiny, was stirred up among us. At last the matter was brought to a point We had lived for a while in the same barracks with the Sixty-First Infantry, and had witnessed, with horror, the frequent application of the cat: but never dreamed that to us, brought up under a different system, that species of punishment would be applied. Our major, in an evil hour, determined to show us, that we were, not less than the Sixty-First, subject to the English military code. One of our men, having committed some depredation, was brought to a general court-martial, and sentenced to receive five hundred lashes; the whole of which were inflicted, in our presence, at a stable-dress parade, within the barrack square of the sixty-first, which stood all the while under arms to watch the event

We returned home from witnessing this spectacle in a state almost of desperation; and three or four laying their heads together, resolved to deliver their comrades, if it should be possible, from their thraldom. For this purpose we sought out an attorney in the town, and caused him to write in our names a letter to his Royal Highness the Duke of York, in which all our grievances were set forth. Among other things, we informed the Duke of the amount of bounty which we had received, and implored him to receive us as volunteers into the York Hussars, a foreign regiment, which, being then in process of enrolment, took from the commander-in-chief its distinctive appellation, inasmuch as his Royal Highness had been appointed to the command of it. The letter was despatched the same evening, and we returned home well pleased with the step that had been taken; though, when day after day, and week after week, passed by, without any reply being vouchsafed, apprehensions began by degrees to be entertained that we had been unfairly dealt with. At length, however, we received satisfactory proofs, that our memorial had reached its destination. The major summoned us to parade one day, and appeared before us with a face flushed with anger. He declared that he would know the name of the rascal who had dared to memorialise the commander-in-chief, and conducted himself throughout more like a madman than an officer of rank and some reputation. At last he wound up by exclaiming, "You have applied to be received into the York Hussars: your petition is granted, and to the York Hussars you go; but mark my words: it is the worst day's work ever you did in your lives. For I go with you, and by my soul you will live to repent the day that you ever withdrew yourselves from under my command." To all this we listened with perfect unconcern, which was converted into mirth when we found, that one of the first effects of our petition was to wring from the worthy major the residue of our bounty. Yet such is the fact; for previous to our embarkation, each man received, either in money or clothing, not less than three pounds fifteen shillings, which though described to us as an additional gratuity from the Crown, we accepted as nothing more than what was strictly our due from the outset

Before I quit the subject of Guernsey, it may be as well to state, that while we did duty there, a Russian fleet, having on board the residue of the army which had served under the Duke of York at the Helder, put in. As the ships were in want of stores, and their fresh provisions exhausted, the delay of the squadron was of necessity considerable; and the troops being disembarked, were placed, some in barracks, others in private lodgings among the inhabitants. We saw a good deal of their officers, who appeared to me to be a quick, intelligent, and brave set of men; though their sense of honour was not in all cases very acute, as the following anecdote will prove. In the town of St Helier was one Mr. Mollet, the keeper of a tavern, and a man of some substance, whose only daughter, Elizabeth, was perhaps the prettiest girl that in any country, or at any period, I have seen. So attractive, indeed, were both her appearance and manner, that she drew a prodigious custom to her father's house, while her principles were so correct that she resisted at the outset every approach to a degree of familiarity that was not compatible with the strictest virtue. Such a creature could not fail to receive numerous offers of marriage; yet these, too, she invariably declined, till a Russian captain of infantry paid his addresses to her.

My reader is not perhaps aware that there is a regulation in the Russian army, which prohibits any woman, whether married or not, from accompanying a body of troops upon foreign or active service. So rigid, indeed, are the Muscovites on this head, that at the period of which I am speaking, the wife of a field officer having been detected in her husband's quarters disguised as a page—she was sent home with ignominy, and he reduced to the ranks. It was of course impossible for Elizabeth's suitor to hide that fact from his mistress, because the occurrence took place in St. Helier, and the whole island rang with it But being master of her affections, he persuaded her to believe, that provided they could contrive to get her removed from Guernsey in one of her father's schooners, it would be easy enough when at sea, to pick her up, and hide her in the Russian transport Accordingly, the poor girl consented to fix the day for the wedding, which was celebrated with all solemnity according to the rites of the established church, and toasted by my. self and a crowd of her friends besides, with great zeal after supper.

About a week had passed in marriage festivities when the Russians were ordered to embark; and the bride was reduced to the necessity of making her own arrangements for the purpose of not being separated from her husband. At his suggestion she sent all her property, amounting to some hundred pounds, all her clothes, trinkets, and valuables of every description, to his ship; while she herself, with a stock of apparel barely sufficient for a few days' wearing, took her berth in a schooner which her father manned, and made ready to follow the squadron. On the appointed day the whole put to sea, the schooner keeping as near as possible to the husband's vessel, and steering for the coast of England. Elizabeth naturally expected that then, during the bustle of a general rendezvous, she would be enabled to join her lover. But she was cruelly deceived. The scoundrel never meant that she should join him. He had obtained all that he coveted of her little dower, and now made no effort whatever, during three days and nights, so much as to communicate with the schooner, though all the while within hail. I need scarcely go on with my tale. The Russian admiral perceiving the schooner at last, ordered its crew to sheer off or he would sink them; and poor Elizabeth returned to Guernsey a widowed wife, forlorn, and well-nigh broken-hearted. Many years elapsed ere I heard of her again, though I never failed, as often as an opportunity offered, of inquiring into her fate; and then the bitterness of grief was past. She had given birth to a son, of whom the Russian captain was the father; and long devoted herself to the child's education. But the entreaties of her parents, and the devotion of another lover, overcame her sadness at last; she married a second time more prudently, and succeeding to the business at her father's decease, carried it on at once respectably and profitably. The York Hussars, composed of recruits collected from prison-ships, and the wrecks of almost all the foreign regiments in the English service, lay, at the period of the breaking up of the Guernsey squadron, In Weymouth, whither, as soon as ships were provided for our accommodation, we proceeded to join them. They were in a miserable plight; half naked, without arms, without horses, and totally ignorant of their duty;—such scarecrows, in short, that the Colonel, M. Jassar, a fine Swiss soldier, would not permit them to go beyond the barrack-gates, or show themselves in the town. It was different with us, who came fully equipped, and to whom all the indulgences to which soldiers are accustomed, were freely granted. Neither were these denied to our comrades so soon as they came into such a state as to bring no discredit on the regiment to which they belonged; for Colonel Jassar was a man who loved to govern with mildness, and whom his men obeyed as much from affection as from fear. Unfortunately for us, however, Colonel Jassar had made up his mind to retire, and he was succeeded by an Englishman, Colonel Robert Long, who lost no time in setting aside all our old usages, and introducing English drill, English habits, English distinctions, and English punishments. Now I do not mean to speak against Colonel Long: he was an excellent officer in the field; but to us who knew our duty thoroughly, as such duty is practised on the Continent, his proceedings were vexatious in the extreme. For example, our horses were always in the best condition, yet our custom was simply this: that every man ran to the stables when the trumpet sounded, and fed or cleaned his charger. From the first day after his arrival, we were paraded by troops for this purpose, and made to fall in, with sponges suspended from our buttons, curry-combs in our hands, and brushes so disposed that the orderly-officer might see them. Then, after standing for inspection in open ranks, we were wheeled to the right, and marched, squad by squad, to our stables. Moreover, there were foot and horse parades, carbine-drill, sword-drill, and pistol-drill; in a word, one continued series of drills and parades from break of day, till it was time to lie down again. All this harassed us exceedingly; and it became the more distressing, that our new colonel not only introduced the cat-o'-nine-tails, but made exceedingly free with it. Our men began to desert, and the more they deserted, the faster flew the lash, till there were comparatively few among the privates to whom it had not been applied. But this state of things could not go on.

We had often talked among ourselves of the necessity of doing something to put an end to this horrid system; yet we knew not how to proceed, till four men more resolute than the rest made up their minds to risk their own lives for the benefit of their comrades. These went to the colonel's quarters one morning, demanded, and obtained admission, and closing the door, told him their minds in language of which it was impossible to mistake the meaning. Little Bobby, as we called him, was not the sort of man to be bullied, so he resolutely refused all their demands; and raising the window, called in some of the guard, who carried the four delegates as prisoners to the black hole. They were brought to trial, found guilty of insubordination, and condemned to receive each, eight hundred lashes; and the punishment was inflicted with as much severity as ever I beheld on like occasions. Nor was this all. As soon as they were taken down, they were marched to the barrack-gate, the trumpeters playing the rogue's march behind them, and then having had their buttons cut off, and their facings taken away, they were told to shift for themselves, as being no longer worthy, to serve in the corps. Yet either their remonstrance, or some compunctious feelings of his own had wrought upon the colonel's mind. The cat-o'-nine-tails fell into disuse, the men were kindly treated, and the duty was done, not only with as much, but with greater alacrity and good will than had been displayed since Colonel Jassar left us.

Before I quit this subject, it may not be amiss to state a

circumstance which many years after the occurrence just described, befell me. I had occasion once to visit Chichester barracks, where the Queen's Bays or Dragoons lay in quarters, and entered the square at a moment when the sergeant-major was busily engaged drilling some recruits. The man's air and appearance struck me as being those of some one with whom I had formerly been acquainted, and approaching to examine him more closely, we recognised each other almost at the same instant He was the ringleader of the mutineers who had entered Colonel Long's apartment, and to whose terrible punishment I had myself been a witness; and he hastened to assure me, by a cordial grasp of the hand, that our old acquaintance was not forgotten. I accompanied him home, and heard that he had undergone some strange vicissitudes of fortune. Being dismissed from the halberds, and ashamed to seek shelter in town, be had wandered some way into the country till he came to a cottage, the inmates of which took compassion on him, and dressed his back, and gave him food and lodgings. He then wandered about till the marks were somewhat effaced, finding labour here and there, and subsisting on alms, where such was not to be had, till at last he fell in with a recruiting, party from the Bays, and offered his services. He was accepted, and by steady good conduct. and great intelligence, he forced himself on; till he obtained the rank of which I found him in possession.

He of course entreated me to keep his past history a secret, which I promised to do; and we lived together for some days very happily, I being his guest, and he my kind and hospitable entertainer.

I had well-nigh forgotten to mention, that one of the first men who met me on my arrival at Weymouth from Guernsey, was the identical Sergeant Bliss, of whom I have already spoken, as deserting from us to the French, when in position in front of Port-au-Prince at St Domingo. He had grown weary, it appeared, of his new friends, and ascertaining that the Prince of Wales's Hussars were gone, he came over again to the English, where he obtained a free pardon from the general. Upon this he joined the York Hussars, and returned with the remains of the regiment to Europe. Bliss never ceased to brood over the severities of which Colonel Long had been guilty, nor to complain of them even when they had passed away; and now he prevailed upon five of his comrades to join him in an attempt to escape across the Channel, into France. With this view they had in a small stock of biscuit and water, after which they seized, one dark night, a boat in the harbour, and passing both guardship and revenue-cutters, gained the open sea, without either compass or rudder, or any thing except oars and sails to guide them. By us, of course, the direction which they had taken was unknown, and we had ceased in some degree to speculate about them, when, about a fortnight afterwards, intelligence was received from Jersey that they had been picked up by a King's cruiser in great distress, and carried into that island. To forward them to Weymouth was the peremptory duty of the authorities there; to bring them before a general court-martial was the duty of Colonel Long: and the result of the trial was that Bliss and another were sentenced to be shot, the remainder to be flogged and, sent to a condemned corps. Having elsewhere described a military execution, I will not again enter into the particulars of this, further than by stating, that all the regiments in the district assembled to witness it, and that the men died without a struggle. In a military point of view, they unquestionably deserved their fate, though probably no man has ever yet seen a fellow creature put to death without experiencing a wish that his life had been spared.

Chapter 6

Disbanded

It was now the summer of 1801, and a report began to circulate amongst us, that his Majesty King George the Third, with the Queen and the royal family, intended to visit Weymouth, and to view the troops that were assembled in the vicinity. The report obtained the more ready credit in consequence of an order which went forth, to form an encampment on the high grounds that overlook the town: and splendid indeed was the spectacle, when along these ridges tents were pitched, for I know not how many regiments of cavalry and infantry, as well as for a considerable detachment of artillery. It is needless to state how, day by day, public curiosity was kept on the stretch, or how joyous was the news when every bell in the place gave notice that the King had at length arrived. Immediately a strong picket, consisting of detachments from all arms, was ordered to mount every day in front of the Royal Hotel; so that each of us in his turn, had the honour to be inspected by Royalty, the King himself making it a point to be present at the accustomed hour, in order that he might receive the salute.

His Majesty's common custom was to ride along the front of the troops, and to inspect them cursorily, as Kings are wont to do, without making any remark. It happened, however, that on one occasion, he deviated from this practice, and the following scene occurred. A portion of our corps, forming the cavalry picket, held the right of the line, which rendered it necessary for his Majesty to begin his inspection with us. The appearance, first of one man and then of another, struck him, and he stopped to ask questions. "What countryman are you?"

"A Saxon."—

"Oh! a Saxon, a Saxon," replied the King "a fine nation, a fine nation—very good soldiers, very good soldiers."

He then passed on to another. "What countryman are you?"

"A Swede."—

"Good, good, excellent men the Swedes—very good men the Swedes."

A third arrested him, and the same question was repeated; the answer was, "A Hanoverian."—

"Oh! my own country, my own country—all good men the Hanoverians, all good men, all good men."

Now came a fourth, and he was, in truth, as noble a looking fellow as ever mounted a horse. He was very tall, beautifully formed, with a dark complexion, piercing black eyes, hair like the raven's wing, and an enormous pair of mustaches. The King gazed at him for some time, and then demanded "What countryman are you?"

"A Hungarian," replied "Forksh," whose name being rendered into English signifies a wolf.

"All excellent soldiers the Hungarians," cried the King, "all excellent soldiers;" and then, as if attracted by the peculiar curl of the man's mustaches, he put forth his hand and began gently to twist one of them. It is impossible to say what motive could have actuated Forksh, for he never gave a satisfactory account of it; but the King had hardly seized his moustache, when he made a sort of snap like a dog, at the royal hand, which was instantly withdrawn. In my life I never witnessed such a scene. The whole parade was convulsed with laughter, in which, after his first surprise, nobody joined more heartily than George III. As to the Prince of Wales, who rode next to his father, I thought he would have fallen from his horse. But he did not forget, as he passed by, to slip a guinea into the man's hand, who never permitted a muscle of his face to relax, nor swayed, even for an instant, from his upright and soldier-like attitude.

I do not know whether this incident, in itself trifling, was or was not the cause, but we became from that day mighty favourites with the King; and he took, as he was apt to do, a singular mode of showing it. One fine summer's morning, about seven o'clock, when we were all busy in stables, there arose a cry in our camp that the King was approaching. The officers ran out, and looking with their telescopes through the streets of the tents, they saw, sure enough, the King, the Queen, the Duke of Clarence, and a large suite walking towards the lines. The trumpets, of course, sounded, and we ran in our stable-dresses to the parade, but his Majesty would not look at us. He had no intention to trouble us, he was only abroad for a little morning's exercise; still, as the sky had become overcast, and a storm of thunder and rain threatened, he would take shelter in the officers' mess-house. Thither, the whole retinue accordingly repaired, and no great while elapsed, ere our good King began to evince both his curiosity and kindly disposition. He desired the colonel to bring in all the Hungarians belonging to his regiment, and as the band was playing in an adjoining room, he requested that it might be silenced. This done, he desired the men to sing a Hungarian song. They sang, and were next requested to dance a Hungarian dance—of course that wish was in like measure gratified, for the band instantly struck up, and the men did their best to set themselves off to advantage, and to please the King. A similar process was gone through with the Poles, the Germans, and others, till almost all the varieties of continental singing and dancing, had been exhibited. The King was much delighted, and the storm being abated, he made a movement to go, but Queen Charlotte interposed—"Your Majesty has had your pleasure, now I must have mine," and forthwith all the women and children belonging to the regiment were sent for. Great was the washing of hands and faces, prodigious the adjusting of bibs and tuckers, and forward they at length came, not all of them in court dresses, but, generally speaking, clean and tidy. Her Majesty had a kind word to say to each, and desired that each should have a guinea. But when, at last, she came to one—the native of her own country—she drew forth her purse and gave her five guineas. Finally, the King ordered a hogshead of beer and an ample supply of pipes and tobacco for every troop, and departed. Yet, for this act of kindness, both King and Queen were abused in the prints of the day, as if their affections had pointed only to foreigners, and the English regiments were neglected.

Thus passed the summer, at the close of which the royal party returned to London, and our camp being broken up, the several regiments returned to the barracks or quarters which they had previously occupied. The winter, too, went by, without bringing any event to pass, in the relation of which it is necessary to waste time; and with the spring of 1803 came a report that the war was at an end. Day by day and week by week the statement was repeated, till it produced, at last, an expectation in our regiment that the hour of disbandment could not be very distant. We were not deceived in this surmise. First, a rigid examination of our horses took place, and two-thirds being cast, we got no remount. By and by the remaining third was taken from us—then we were ordered on a certain day to carry our arms and appointments into store, and last of all, to embark on board of transports for the Isle of Wight. To the Isle of Wight we accordingly sailed, where though we still held together and wore our Hussar uniform, the regiment was, to all intents and purposes, disbanded.

It had been announced to us on one of the parades, which from time to time took place, that such of us as chose to enlist in an English regiment should receive a fresh bounty—and that transports were provided for the purpose of conveying to Germany all those who preferred returning home. For my part I was yet hesitating how to act, when Captain Quentin visited our barrack-yard, and informed Colonel Long of his desire to procure from us a certain number of non-commissioned officers and privates for the Tenth, or Prince of Wales's Hussars; Colonel Long did me the honour to recommend me to Captain Quentin as his recruiting-sergeant, and the Captain, after objecting a little to my height (for I measured only five feet seven inches), offered me the situation. I expressed myself willing to accept it, provided my rank as sergeant were permanently secured to me, and I was permitted to offer to my comrades a fair bounty: and though Captain Quentin could not say positively to what the latter would amount, he assured me that it should not fall short of four guineas. Still, I was to practice the most rigid economy in dealing with the volunteers. A few shillings in advance he would not object to, but beyond this he judged it altogether inexpedient to proceed. Thus instructed, I applied myself to my new task, and succeeded the same night in getting two excellent men—such men as answered in every respect the pattern which had been set for me. They were both good soldiers—they measured five feet nine inches—and they were under twenty-six years of age. I was well pleased with my evening's work, and made no doubt of gaining, with proper management, the whole amount which it was his wish that I should provide.

Captain Quentin did not remain in the island to watch our proceeding. He departed the day after my engagement, leaving me instructions, not indeed to get the men attested, but to keep them in good humour till he should return and approve of them. Now, there is no keeping a recruit in good humour without a certain expenditure of money, and as my purse happened at the time to be particularly well filled, I made no hesitation in advancing from its contents the necessary supplies. By these means my recruits grew continually more numerous, till at last I could muster twelve—with whom an agreement was actually made,—besides many others who waited only for an invitation to join their comrades. When things were in this state I did net hesitate to give to each man what I thought a fair allowance, in his peculiar circumstances. The shilling they took, of course, from the King, and I added to it over and above a pound note— so as to put a guinea into every man's pocket

There was, of course, no end to the mirth and dancing of those three days. Our rendezvous was at the Star Inn, East Cowes, where fiddles were kept going all night long, and our cash being abundant, we received from the landlord and his family the most liberal treatment. But soldiers, when bent upon frolic, scarcely know where to draw the line or to stop short. We determined to have a regular spree one day, and the following were the arrangements which we made, in order to fill up the measure of our happiness.

We hired fourteen hacks—some with three legs, some with four—accoutred with or without saddles, just as the case might be; and ordering them, as well as a gig, to be in readiness by nine in the morning, at about half past nine we were all mounted. On me, as master of the ceremonies, devolved the care of arranging the cavalcade, and I paraded it thus. In front of all rode two trumpeters—excellent musicians in their way; behind them, with an interval of perhaps twenty yards, rode six of my recruits; then came the gig at a like interval from the advanced guard, in which I, with a young woman, took our stations; while, last of all, about twenty yards off, marched the rear-guard, consisting of the other six men mounted. At a given signal the trumpets sounded, and we rode through the streets of Cowes—men and women turning out to cheer us, and crowds of children following—and then away towards Newport, making frequent halts, as maybe imagined, at such public-houses as met us along the road. We had determined to dine at Newport, and we did so, very much to the astonishment of the inhabitants, who were quite at a loss what to make of men, dressed as we still were, like cavalry soldiers, yet destitute of arms, and mounted on such wretched cattle. I need scarcely add that the consumption of wine and punch at that dinner was immense. Nevertheless, we had all our wits about us, when after drinking our last bottle at the inn-door, we resumed our order of march, and departed amid the braying of our own trumpets, the laughter of the crowd, and the incessant shouts and cries of the children.

We were not drunk, though all had taken as much as they could carry, consequently my advanced guard kept order tolerably well till we had cleared the town, when, recollecting that I had appointed another rendezvous at the White Hart, about a couple of miles from Cowes, they set off at a brisk pace, and left me and my rear guard behind. On we went, however, at our own jog trot, and were passing the infantry barracks on the common, when a foot soldier, excessively intoxicated, came staggering across the road, and ere I could provide against the accident, ran right between my horse's feet. The man fell and cut his cheek and nose on the gravel, both of which bled profusely; but by a sudden wrench I threw my horse back so completely on his haunches, that not a hoof touched him. Still he was so drunk, or so sulky, that he could not or would not rise, and while I was yet consulting with my comrades, who had closed up, as to the best course to be pursued, a party from the barrack-guard came out and made me prisoner. Now then, thought I, here is a nice conclusion to my frolic—I am in a scrape at last, if I never got into one before; yet I collected my thoughts, became as sober as a judge, and told the truth, both to the adjutant and the surgeon, who ran out among others to ascertain what was the matter. For the cry was that I had driven over the man; and as he was carried in by his comrades, a feeling became prevalent among them that his legs were broken. He was conveyed to the guard bed, his face washed, and his body examined, a proceeding of which the result was to satisfy those present that he had sustained no serious injury; and the adjutant had already told me to go in peace, for that no blame attached to me, when a scheme came into my head which was immediately executed. "Get up my man," said I to the drunken soldier, "you are not hurt. Get up and jump over the bench, and I'll give you five shillings.

"Will you," cried the rascal—looking me full in the face—"then it's done," and done sure enough it was. He sprang to his feet, cleared the bench, and demanded the sum; but I told him he should have it the next time we met and drove off amid shouts of laughter from the bystanders.

Misfortunes, they say, never come single, and I was doomed this day to experience the truth of the proverb. We found our advance waiting for us at the White Hart, to whom we told our story, and in the delight of our hearts we indulged somewhat more than might be prudent, of which the consequence was, that when driving into Cowes, the wheel of my gig took a large stone and over went the vehicle, tossing my fair companion into the kennel and throwing me above her. Shaft, wheel, and trace, all gave way, and the wreck of the landlord's carriage was carried upon men's shoulders into his stable-yard.

We had spent some weeks thus, when Captain Quentin, true to his promise, returned to Cowes, bringing with him the sergeant-major of his regiment, a Belgian, by name Du Pré, and as thorough a coxcomb as I have ever chanced to see in his station. Covered with silver lace and gorgeously apparelled, he would scarcely stoop to notice so humble a personage as myself, and as to the recruits, with them he would hold no intercourse, farther than was requisite in parading them for inspection. It struck me, likewise, that the captain's manner was altered for the worse. He was captious and inquisitive, asking as many questions about the men's history and past conduct, as if he had suspected me of a wish to deceive him. But that which astonished me most of all, was the manner in which both he and his sergeant-major received the statement of the money which I had advanced out of my own pocket. The latter pronounced me decidedly wrong—the former swore that I might seek repayment where I could, but that from him I should never receive it I was nettled, and reminded him in few words, that neither I nor my comrades were as yet attested, and that I had only to tell them of the treatment which I had received at his hands, and to a man they would withdraw from their engagement. Upon this the captain lowered his tone, observing that he never meant to keep me out of my money—that I had done wrong in having so far exceeded the license which he had granted me, but that if I would call at his quarters that evening, he would settle with me. I did not call that evening, for I devoted it to reflection, which ended in a persuasion that it would not be for my advantage to join the Tenth, and that the sooner I withdrew myself from the Isle of Wight the better. Accordingly, having ascertained that a vessel would sail next day for Weymouth, I engaged a passage in her, after which I merely visited my recruits, and went quietly to bed. Next morning about nine o'clock I waited on Captain

Quentin, who handed me my twelve pounds without scruple, and then he told me, his sergeant-major being present, that I would not suit him, and that he should thenceforth dispense with my services.

"I am very glad to hear it, Captain Quentin," said I, "for to be plain with you, it was my intention to take the very step in which you have anticipated me. Neither you nor your sergeant-major will do for me, so I wish you good morning."

I went straight to the *Star*, ordered the porter to convey my trunk on board of ship, informed my late comrades how the case stood between me and the captain, and bade them farewell. They accompanied me to the sea-side very much cast down at the separation, and I have never seen any of them since.

CHAPTER 7

I Join the 20th Light Dragoons

I had been, while serving in the York Hussars, on intimate terms with the master of our band—a German like myself—who, when the corps was disbanded, went straight from Cowes to London, and soon got a place in the band of the Coldstream Foot Guards. Though I brought with me to Weymouth a considerable stock of ready money, I was yet anxious about the future; so I wrote to this man and requested that he would look about for some cavalry regiment into which I might be likely to be received as a sergeant. The return of post brought my friend's answer, expressing a wish that I would come up to London without delay, and stating that as the town was full of recruiting parties which all paraded once a day in rear of the Horse Guards, it was next to impossible that I could fail with one or another to gain my object. The advice appeared judicious, so I mounted the top of the coach, and in due time was transported into this mighty capital, of which I then knew nothing, but with which I have since become familiar. I took a lodging fer myself in one of the streets that lead off from the Strand, and being ignorant of my friend's address, repaired next day to the parade ground in St James's Park. He was there, as I expected to find him, and the meeting between us was on both sides very affectionate. Moreover, I learned from him that the 20th Light Dragoons was just returned from Jamaica, a perfect skeleton and in indifferent order, and both he and I concluded that its colonel would not be averse to take advantage of my experience in drilling his recruits, and fitting them for active service.

With this idea in my mind, I presented myself to the recruiting-sergeant, one of your thorough-paced, rum-drinking, yellow-visaged West Indians, and stated my case. His answer was, "We don't enlist sergeants; however, you may be an exception to the general rule, so we had better go and see the officer." We went accordingly, and Captain Hunt (for such was the officer's name), after putting a few questions to me, expressed himself anxious to treat with me on my own terms: with which, however, he could not undertake to comply, till he should have obtained the colonel's sanction. He therefore proposed that I should accompany him to Lord Heathfield's house, and I went For a few minutes Captain Hunt was closeted with his lordship, during which interval, Sergeant Goodall and I remained in the hall: but by and by I was called in, and some such scene as the following occurred:—

"Ha!" said his lordship, "You wish to join my regiment, and to retain your rank of sergeant."

"Yes, my lord."

"Do you understand English?"

"Pretty well, my lord."

"Can you give the word of command in English?"

"Yes, my lord."

"Well then, let us see. Now, speak out; don't spare your lungs, but imagine that you are standing in the centre of Guilford Barracks, and the wind blowing great guns. Say as I say, 'Right face!'"

His lordship spoke audibly enough I must allow, but I was determined to beat him.

"Right face!" hallooed I, as loud as I could bawl.

"That's good, that will do. Now try again, 'Halt, left wheel!'"

"Halt, left wheel!" shouted I, with a voice that made the window rattle in its frame.

"Hunt, this man will do," said his lordship, turning to the captain: "he's just the man for us, and you shall have him in your own troop. But look ye, friend," addressing himself to me, "we don't take recruits as sergeants: you must go today and be attached as a private; tomorrow, I will make you a corporal; and the next day, yea shall become a sergeant That's the way we do business here!"

Lord Heathfield was as good as his word. I was but a day and a half a private, ere I became a sergeant in the 20th Light Dragoons.

For about nine months after this I remained in London, recruiting, with some little success, as far as the regiment was concerned, but at a prodigious cost to my own finances. I came to the metropolis with seventy-five pounds in my purse; and my new comrades no sooner ascertained the fact than they made a dead set at it. I had this party to treat, and that party to treat; not once in a way, but continually, till my money melted away, and my indignation became roused at the gross deceits that were practised upon me. At length, when my stock was reduced to about fifteen pounds, I told the captain that I was weary of recruiting, and that I wished to join the regiment. Now it so happened, that this was precisely the step which he was anxious that I should take; for the quarter-master of his troop was very young, and the rest of the non-commissioned officers were without experience. He therefore cordially approved of the determination, and giving me letters to Major Wallace, the commanding officer, and to the adjutant, expressive of his entire approbation of my conduct, he sent me away. I joined the regiment in Guilford, where both officers and men behaved to me with the greatest kindness: and, in spite of perpetual drills, parades, receiving stores, and all the other annoyances which are attendant on the formation of a new corps, I spent my time for a season very pleasantly.

From this date, for the space of perhaps a year and a half, I have nothing to relate, except such incidents as befell in the course of our movements from one cavalry quarter to another. We passed, for example, from Guildford to Northampton, from Northampton to Romford, from Romford to Dorchester, and from Dorchester to Chichester and Southampton, without meeting with any adventure that seems to demand description. It is true that we changed our commanding officer in this interval more than once; for there came a Colonel Taylor from the 7th to supersede Major Wallace, who again was superseded for a brief space by Colonel R. Gillespie. In like manner, Colonel Gillespie, being desirous of joining the 19th in India, effected an exchange with Colonel, now Sir Robert Wilson, under whom the discipline of the regiment was well kept up, without a single appeal to the cat But these are matters with which, as the narrator of my own career, I have comparatively slight concern. Let me, therefore, describe only two circumstances, both of which took place at Dorchester, and then pass on to matters of a more stirring kind; such as are witnessed only by soldiers who have had an opportunity of learning what war really is.

There was in our regiment a man called Fitzgerald, an Irishman of great stature, but quite unfit, from that very circumstance, for a Light Dragoon. He had been enlisted by Lord Heathfield himself as a fugleman, and seldom discharged any other duty than that of orderly to the officer commanding. He was married; received every possible indulgence, was highly esteemed by the colonel, and did pretty much as he liked. When we lay at Dorchester there was a continual complaint among us that some article of our clothing was stolen. Now, a pair of boots, now a pair of leather breeches; now this thing, and now another was missing; and the most provoking part of the business was, that nobody knew what had become of them. At last one of our men, happening to look into a pawnbroker's shop, saw a great coat rolled up en the counter, and recognised the regimental mark upon the cape. He went instantly to the adjutant, who causing a search to be instituted, found a large portion of the articles which had been stolen from the barrack-rooms, in the pawnbroker's possession; and learned from the knight of duplicates, that they all came from the same quarter, namely, from the tallest man in the corps. Fitzgerald was sent for to the orderly-room, and charged with the theft.

"You're mistaken, sir," said he to the adjutant, "I am not the thief, but I know who is, and will fetch him."

"Go, and do so, then," replied the adjutant.

Fitzgerald went, but not a foot did he move to return. On the contrary, he bolted through the barrack-gate, away into the corn-fields, and for some time we saw no more of him.

Fitzgerald was a daring resolute fellow, and having his wife in lodgings in the town, not only did not make off as deserters generally do, but had the hardihood to visit and sometimes to spend the whole night with her. The circumstance was reported to the colonel, who flew into a passion, and directed all the, non-commissioned officers to go with pistols and carbines in pursuit, and to bring him in, dead or alive. There was as nice a hunt through the fields as ever was seen, for the country is open for miles round the town; and Fitzgerald, being warned of the danger, got the start, and long kept it. But he was gradually headed here and there, and driven back towards a wooded avenue, which, like the boulevards of many of our continental towns, begirts the place, where each behind a tree, stood corporals and sergeants without number; most of whom being unwilling to take his life, strove to master him with the butts of their carbines, but were beaten off. At last one, a foreigner like myself, levelled his piece, and exclaimed, "Stop, Fitzgerald, or I'll fire."

"Fire, and be d——d!" was the answer. He did fire; and the ball passing beneath the man's arm, and out through his left breast, killed him on the spot. There was of course an inquest, and a verdict of manslaughter, followed by an imprisonment and trial. But the imprisonment was rendered light by the attentions paid to the captive by his officers, and the jury acquitted him.

The other circumstance was this. When we occupied the barracks at the same place, one of our men got a pass which permitted him to be abroad at roll-call, and to remain as late as twelve o'clock. He went to a public house, drank too freely, and rose to come away in good time; but in his confusion let the pass fall from his hand, and returned to his room without it. Next morning some constables came and took him out of bed, on a charge of robbery. The bank, it appeared, had been broken, into overnight, and this man's pass was found on the counter by the persons who first came to investigate the circumstances. He was committed to prison, as a matter of course, and put upon his trial; but no harm overtook him. It was sworn to that there was barely time for a man to pass from the public-house to the barrack gate in the interval which elapsed between his settling his bill and his admission by the guard; while his comrades all attested that he lay down in a state of intoxication, and never raised his head from the pillow till the constables came for him. Moreover, it appeared on closer examination, that the entry had been effected through an aperture which was incapable of admitting, I do not say the man himself, but his head. On such evidence he was acquitted. Yet his escape was a narrow one; nor could it ever be ascertained by whom his pass had been used in a matter so well calculated to screen the real culprit, and bring an innocent man into trouble.

I pass by the feelings which bowed down the members of the two left squadrons, when after a march to Southampton, they beheld their comrades of the right squadrons embark under Major Butler's orders, for foreign service. They went joyously on board, and we attended them to the pier with band playing, and every other demonstration of respect; but when they were gone, we returned to our barracks like men on whom some slight had been passed; so reluctant were we to separate from our old messmates, and so chagrined at being denied our share in the honour that was before them. Neither need I describe the sort of life which we led at Ipswich, where Lord Paget, now Marquis of Anglesea, commanded a cavalry brigade, and gave them, in fair weather and foul, both early and late, ample occupation. Rather let me hurry on to the moment, on our parts long and anxiously desired, when being commanded by Colonel Wilson, we were marched to Portsmouth, and, after delivering over our horses to persons appointed to receive them, removed on board of ship. Whither we were going nobody knew, and few took the trouble to inquire. It was enough for us to be assured, that now at length there was a prospect of service before us; and though the removal of our horses seemed to point to a distant field of operations, even that anticipation nowise damped our spirits. We gave three hearty cheers to the crowds who thronged the shore to witness our departure, and rejoiced exceedingly, when, the anchors being raised, our squadron moved slowly down Channel.

The armament to which I was now attached, had at its head Admiral Popham and General Sir David Baird; the former in command of the fleet, the latter of the troops. Our first rendezvous was the Cove of Cork, of which it is unnecessary that I should give a description, further than that the wretched appearance of the boatmen and people on shore struck me very much. But I saw little of them, and nothing of their neighbours; for, after a brief sojourn for the purpose of taking in stores, we again weighed anchor, and stood beyond the harbour's mouth, under a gentle breeze, with not fewer than seventy-five sail in company. Neither did our fair wind leave us all the way; to Madeira, where we touched and lay a little space for refreshment; after which we again pursued our voyage, without meeting with any adventure, till the port of St. Salvador lay before us. I soon found that our sojourn here was likely to be protracted a little, for the colonel went on shore avowedly to purchase horses, and both water and fresh provisions were exhausted; I therefore requested, and obtained permission to land; and as the circumstances attending this ramble appear, at least to myself to have some interest, I shall perhaps be pardoned if I shortly describe them.

St Salvador is divided into two towns, the upper and the lower, of which the former stands beautifully on the ridge of a hill; while the latter, full of filth and the fumes of the coarsest tobacco, runs along the margin of the water. There are plenty of convents and monasteries in both, but particularly in the upper town; into the chapel attached to one of which I, with two of my fellow-sergeants, entered. It was the hour of vespers, and the monks all sang, with might and main, the chants peculiar to the day, to which we listened with imperturbable gravity, till one, more corpulent than the rest, came to us, and desired to know whether we were Christians. We said "Yes, of course"; upon which a second question was put, "Whence come ye?"

Now, I had my wits about me, and replied, without hesitation, "From Ireland." That was as it ought to have been. Ireland was indeed a Christian country; and we should get into favour at once, provided it could be shown that we understood what was going on around us. Accordingly, the Abbot (for such he proved to be) opened a mass-book, and requested me to read. I had not forgotten my Latin, but read with each correctness, that the fat man was quite charmed. We were carried into the refectory and feasted on sweet-meats and fruit, well washed down with wine of the best quality; after which we took our leave, and returned to the inn where we had ordered a dinner to be in readiness. Neither did we fail to make the same answer to our host, who was just as inquisitive touching the state of our belief, as the Abbot. Finally, the cloth was laid, the dinner served, and we made ready to begin.

But there is a custom in St Salvador which could not be omitted. At the head of the table, between two lighted tapers, a wooden crucifix was placed, towards which the waiter looked with all possible earnestness while he said grace; and when the meal was ended the same ceremony occurred, with this remarkable addition. Having returned thanks, the waiter took the crucifix and kissed it; he then handed it to us, by whom it was kissed too. And well would it have been, had all who visited St Salvador acted with as much discretion as we did. But we had in our regiment two wild thoughtless officers, one of whom was always followed by a poodle-dog, and he had the great imprudence to apply the crucifix to his dog's mouth instead of kissing it himself, as he had been requested to do. Immediately there was a rising throughout the whole town, the consequences of which these gentlemen escaped only by flight; while the same night, two persons, a sailor and a woman, were murdered; doubtless in revenge of this wanton insult to the people's prejudices.

Having procured about one hundred horses, and recruited our sea-stock, the fleet again weighed anchor, very much to the satisfaction of those on board, between whom and the shore all communication except on duty was prohibited. I did not, however, continue my voyage in the transport which had brought me thus far, for the captain of the *Diomede* 64, having requested the loan of a sergeant to instruct his midshipmen in the broad-sword exercise, Colonel Wilson was good enough to recommend me, and I got a berth in his vessel. While passing in the *Diomede* from St Salvador to the Cape, I witnessed, on a calm day, the loss of two Indiamen, which were wrecked on an island that rises so little above the level of the water, as to be covered whenever the wind blows high. How they got on shore it was difficult to imagine, for the breeze was of the lightest; indeed, so smooth was the sea, that, except three persons, all, both passengers and crew, were saved without difficulty. Nor would these have perished, but for the intemperance of two, and the misguided and fatal avarice of the third. It is well known that Brigadier General York perished because he had so loaded himself with *doubloons*, that falling short in his leap from the ship's bowsprit to the rock, he sank like a stone, and never rose again.

With the exception of this misfortune, and the usual rough sports in crossing the line, there happened nothing in the course of the voyage from St Salvador to Table Bay particularly deserving of notice. Once, indeed, our ship, which formed the rear-guard of the convoy, cleared for action; and the first-lieutenant placed me as captain at one of the guns. But the alarm proved to be groundless, for the strange fleet, which refused to answer our signals, even when we fired into their leader, showed at last the Portuguese colours, very much to our chagrin. Though, therefore, there was much lamentation over bulk-heads knocked away, and sea-stock displaced, no bones were broken; and we steered our course again, only half pleased with the result But our mortification ceased to be remembered, when at length the lofty peak of Table Mount loomed above the waters. For two days we saw these bold heights rising before us, the resemblance to a lion *couchant* becoming hourly more and more distinct as we neared them; and on the third, keeping clear of the Dutch batteries, which vainly sought to annoy us, we steered into Table Bay. There, about mid-channel, in a station which we compelled some fishermen to point out, the admiral took his berth, while round him the convoy, as by ones and twos the vessels got together, dropped anchor, and furled their sails.

CHAPTER 8

Service at the Cape

We were now at the end of our voyage, and had nothing farther to seek than the opportunity of making good our landing, the signal to prepare for which soon floated from the commodore's masthead. Three days' provisions were ordered to be cooked, and all boats to be got in readiness; while armed launches, and such vessels as drew the least water, were moved as near to the beach as seemed compatible with a due regard to their own safety. Meanwhile, the enemy were not idle. Their batteries along shore, both numerous and heavily armed, kept up an incessant fire, particularly upon our reconnoitering frigate the *Leda*, which never seemed to regard such salutations; while large masses of men showed themselves on the heights, as if determined to push us back into the sea. Nevertheless, the boats were manned and filled with troops; and the whole, rowing as close inshore as the heavy surf would allow, there halted. I do not know why this move was made, for nothing came of it; indeed, after the loss of a barge and half a company of grenadiers, the whole of whom went down as soon as the boat upset, we were recalled by signal from the commodore, and returned each corps and troop to its respective vessel.

There had been several councils of war previous to this attempt—they were renewed apparently with fresh spirit as soon as the attempt failed; and it was determined by those in authority to divide the force, by sending a portion, with Brigadier General Beresford at their head, round to Saldana Bay. It chanced that the 29th Light Dragoons formed part of General Beresford's detachment, which put to sea at sunset with a fair wind, and were, at an early hour in the morning, at their place of debarkation. Here very little show of opposition was made. A few Boers, supported by a handful of French troops, rather watched our operations than strove to interrupt them; so that before dark we were all safely on shore, our piquets planted, and our bivouac formed. Yet were we not without our difficulties. The horses, unaccustomed to the sort of food laid in for them at St. Salvador, had fallen into such wretched condition, that they were incapable of doing service; and the guns it was necessary to drag by sheer manual labour over the trackless sands of which the soil of this part of South Africa almost entirely consists. Accordingly, though we began our march next day, our progress was of necessity slow; while our sufferings from heat, and still more through the want of water, proved to be considerable. Still, as the enemy never showed a front, nor, indeed, approached nearer than a day's march of us, we had, as a military body, nothing to do: and we found, on our arrival at Cape Town, that it was already in possession of the English.

The tale of the capture of the Cape of Good Hope has been so often told already, that I may be excused from entering upon the subject now, more especially as the operation presented but few incidents by the description of which a common reader or listener is likely to be attracted. A trifling skirmish opened the gates of the capital to our people; after which General Jansen, unable to maintain himself in the interior, became, with his army, prisoners of war. Neither is it necessary to linger long over the details of my own life, during the few months which I spent in South Africa, One or two anecdotes, such as occur to my recollection at the moment; will probably suffice to fill up what might otherwise be a blank in my narrative; and then we pass on to other and more curious matters, in which it was my fortune to bear a part

The duty in Cape Town resembled in almost every particular the order of service in a common garrison-town in England. Sir

David Baird, being a mighty disciplinarian, had all his infantry-officers at the balance step; and, watch in hand, appeared himself on the drill-ground, regulating their movements as if he had been the adjutant of a regiment. So passed the time from six to seven each morning, after which came regimental and brigade parades, from which the men never retired before nine, and sometimes not for an hour or two later. Meanwhile, in barracks, pipe-laying, heel-balling, and the other amusements peculiar to the soldier in those days, went forward; which were diversified by guard-mountings, field days, roll-calls, and a system of drill, to which there seemed to be no end. It was otherwise with us of the 20th Light Dragoons. Our Colonel, Sir Robert Wilson, gave us as little trouble as possible. We took our pickets, to be sure, and paraded once a day, besides attending faithfully to our stable-duty, and preserving good order; but he never harassed us with work that was not called for; and as to punishments, there were none, because they were not needed. Nay, more—he used to march us two or three times a week, in our stable-dresses, to an elevated plain; about a mile from the town, and there encourage us to play at all sorts of athletic games, himself and his brother-officers taking part in them. This latter proceeding, however, accorded not at all with the rigid notions of the general. Having come upon us one day, while engaged in our sports, he took no notice of the circumstance at the moment, but the very next morning a general order appeared, which left us no leisure for a repetition of the scene. The riding-school was brought into play—we had our parades and drills as well as the rest of them—and were made to feel that, under what is called a smart commander, the English soldier must cease to think of aught except the drudgery of his profession.

While the main body of our force occupied Cape Town, a line of outposts was established about seventy miles in the interior, which were relieved, from time to time, by detachments both of horse and foot, sent up for that purpose. It came to my turn, among others, to be employed on this service; and I found myself, with a captain of my own regiment, a cornet, a lieutenant of artillery, about forty men, and two six-pounders, occupying the house of a wealthy Dutch farmer. Our host was exceedingly civil, particularly to me, who acted as interpreter between him and his guests; and being rich in flocks, and liberal in his ideas, we fared well. We had plenty to eat and drink, excellent stabling for our horses, little or nothing to do in the way of duty, and a good deal of amusement. For example, we all became hunters of wolves, of which we destroyed great numbers; though, at the outset, our acquaintance with these animals had well-nigh proved too intimate. The case was this.

Our host was in the habit of collecting his flock every night, within a large *kraal* or pen, round which his slaves kept fires burning, in order to scare away the wolves. Not being aware of the boldness with which these animals make their attacks, I had gone, with a number of my comrades, to sleep one night among some straw, about fifty yards in front of the *kraal*, for the weather was hot, the rooms were close, and we fancied that we should be more comfortable without doors than within. We made for ourselves excellent nests among the litter, which we drew over us, and were sound asleep, when suddenly a whole troop of animals came rushing along, numbers of which trod upon our chests, heads, and limbs, without, however, doing us any injury. We awoke, of course; and to our great astonishment, heard several shots fired, after which, back came our four-footed visitants, again dashing through our capacious bed without ceremony. This was too much, so we sprang to our feet, and learned, to our amazement, that the *kraal* had been attacked by a pack of wolves, a large portion of which had galloped over us as we lay asleep. Immediately an impulse was given, under which we acted during the remainder of our sojourn, at the outposts. We watched for the wolves night after night, the artillery-officer planting one of his guns so as to give them a salute—and once he fired, and, with the grape with which he had loaded, killed two of them. But the alarm throughout the line, occasioned by that shot, was indescribable. All night long patrols were coming in to ascertain what was the matter; so that our officer was never again tempted to repeat his experiment, which, indeed, was little needed, for we soon found out a more convenient method of dealing with them. There were in our vicinity three wolf-towers—that is to say, circular buildings, hollow in the midst, and about ten feet in height—having a sort of trap-door in each, similar in its construction to those which are used in rat-traps—and a place within where the bait, a rotten sheep, could be fastened. Into these the wolves were tempted every night, the trap-door falling down upon them the moment they touched a particular spring; and in the mornings we used to go, with muskets and carbines, to shoot them from above. We destroyed by these means some hundreds of those mischievous animals.

Our tour of duty being ended, we returned to Cape Town, where matters continued to be managed so as to disgust our commanding-officer, and to our great grief he left us. Before he went away, however, he assembled both officers and men upon parade, and assured us that his first proceeding after he should reach England, would be, to apply for our recall. He then entreated the major, on whom the command would devolve, to act up to the system of internal economy which he had established, and expressed a hope that when we met again, he should find the defaulter's book as little blotted with entries as It was at that moment Colonel Wilson was not yet out of sight of land, ere his parting admonition was forgotten. The officer to whose tender mercies he committed us had been educated in a different school, and he preferred that lessons learned in his youth to those which he had acquired in manhood; so the cat-o'-nine-tails which had fallen among us into entire disuse came immediately into play. I am quite sure, that with all this severity the duty was not better done; and I know that things which used to be accounted an amusement, were now felt as a hardship.

Our only hope thenceforth was that Colonel Wilson would perform his promise, and that we should be recalled from a station which our superiors were determined to make as little agreeable to us as possible. Neither were we disappointed in that hope. The Colonel quitted us on February 18, 1806, and in the month of August in the same year, there arrived two squadrons of the 21st Dragoons, to whom we were commanded to make over our horses. It was a bright day for us in which we obeyed that order, and our imaginations were busy with the delights of England, when a large black ship made her appearance in Table Bay, and our destination was immediately changed.

    I had forgotten to state, that not long after the fall of the Cape, an expedition against Monte Video and Buenos Ayres was planned, and that a force under Brigadier-General Beresford had proceeded with Commodore Popham to attempt the reduction of these places. At first, all went well with them. The enemy opened their gates, and the inhabitants submitted; but by and by, a change for the worse occurred; and the vessel, just alluded to, was the bearer of despatches which announced the imminent danger to which our comrades were exposed. Immediately reinforcements of ships and men were directed to proceed to the Plata; along with which we, being now dismounted, and one squadron of the 21st, to which our horses had been made over, received orders to take our passage.

    Before I enter upon the narrative of our operations on the River Plata, it is necessary that I should guard myself against the risk of being thought to speak in terms otherwise than respectful of Sir David Baird. He was undeniably too much addicted to the harassing system, and sometimes mistook the duties of an adjutant for those of a general: but he was impartial, paid no respect to persons, and never deprived the soldier of his dues. The treasure found at Cape Town (and it was considerable), he divided on the spot between the fleet and the army; and he knew in dealing with individuals how to show mercy, as well as how to be severe. For example, there was one of his orderlies, a corporal of the 20th, who, though a good man on the whole, forgot himself so much at to get twice drunk, in spite of the general's admonitions to the contrary. Now there was no crime which Sir David hated so much as drunkenness, out of which, he was accustomed to say, all other crimes took their rise; and Corporal Marshall, after the second offence, was sent back to the regiment, with directions that he should be tried by a court-martial. The sentence implied, as might be expected, reduction to the ranks, to be followed by corporal punishment. The first of these punishments General Baird permitted our commanding-officer to carry into execution; from the last he desired that the culprit might be excused; and knowing his worth, he took him again into his family, where the man conducted himself ever after with the utmost propriety. He was accordingly restored to his chevrons, and I shall have occasion to speak of him again in the sequel.

I return now to our voyage, which proved to be tempestuous, insomuch that the fleet soon became scattered in all directions, and the ships were compelled to steer their coarse, each independently of its consorts. That in which the 20th Light Dragoons happened to embark, was the first to reach the Plata,—a magnificent riser, in point of width, and so soon as you ascend beyond the influence of the tide, remarkable for the excellence of its water. Of the scenery that adorns its banks—the wide and open plains, bounded afar off by lofty mountains, it is unnecessary that I should speak. When you first enter the mighty stream you see, to be sure, nothing of these things, for the space from shore to shore measures upwards of one hundred miles; but as you draw towards MonteVideo the panorama becomes attractive in the extreme, particularly to persons, who, like ourselves, had suffered much from the effects of a rough sea. We were all therefore deeply interested with the objects around us, though our surprise was a good deal excited, when we found no vessel waiting with orders, nor other signs of our predecessors in the river. But at last, a small King's cutter hove in sight, which signalized us to come under her stern, and communicated to our captain the sad intelligence that General Beresford and his troops were cut off. "I am sorry to say," added the officer who spoke, "that we have not a foot of ground to stand upon; nevertheless, you must continue your course till you reach the admiral's station, where directions will be given as to your future arrangements."

On we went, grievously chagrined by a communication so little expected, till at the close of another day's sail, we beheld the fleet lying at anchor in the middle of the river. Casting our eyes landward, we saw at the same time that the Spanish flag waved upon the battlements of Monte Video; while an occasional shot from the batteries, as a boat or light craft ventured near, gave proof that the garrison, was on the alert. As the commander of the cutter had forewarned us, we were immediately brought to by the admiral, who confirmed the intelligence of General Beresford's defeat, and directed us to take up a convenient berth while our consorts were assembling. We obeyed his orders of course; and during several days our sole occupation consisted in watching the arrival of one straggler after another, and in speculating, as men so circumstanced are apt to do, touching the probable designs of our superiors.

The fleet came in at last, and no accident having occurred to any portion of it, was collected round the admiral's ship in the order by him pointed out. Then followed signals for officers commanding regiments and the heads of departments to attend a council of war, the result of which was, that an attempt ought to be made, first to silence the enemy's batteries which commanded the coast, and then to force a landing. As good luck would have it, too, there had arrived in the *Plata* a three-decker bound from India to England, which the admiral pronouncing unfit to undertake so long a voyage, added to his own squadron, and resolved to employ against the town. Accordingly she moved in support of a flotilla of schooners and ships' launches towards Monte Video, in order to reduce which, several transports had at the same tone been fitted up as bomb-ships. But there was not sufficient depth of water to bring the *Lancaster* within ranges and the rest were too light to do damage to the enemy's works. A couple of hours' useless cannonading sufficed to show that this scheme would not answer; and the battering vessels being recalled, new councils were held, and new determinations arrived at.

The senior officer present with our armament, was lieutenant-Colonel Backhouse, of the 47th regiment; the second in command was Lieutenant-Colonel Vessel of the 38th. Colonel Brownrig acted as quarter-master-general, and was assisted in the adjutant-general's department by Captain Ebrington. By these gentlemen— the whole staff of the army—it was judged expedient to get possession of Maldonado, an open town at some distance below Monte Video, where the troops being delivered from the inconveniences of a long imprisonment on board of ship, might establish a post, and wait for reinforcements. Accordingly at daybreak one morning the fleet weighed anchor; and keeping out of reach, of the guns of a strong fort, which the enemy still held is the middle of the stream, brought up, after a few hours' delay, as near to the bank as possible. Immediately the boats were hoisted out, and the troops having been already prepared for the movement, stepped without confusion into their places, and the disembarkation was effected. For there were no batteries here to harass us, and the ships' launches with carronades in their bows, soon cleared the level strand of the few musketeers that showed themselves; yet were the enemy not unprepared to give us a welcome. About three or four hundred yards from high-water mark, there were some ranges of low sand-hills, behind which, having a couple of field-pieces to support them, the Spaniards were drawn up in force.—Though they did not see this formation, our chiefs suspected that such a thing might be, and they made their dispositions accordingly. The infantry was formed in an echelon line—the grenadiers of the 38th being near the right—the mounted cavalry were in reserve—and we, who had no horses, fell in as light infantry on the left. Two three-pounders dragged by seamen, constituted the whole of our artillery, and considering the difficulties that attended the transport of wheel-carriages through the sand, they were amply sufficient for all purposes.

Such was the order into which we threw ourselves, as soon as the last of our detachments touched the land; and our advance was begun in the highest spirits, and in full confidence of success. Neither did the enemy fire a shot, till the grenadiers on our extreme right had topped the sand-hill, when a volley was thrown in upon them with more murderous effect than I recollect on any other occasion to have witnessed. They fell by sections—almost every man being struck in the head. There was, of course, a momentary confusion, while the survivors recoiled under the ridge, but no serious check occurred. The line formed again, sprang with a rush over the summit, poured in a well-directed fire upon the Spaniards, and overthrew them in a moment. No pause was made, nor time given to rally, for the squadron of the 21st charged home; and a round or two of grape from the three-pounders completed the defeat. We took the cannon and turned them on the fugitives—after which we pursued them into Maldonado, and sweeping from house to house, were in five minutes masters of the town. Then followed a scene of barricading and plunder, such as I have no words to describe. While some ran to fill up the ends of the streets with barrels, cars, and household furniture, others broke into the wine and spirit stores, or ranged through the dwellings of the inhabitants, carrying destruction and terror into all their quarters. For our commandant gave his people three hours' license, and never surely did men make better use of the opportunities afforded them. It was in vain that the officers flew from cellar to cellar, knocking in the heads of casks and pouring out the contents into the street. The soldiers, if they could not get at liquor elsewhere, dropped their canteens into the kennel and were soon in a state which set all subordination and discipline at defiance. It was well for us that the Spaniards did not think of returning to the attack. If they had done so, we should have been cut to pieces, almost without resistance.

Maldonado, though not a fortified town, was a military station—that is to say, there was a barrack there—a gloomy pile, having all its windows secured with iron bars and surrounded by a lofty wall. Into that building we thrust our prisoners, of whom a large number had fallen into our hands, and there kept them till an opportunity offered of sending them on board the fleet.

Meanwhile the few among our own people who were fit for duty, took the outposts, and the rest slept where they had fallen down—some in houses, some in the streets, but all in a state of helpless intoxication. Under such circumstances, the night was, to those in command, an anxious one. But with the morrow came such threats from head-quarters, as, assisted by the provost and his guard, restored order; and the men betook themselves to the work of fortifying and rendering the post tenable. Moreover, the walls of the houses were posted with proclamations inviting the inhabitants to return home, and assuring them, in the common style of such documents, that the English were not come as conquerors but as friends. Still the work of pillage, though covertly carried on, could not be entirely suppressed; and I plead guilty in my own person, of having committed one outrage upon property.

 I have no taste for drinking, and never had. Like other soldiers I enjoyed my glass when it came in the way; but such scenes as were enacted in Maldonado on the present occasion always filled me with horror and disgust. While others were marauding in crowds I accordingly kept quiet; but no sooner was discipline restored than I determined to see whether the wholesale plunderers had left any gleanings behind such as might satisfy my moderate desires. With this view I sallied forth one day from the barrack, into which we were by this time marched, and stealing along by the backs of the houses so as to elude the notice of the provost, I entered a deserted mansion, and began to look about. It was thoroughly ransacked, the furniture was all broken, and every thing of value apparently removed; indeed I saw but one article on the ground floor, a small square table which was entire. I struck my fist upon it, and heard something rattle. This induced me to feel about for the handle of some drawer; but I could discover nothing of the kind, so I turned it upside down, and jumped upon it. The bottom of the drawer gave way, and I beheld a dozen silver-handled knives and forks, of which I took immediate possession, and wrapping them up in my pocket-handkerchief, stuffed them into my bosom, and mounted the stairs. Again, the spectacle that met my eyes was of the most melancholy kind, for the progress of the spoiler was every where visible; yet I again ascertained that my predecessors had left their work incomplete, and my hopes were a second time excited. There was a small door in the wall of one of the bed-rooms which seemed to have escaped notice, for it was closed, and resisted all my efforts to open it. "Now," thought I, "suppose the *Padrone* should have kept his money-chest here. It is exactly the sort of place for a safe"—and money and jewels, it may be necessary to add, were the only species of property which I coveted. Full of this idea I looked about till I discovered a shovel in one of the cellars, with which I attacked the door, now pressing it from below, now forcing my weapon through the narrow side slit, till at last it flew open. I sprang forward and found myself in a well-furnished dressing-closet — in the wardrobes surrounding which were both ladies' and gentlemen's apparel, made after the newest fashion, and of the most costly materials. But I did not want coats or silk gowns, so I looked farther and beheld two trunks, both of them locked, standing at the opposite extremity. Into them, with the help of my friendly shovel, I seen made my way, and was again disappointed to perceive that they, too, were filled with articles of dress. Shirts of the finest linen, chemises flounced with lace, silk stockings, silk handkerchiefs, and ladies' shoes—these made up the lading of the boxes—while here and there I came upon a petticoat of the richest brocade, and a robe of which I could scarce estimate the value.

I gazed long and eagerly on my treasure, lamenting only the absence of means for securing it entire; and pondering within myself what selection to make out of so much that was tempting. At last, after packing up a petticoat or two, I found them too bulky, and was forced to content myself with a dozen shirts, as many shifts, some silk stockings and handkerchiefs. Of these I made a bundle, with which, under my arm, I loitered about till it grew dark, and then stole quietly back, throwing all my eyes about me, to the barrack. I was fortunate enough to reach my quarters unobserved, and soon won the hearts of the women of the regiment, by distributing among them the chemises and silk stockings. The shirts and handkerchiefs I of course kept to myself, and for many years afterwards I continued to wear them, whenever it was my wish to appear in female society to the best advantage.

Chapter 9

I Strike a Few Blows

Such was the routine of our existence, for some time in Maldonado. The provost going continually about with a drummer and guard, he soon became the only successful marauder in the place; for he was a wise man in his generation, and knew how to thrive upon the execution of the laws. His mode of proceeding was this. If he caught a poor devil laden with booty, he eased him of his burden forthwith, tied him up and gave him five and twenty lashes; an amount which he was never known to exceed, unless the culprit proved refractory. For after the twenty-fifth had been applied, his humanity always got the better of his sense of justice, and he would say, "Now be off, I have not seen you, nor have you seen me." Of course the tortured wretch was too happy to fall into these terms, so he departed with the comfortable conviction on his mind, that he had acted as jackal to the man in office, and helped him to make his fortune.

There had been great waste of the necessaries of life when we first entered the town; and a scarcity of provisions began in consequence to be felt. From the fleet, moreover, our supplies came in both irregularly and in small quantities; for there, too, both food and rum began to run short Under such circumstances, inquiries were instituted which led to the intelligence that numerous herds of cattle grazed over the plains in the interior: and spies being hired, it was resolved to send out an armed party, for the purpose of collecting and driving a herd of them in.

To accomplish this object one hundred infantry and fifty horse were ordered to parade at ten o'clock at night, and to march under the guidance of a trusty emissary whither soever he might lead them. They went, and returned next day with upwards of twenty bullocks; a very acceptable booty both to soldiers and seamen, to which, night after night, further additions were made. Horses, too, were by such means got together, in sufficient numbers to mount all the dragoons, while occasionally a mill was surprised, and its contents of flour brought to head-quarters. I was more than once employed on these services; but as nothing extraordinary befell, except twice, I shall content myself with describing those excursions only out of which something like an adventure arose.

Our stock of fresh meat was getting very low, and the enemy, warned by our frequent forays, had driven their cattle to a distance; when on Christmas eve, 1806, Colonel Backhouse heard from one of his agents, that at a particular point, not far from the water-side, though deeper into the interior than we had yet ventured, a drove of some hundreds of bullocks was penned up. He determined, to get possession of these if he could, and the ordinary force, a hundred infantry, and fifty troopers, were directed to parade, at the usual hour, for bullock-hunting. We moved off in high spirits; and with videttes thrown out and other precautions taken, penetrated, without meeting with the smallest opposition, to the point indicated by our guide. We reached it about three o'clock in the morning, and saw, sure enough, between, two and three hundred cattle, with some valuable horses, gathered within a pen. To drive off the keepers, open the pen, and turn the animals' heads towards Maldonado was the work of a minute; and after a short halt to refresh both men and animals, we began our homeward march. But we had not proceeded far, when the day being fully broke, we saw the wide plain through which we were moving, covered with scattered bands of horsemen, who began sounding their cow-horns with all their might, and riding in a direction parallel to that which we with our plunder were pursuing. Of course we pricked up our ears, and moved like men prepared for battle, till suddenly the yelling of cow-horns ceased; and the natives, putting each a finger in his mouth, sent forth a loud and peculiar cry, which the cattle appeared to understand as fully as we did our own language. Up went the tail of each particular bullock straight on end, and away they galloped immediately, one taking this direction, another that, till the whole herd had dispersed to the various points of the compass. Then was there riding and running amongst us—some laughing, others swearing, but all equally failing to head the brutes or keep them in their places; till suddenly there opened upon us, right and left, in front and in rear, a terrible fire of musketry. The Spaniards, it appeared, had laid for us an *ambuscade*, into which our precipitancy hurried us, and nothing now remained but to leave the cattle to themselves and fight our way back to Maldonado But the odds against us were too great. After losing several of our men and an officer—the latter shot through the heart—we were driven back to the water's edge and there surrounded. Some tall rocks that lay within low-water mark afforded some cover to the infantry, while the cavalry had nothing for it but to skirmish at every disadvantage. It was a providential matter that the tide was out, otherwise no exertion of valour could have saved us; and that the Spaniards held us in too much respect, to press us back from our hazardous position.

We maintained the fight as we best could, charging from time to time when an opportunity offered, and then retreating again, so as to be in some degree protected by the fire of the infantry, when the officer who commanded, seeing the impossibility of forcing his way through, sent off three dragoons, one after another, at intervals of five minutes, along the edge of the water towards head-quarters. Happily for themselves, none of them were cut off, though the arrival of one was all on which we ventured to count; and Colonel Backhouse lost not a moment in getting his people under arms, with the whole of whom, a slight garrison being left to defend the works, he hastened to our relief. But the Spaniards did not wait his coming—they retreated on the first appearance of his scouts, and left us at liberty to march back, not a little mortified at the result of an excursion from which we had hoped to derive so much profit.

The second expedition which I have undertaken to describe was somewhat similar to the above, except that the issue of the two by no means corresponded. It fell out thus:—

About sixteen miles from Maldonado, though, like it, but a short way removed from the river, stands the city of San Carlos, an open town, but a place of some importance, being the residence of a bishop, and the capital of the surrounding district It was determined to lay San Carlos under requisition, and to threaten the inhabitants with a hostile visit, unless they supplied us with a certain quantity of cattle. To convey this message the accustomed force was sent out, Colonel Brownrig and Captain Ebrington both being of the party, the latter of whom, by the way, seldom failed to be present whenever any thing like ran or fighting was likely to take place. We arrived as usual, at an early hour in the morning, within a mile and a half of our point; where the party being assembled, a flag of truce was sent in, and the pleasure of the English general explained. No great time elapsed ere the bishop in full canonicals, followed by all the clergy of the place, came out to salute us. They brought with them multitudes of country people loaded with bread, cheese, and wine, and having explained that they could not at that moment furnish the cattle required, they promised, if the party would return on a stated day, that all would be prepared for them. As it was our policy to conciliate rather than overawe, the excuses of the bishop were accepted, and Colonel Brownrig having permitted us to eat and drink of what the San Carlos people supplied, our trumpets sounded to horse, and we withdrew.

By-and-by the day came round at which we had engaged to retire, and it was again my fortune to form one of the intended escort It seemed, also, that though nowise distrusting the bishop, Colonel Brownrig was willing to provide against accidents; for in addition to his infantry and cavalry, he took with him on this occasion, a lieutenant's party of artillery and a couple of six-pounders. As it had happened to us before, so it befell now, we arrived within a mile and a half of San Carlos without opposition; and were scarcely halted, when the bishop and his clergy, without waiting to be sent for, came out to salute us. We planted our videttes and sentries of course, on small eminences at a little distance from the road, after which we dismounted, and bridle in hand, began to eat and drink and be merry—but no cattle came. The bishop was questioned; he expressed his surprise, but assured us that they could not be far distant; nevertheless, as it might be inconvenient for us to wait, he would go and hurry their movements. He went accordingly, with his clerical attendants; after which the country people began one by one to pack up their stores, and slink away. "This is odd," said Captain Ebrington to Colonel Brownrig, "I don't know what to make of it." But scarcely were the words out of his mouth ere the mystery received its solution. First one vidette, then another, held up his helmet in his hand, fired his carbine, and came galloping to the rear; while the infantry who communicated with them, though more withdrawn, followed the example. Now the trumpets and bugles rang out to mount and fall-in ; and never was greater need; for at the distance of perhaps a quarter of a mile, about five hundred horse made their appearance, pushing towards us at full speed, and in excellent order.

"What shall we do?" cried one.

"Do this," replied Brownrig, soon recovering his composure. "You take the cavalry, Blake, and meet them, and charge right through. I will form the infantry and guns on the flanks, and see whether they don't get the worst of it."

It was no sooner said than done. There was no firing no throwing out of skirmishers, but in a trice, draw swords, and at them. Through and through we rode, hacking and cutting and receiving in our turn some hard blows; one of which divided the chain that guarded my horse's head-stall, while two others wounded him in the neck. But we gave much more than we got. Corporal Marshall, to whom I alluded some time ago, engaged the Spanish commandant hand to hand; and, cutting clean through his left wrist with one blow, lent him another on his right temple, which divided the head into portions. The rest of us were levelling over men, when suddenly the bugles sounded the retreat, and we wheeled round. This was done to get us clear from the range of the infantry and guns, both of which were now in position, and eager to take part in the fray. Seldom have grape and musketry told with greater effect than the first volley. In three seconds the Spaniards were rolling one upon another, or scattered like sheep over the plain; and we, having recovered our order, took good care that they should not rally.

The victory was complete, and the loss on our side comparatively trifling; but our commanders were not the sort of men to be content with this. "We'll burn the town about their ears!" was Colonel Brownrig's first exclamation after he got his people together: and he kept his word. We marched to the place, set it on fire in several quarters, and, having helped ourselves to such valuables as could be easily removed, withdrew. We brought back such of our own wounded as could bear the jolting of cars, left the rest, with all the Spaniards, under the care of an English surgeon; and, carrying back a good many prisoners, returned to Maldonado.

The enemy had by this time assembled in great force, and our situation was becoming, day by day, more critical. Provisions were scarce; for the stores in the fleet ran short, and our bullock hunts were now for the most part unproductive; nay, something like apprehension was experienced for the safety of the town; when, to our indescribable joy, a British fleet made its appearance in the offing. Succours, we concluded, were come at length, and all our difficulties were at an end. We had not deceived ourselves in this anticipation. The same evening, about four or five o'clock, Sir Samuel Achmuty landed, and, by his frank and generous bearing, gave an earnest of the kind treatment which we ever afterwards received at his kinds. He caused us to be paraded in our stable and foraging dresses—expressed his high admiration of our conduct—inquired into our wants—and assured us that it would be his business to make us comfortable. He kept his promise; for that very night a supply of rum, which we had not seen for a long while back, reached us—and in the course of the day following, so many men, both horse and foot, joined us, that we believed ourselves capable of going where we liked, and accomplishing any service on which we might be directed. I cannot particularize the infantry regiments which accompanied Sir Samuel; though I remember that the 95th Rifle corps was one of them; but to support us there were the 9th and 7th Light Dragoons, all dismounted. For some of these we speedily provided horses, and Brigadier-General Lumley taking the command, appeared anxious to enter at once upon a wider and more enterprising system of warfare than we had heretofore pursued.

The very night of the day in which the reinforcements landed, our Brigadier informed us that he should push the outposts far beyond their former stations. He accordingly paraded us an hour or two later than usual; and carrying us in the dark far ahead of our old land-marks, told us to keep a sharp lookout, inasmuch as we should probably have something to do. It was a night of incessant and heavy rain; thundering and lightning with all the violence peculiar to the climate of the Plata River; and the darkness was such, that, alter every flash, you could not see the length of your horse's head before you. We had no cover, for our post was the open plain; and fires it would have been imprudent to kindle; consequently we either crouched under our horses' bellies, or, wrapping ourselves up in our cloaks, came to the philosophical determination of getting thoroughly wet, yet not complaining. We were so circumstanced when Captain Du'Cane, being the officer on duty, proposed to me to carry out the relief, and said he would go with me. The exercise would hinder our horses from getting stiff; and, as far as we ourselves were concerned, we should be just as comfortable in front as in rear. I assented at once, and we took the field; but not a vidette could we discern; so we kept circling and circling, hour after hour, to no purpose. We dared not shout, for the enemy were close at hand: it was impossible that we could have mistaken our line, for that was straight enough: what then could the matter be? The return of light satisfied us on this head. We had passed clear through, not only our own chain, but that of the Spaniards; and were now riding backwards and forwards about a hundred and fifty yards in rear of their sentries, and within less than half that distance, from one of their pickets. There was some staring on both sides, but little disposition to parley on ours; we clapped spurs to our jaded animals, and rode off; yet we should have been probably overtaken, had not our videttes observed our danger, and made signs to the picket to advance. The enemy did not desire a fight, so we escaped.

The whole army was now assembled, and the general, after well weighing the matter, came to the conclusion that our position was a false one, and ought to be changed. The post to be attacked was Monte Video; and the more remote the scene of our operations, the greater would, of course, be the obstacles which a numerous, if not an enterprising enemy, would be able to throw in our way. He therefore determined to embark his troops, and to effect a landing at some point within a single march of the town. With this view we were instructed to evacuate Maldonado without beat of drum; and so judicious were the arrangements of those by whom the plan was concocted, that every man and horse returned on board of ship ere the Spaniards were made aware of our intentions. Some little delay occurred after the embarkation, but it was not great; and then the fleet, raising its anchors, steered with a light breeze for a place called Brest Florence, about eight miles from Monte Video. We reached our new anchorage in the morning, and the very same hour the boats were hoisted out The consequence was, that altogether unopposed, and without inconvenience or the loss of life, the troops lay that night upon the downs and sand-hills that close in the Plata in this direction.

All night long the boats of the fleet were in motion; and guns, stores, ammunition, and all the materiel of an army were landed in abundance. An hour before dawn, moreover, we stood, according to custom, in our places; but, as the day broke, we received very satisfactory proof that the Spaniards had not been idle; for a formidable array of infantry, cavalry, and artillery, was already in our front They were drawn up on some heights about a couple of miles in the interior, and formed, with their wings thrown forward, three sides of a square; while their cannon, dragged by bullocks, were so disposed as to bring a cross fire on every point by which we might be expected to approach them. Sir Samuel examined their array carefully for a minute, and then ordered the advance, which our troops obeyed with the alacrity which English soldiers always exhibit when about to be led into action.

Our dragoons were not yet entirely mounted. The squadron of the 30th, with the 21st, and such of the 9th and 17th, as landed, had horses; and a portion of them, including our troop, were directed to move forward: but we were not well handled. The officer in command led us to the brow of an eminence, just within point-blank shot of the enemy's artillery, and there, finding that they had got the range, he halted. Several men and horses were killed and wounded in consequence, and more would have suffered had not Sir Samuel rode up. He rebuked our commandant in good round terms, desired him to move down into the hollow, and keep his wits about him, as he would be needed very shortly. The old man was yet speaking, when a shot took his horse in the hip, and knocked the leg to shivers. Of course, Sir Samuel fell to the ground as if slain; and his staff (all of whom were with us prodigious favourites) crowded round him, to ascertain whether he was hurt "There's nothing the matter," said the gallant old soldier; "I'm not hurt in the least. Just help to get me from under this horse; and John," calling to his groom, " fetch my charger." It was done in a moment; and I need scarcely add, that the perfect unconcern of our brave chief was not without its effect on the courage of his followers, For, no sooner was he on his legs, than he gave us some work to perform. "Charge that gun, and that, and that," said he, "they will annoy the infantry as they come up." On we rushed at a gallop; and sabring the cannoneers, was in possession of three pieces ere another shot had been fired. Meanwhile, the rest of the troops were advancing to the attack with all the regularity and precision of a field-day. The 95th, spreading through the sand-hills opened the ball; other regiments followed in column; and the enemy's wings being driven in upon his centre, a scene of fearful confusion ensued. They fled in all directions, our people marching after them, as fast as was consistent with the preservation of their ranks.

We pursued them that day under the very guns of Monte Video, and halted merely because the city gates were shut So close, however, were we to the walls, that we could distinguish the muzzles of the enemy's cannon, from which, it is greatly to be wondered at, that we met with no annoyance. For we stood till it grew dusk within light field-piece range, yet not a shot was fired. We then fell back to an advantageous position, about a couple of miles to the rear; whence, after stationing our outposts, and making other necessary arrangements, we entered on the business of a siege.

CHAPTER 10

The War & My Own Adventures

Monte Video, of which our object was to recover possession, is justly said to form the key of the Plata; its harbour being by far the most commodious throughout the coarse of that river; and its fortifications possessing strength enough to hold out against any sudden or ill-arranged attack. At the period of our arrival under its walls, the government of the town rested with Admiral Leniers, who had served on board the Spanish fleet at the battle of Trafalgar, and was accounted an able and determined officer. I do not know the exact strength of the garrison, which was, however, numerous; and remembering its recent triumph over General Beresford and his brigade, was inspired with the most resolute spirit; while outside the ditch was an army of observation, which was by us considered to amount to full thirty thousand men. In carrying our estimate to this height, it is not impossible that we may have been mistaken. But however this may be, it is certain that, to conduct the siege, and at the same time hold the enemy's field-force in check, required all the daring and other soldier-like qualities of a British army that scarcely exceeded five thousand combatants.

For several days after the battle, the troops were employed in throwing up batteries, unto which the seamen from the fleet cheerfully lent their assistance in dragging the guns. The fire of the place, however, proved so far superior to any thing that we could bring against it, that there seemed to be but a slender prospect of effecting a breach—till an artificial mound was occupied within musket-shot of one of the bastions, and a battery for six pieces established under its cover. The mound in question had, it appeared, been raised by the natives, as a sort of butt or embankment to catch the balls which they might fire at a target; and now it was converted, by our engineers, into a blind, from the rear of which the town might be bombarded. Of these matters, however, it becomes me to speak with caution. As a cavalry soldier I had no share either in the labours or the honours of the siege—my duty requiring me to watch that my comrades were not attacked when they least expected it by the enemy in the field.

It was at this stage in the blockade that the enemy hazarded a sortie, to themselves eminently disastrous, to us, as a mere spectacle, peculiarly shocking. We had heard, all night long, the noise of mirth and revelry within the town; and, not long after dawn, beheld a sally-port near the water's side thrown open, and a prodigious crowd of men, all of them mounted, pour forth. When I speak of a sortie, let me not be misunderstood. Never was there such a scene of confusion—for the men were all drunk—and they rode, some horses, some mules, and some asses, and, totally free from restraint, as if there had been no officer among them, they pushed towards our lines. Poor devils! they were mowed down by hundreds; for some of our gun-boats had concealed themselves under a sand-hill, so as at once to be protected from the guns of the town, and themselves to command this road; and they threw in such a ceaseless shower of round grape and canister, that the carnage was dreadful. Those who did arrive within range of our infantry fire were all cut to pieces. The road was thus literally heaped with slain, insomuch that, if one-half escaped within the gate to speak of the result of the movement, the multitude that came out must have been prodigious.

Meanwhile we who were not employed in the trenches at in working parties, had plenty to do at the outposts. We were on duty almost every other night, and the Spaniards being very numerous, presented so bold a front, that our utmost vigilance was required to hold them in check. There was one picket in particular, at which on several occasions I found myself, where they proved singularly active. It was a deserted farm-house, with a sort of *kraal* or pen about two hundred yards in front of it—a square enclosure composed of the trunks of felled trees, and of considerable dimensions. The post in question was a sergeant's picket, having an officer's guard on each flank of it—from one of which, indeed, commanded by a captain—it was but a detachment I had held it several times without meeting with any adventure, and had begun to question the fact of its peculiar difficulty, when the fool-hardiness of a thoughtless trooper brought on a crisis, which might have been attended with very serious consequences.

The battery at the target mound had done its work so well that a breach was at length effected, and the enemy having rejected the terms that were offered for capitulation, the whole army knew that the hour of assault could not be far distant I took the command of the perilous picket, on the morning of the day which we guessed would usher in the storm; because the slow firing both then and afterwards seemed to indicate, that, to keep the chasm clear of workmen, was all that was on our side desired. Moreover, it was communicated to us when marching off, that an unusual degree of vigilance would be necessary, inasmuch as there was reason to suspect an attempt on the part of the Spaniards to raise the siege. Thus warned, I went to my post fully alive to the delicacy of my situation; and so anxious was I that no accident should occur, that I had the only light, which it was esteemed prudent to burn within the house, shut up in a remote closet. One of my men, however, entertained ideas on this head widely different from my own, for scarcely was my back turned to visit the videttes after the night had set in, than he brought forth my candle, lighted about a dozen more, and distributed them through the house. The consequences were not slow in displaying themselves. The enemy, creeping forward into the *kraal*, opened a fire of musketry upon the picket, the first effect of which was to kill the sentinel, whose post lay nearest to the log fence. An alarm immediately spread throughout the line. For myself I hurried back, caused every light to be extinguished, and making my men mount, drew them up in such a position, as that they were clear from the line of fire; at the same that they were ready to act with effect, should an effort be made to bring on a closer encounter. But after a useless fusilade, which was soon put a stop to, when a few of our men dismounting, stole with their carbines up to the *kraal,* the fire ceased, and the officers on the right and left, who had hurried to the spot, returned with easy minds to their own stations.

About an hour elapsed after silence was restored, and we were thinking of a return to the picket-house, when an orderly from the rear came up with directions that the outposts should fall back. Silently and cautiously we drew in our videttes, and formed by threes in a column, after which, giving the word in a half whisper, I put my men in motion. We soon fell in with and joined ourselves to the captain's picket, upon which other detachments in like manner rallied; and then all, at a slow pace, moved in a direction to cover the target-mound battery. Neither were we long left in doubt as to the object of this movement The infantry were already under arms to assail the breach, and it was our duty, as well as the duty of their own reserves, to guard the rear.

It was still dark when we reached our halting-ground, an elevation just sufficiently exalted to give us a complete view of the fort of Monte Video, which was about to be assaulted. There was no moon, but the stars were out in thousands; while from time to time the enemy, as if in anticipation of what was going to happen, caused a splendid illumination of the breach, and the glacis beyond it, by a discharge of blue lights. Except the bursting of these fire-balls, however, there was no sound to break in upon the stillness of the night: for our batteries were mute, and those in the town, doubtless reserved their fire, till living objects should be presented at which to diced them. Not long, however, was this state of things permitted to continue. There was a murmuring sound, as of men rising from the earth—then followed the measured tread of feet—and by-and-by the face of the town next us seemed to be on fire, with an incessant discharge of musketry and cannon. It is impossible by any language to convey an adequate representation of the scene on which I then gazed, or to describe my own feelings, or those of my comrades, as in breathless silence we waited for the event. Minutes grew into hours, hours into ages, as the assailants pressed on to the breach; now gaining, now losing, as, we feared, their ground, while their shouts mingling with the roar of fire-arms, sounded awfully. But while we thus held our breath, events were going on in a different quarter, of which we knew nothing. The 40th regiment, led on by Colonel Brown, having been directed to threaten an escalade, converted the false attack into a real one; and gaining the ramparts almost unopposed, pushed forward to the assistance of their comrades on the breach. Then could be distinguished the yell of the victors rising above every other sound; while the light of burning houses made manifest the columns of red-jackets moving down into the streets. Yet was the victory far from being secured. Every street in the place was barricaded and each barricade sustained one gun or more, the discharges from which cut down whole sections, and was not without difficulty silenced.

As I took no active part in this assault, I must now attempt to describe it Let it suffice to state that the action was very gallantry sustained; but that the indomitable courage of the English prevailing over every obstacle, the enemy at last laid down their arms, and the town was taken. The citadel, to be sure, still held out and a powerful force was in our rear; which, had it advanced during the progress of the assault, ought to have destroyed us. But there was no disposition on the part of the enemy to risk another battle, and the Governor conscious of his incapability to hold out, cared not to keep the citadel after the town had fallen. The consequence was, that by noon next day a white flag was hoisted, and Monte Video, with its harbour, works, and shipping, passed once more under the power of the English. In speaking of the shipping, I must indeed make one exception; for there was a French frigate in the roads whose commander would not submit On the contrary, having loaded his guns, he set fire to a train that communicated with his powder magazine, and the ship blew up with a crash which shook the ground like an earth-quake.

There occurred little during a space of some weeks, which were spent by us peaceably in Monte Video, of which it is necessary to take in this place any particular notice. The government was carried on under Sir Samuel Achmuty, with a mixture of vigour and mildness, which at once insured the safety and won the respect of the natives; while the troops enjoyed as much of leisure as was consistent with a regard to their own security and a maintenance of a proper discipline. A single act of perhaps necessary severity was indeed perpetrated in the place. I know not how far any discovery might have been effected of treasonable practices in contemplation; but there came forth one morning an order that every house in the city should be searched for arms, and that all weapons, as well swords and daggers, muskets and pistols, should be removed on board of ship. I shall never forget the store of superbly mounted arms that search brought to light. Fowling-pieces inlaid with gold and silver, pistols mounted in the most costly manner, swords and daggers having gold or silver handles, and in some instances, scabbards of the same material were gathered together in heaps, and transferred to the admiral's ship. There was of course a good deal of murmuring among the parties thus deprived of their weapon, many of which had been valued as heirlooms in the families of the owners; but the measure was, doubtless, dictated by a regard to self-preservation, otherwise, by a chief so humane and considerate, it never would have been enforced.

While the bulk of the army lay in Monte Video itself, or encamped in the vicinity, the outposts, both of horse and foot, were pushed forward in the direction of Buenos Ayres; the main body of the advanced guard occupying the town of Los Pedros; while the patrols extended from Canalon in a sort of semicircle as far as St. Joseph. It so happened that the squadron to which I was attached took up its quarters in Canalon, a town or large village, in which is a handsome church, with several houses that were occupied by families of wealth and consideration in the province. Nothing could exceed the degree of comfort which we enjoyed at this station. Before us, and on every side, the country was open and level, so that the approach of an enemy could be distinguished at any time; while his columns were yet some miles distant and as to provisions, there was a risk that our men would injure their health by eating to excess. For the vast pampas which spread around were covered with herds of cattle, the owners of which took so little account of them that they slaughtered them by the score, for the sake of the sake of the hides and tallow. Of course an army, thrown into such a position, could not fail to fare well; indeed the work of frying, and stewing, and roasting, and eating, went on so perpetually, that we came in the end almost to loathe fresh beef, no matter how disguised in the dressing. Neither were vegetable, and especially onions, wanting. In short, with a regular allowance of wine served out to us, and more to be had for purchase, and the choicest morsels taken day by day from a whole carcass we not only never knew what hunger was, but became profuse in our expenditure of victuals; regular working parties being required to remove and bury the remains of animals which we could not consume after we had slaughtered them.

I was by this time promoted to the duty of serjeant-major; consequently, I neither mounted picket, nor had to look after the internal economy of my troop. My business, indeed, was over as soon as the reports were collected,, and I had a great deal of time at command. Nor did it make the slightest difference in my situation, whether we lay, as at first we did, under canvass, or occupied, as was by and by considered expedient to do, quarters in the village itself. I was free to go where I chose, and do what I liked, so soon as parades were ended and states given in; and having been always of an inquisitive temper, it was not very long before my search after novelty brought me into a peculiar and most interesting situation. Let the truth be spoken—I was weary of beef, and longed to diversify my food; and I went forth one day on a cruise, of which it was the object to find either some new milk, or a *gallinea*, or fowl of any description. I had, of course, a haversack on my back—for your haversack is of most capacious swallow; and all things, living or dead, that find their way within its jaws settle down, and are turned to account. Forth, then, I sallied, one morning, thus equipped; and having been often struck by the height and extent of a wall which surrounded, as I supposed, the domain of some wealthy *hidalgo*, I turned my steps in that direction, and looked anxiously about for some means of ingress. I was fortunate enough at last to discover a low door, which proved, on trial, to be only on the latch, and which, opening to the pressure of my hand, admitted me at once within the sanctuary. I looked round, and saw a magnificent lawn, interspersed here and there with numerous flower-beds, about which clumps of trees of every description were collected with the greatest taste, Moreover, the mansion which adjoined to these pleasure-grounds was on this side very striking. Like almost all other houses in the province of La Plata, it stood but one story from the ground; but a handsome colonnade gave a finish to its architecture, and a grand flight of marble steps led up to the glass doors by which it was entered.

I was gazing with much admiration on the whole scene, not, I confess, without a hope that for my haversack some store might be discovered, when an elderly lady, well dressed, according to the fashion of the country, came forth and made me a low curtsey. I returned the salute as in duty bound, upon which she advanced towards me, and in a tone of great civility requested to be informed whether I was in search of any thing. I was not much of a Spaniard then—yet I understood enough of the language to assure her, that an idle curiosity had alone tempted me to intrude, and that the extreme beauty of the place must be my excuse for all that followed. She immediately begged me to come in, and offered to conduct me all over the grounds, after I had refreshed myself The invitation was a great deal too agreeable to be declined, so I followed her into a snug parlour, where sweet cakes, dried fruits, and some excellent wine were soon served up.

Having partaken sparingly of her good things, the lady became again my conductor, and led me into another room, where, upon a sort of bed lay an elderly man measuring at least six feet six inches in length, and of a solidity that was fearful to look upon. He laboured then, and had laboured for some years, under a dropsy, which had swollen him to a size that was quite portentous, and rendered him so helpless, that, when moved at all, he was lifted by means of a crane from his couch and placed in a sitting posture, in a huge arm-chair. The *hidalgo* informed me that he was the owner of the mansion, and that he had several sons and daughters, though they were all resident in Buenos Ayres, and engaged me in a conversation, which to him, at least, proved so agreeable, that I was pressed to return and dine with him at five o'clock, This invitation, also, like that originally given by his Seigniory, I did not think it necessary to decline; so I took my leave, with a promise that I would be punctual to the time appointed.

I returned to dine with my two friends, and found two guests besides myself—a young gentleman about sixteen or seventeen years of age, and an elderly lady. The evening passed pleasantly enough, for if I could not converse much I had an excellent appetite, and the viands served up were greatly to my mind. Moreover, if to me the day's adventure had proved acceptable, there were others who seemed to be at least as well pleased with it Not only my dropsical host and his wife, but the youth became greatly attached to me, and insisted that I should accompany him to his mother's house, and be introduced to her and to his sister. I went accordingly next day, and out of that introduction events, to me, of no trivial moment arose.

The young man who thus pressed his friendship upon me, was called Antonio de Mendoza. His father was dead, and he lived with his mother and sister, in one of the best houses in Canalon. They were wealthy people, and very much respected; for I found constantly at the table the rector of the parish, the vicar, the *alcalde*, and all the principal dignitaries of the place. Every around them, likewise, bore testimony to the independence of their condition. They had a numerous retinue of slaves. Their table was both bountiful and elegant, and all their habits were those of persons who have enough and to spare, without being obliged to labour. Their hospitality, too, especially towards myself, was boundless. I could not be with them too much; I could not accept their invitations too frequently; nay, young Antonio seemed determined that I should live with them altogether; for if I was not in his mother's house, he was sure to be with me; indeed, there were times, when, but for his great gentleness and the devotion which he expressed towards me, I should have felt his presence as a restraint, for not even at stable-hour could I shake him off. Nevertheless, the lounge was, to me, an exceedingly agreeable one; though, by and by, the acquaintance took a shape, which put me to uncommon embarrassment and difficulties.

I have stated that besides the mother and son there was a daughter in the house. Donna Maria Eusepha de Mendoza, a beautiful creature, about eighteen years of age, and very highly accomplished. She played the harpsichord and sang sweetly; she was singularly winning and gentle in her manners, and altogether appeared to take so much delight in my company, that it would have been extraordinary had I proved insensible to her merits. For it was one of her chief amusements to teach me the Spanish language, not only in conversation, but by writing; and as I copied her lessons and gained from day to day an increased command of the idioms, her joy seemed to enlarge itself. Moreover, the gentlemen who frequented her mother's table appeared to encourage her in her predilection for me, a circumstance which may, perhaps, be in part attributed to the following cause.

The Spaniards had no love for the English. They despised them as unbelievers, and hated them as robbers and plunderers. Now I was not an Englishman, and the first time I was questioned respecting the place of my birth, I had tell the truth—nay more. I communicated to the priests a great deal of information as to the geographical position and ancient history of the Rhenish provinces; which being new to them, set them on the search, among all the books which they could command, for a confirmation or contradiction of my statements. I was not aware of this fact till one day at dinner, the rector produced a volume and a chart, the former of which bore me out in all that I had told him, while on the latter be was able to trace the situation of each town. From that hour, I was in his eyes, and in the eyes of others who took their cue from him, every thing that was excellent. The Germans were a noble people, great things had been done by them; they were a trustworthy people, they were superior to all other people in Europe. In a word, priests and ladies, the *alcalde* and notary public all became my friends, and all expressed their desire to see me happy and respected.

Things went on thus for some time, Maria and I taking our walks together in the garden, and the old lady praying when we came in that all the saints in the calendar would bless us. Still we had dealt as yet only in general expressions, for though I admired the girl and liked her ways, I was not in love; though at each successive visit, the tone of my friends became more confidential, and at last the truth came out. The old lady proposed that I should marry her daughter, and quit the English service. She told me that one of her brothers commanded a regiment of cavalry in Buenos Ayres, in which her eldest son was a captain; and that if I would wed Maria, and flee with her to the capital, she would undertake to get me a commission in the same corps. I treated the proposal half in jest and half in earnest, expressing my great admiration of her daughter, but objecting to her proposition, my own poverty, and the risk which I should run if I deserted. My poverty she scouted. They had abundance of wealth; more than I should require all the days of my life, and as to being taken, that was impossible. For as soon as the ceremony was over, there would be guides to escort and carry us off, and all the pursuers in the world could never overtake us. I smiled, shook my head, and said I would consider of it; and for that day the subject was dropped.

From this time forth, and during several weeks, I was continually assailed, not only by the mother but by the priests, by Antonio, and even by Maria herself, to make her my wife —The confidence which they reposed in me, too, was wonderful; for not only was Maria with me alone at all hours, and in all places, but of their very riches they made a display to me. I thank God that I never wronged the girl, nor polluted myself by accepting a bribe, though the temptations to both offences were very great, as may be seen by the following statement. One morning the old lady and I had as usual been arguing the point of the marriage, and I again made the objection of my own poverty; asking her, how both she and I would feel should I, a stranger in Buenos Ayres, fail to find employment, and prove incapable of supporting Maria in the style to which she was accustomed?

"Come with me," replied the old lady; "you seem to doubt that we have money enough for your purposes as well as our own. Come with me and be convinced. I would not treat an Englishman so, but with a German, and especially with you, I feel that I am safe."

So saying, she led me into a back parlour, in the floor of which was a trap-door, on descending a stair from which, I found myself in a large cellar, well-stocked with the wines of every country and almost every vintage. The old lady carried a lamp, by the light of which I observed two ponderous iron chests, each of which was fastened by three locks. The largest of these she opened first, and its contents were, services of massive silver plate, dishes, candlesticks, plates, coffee-pots, spoons, forks, knives, every thing in short, that could be required to set out a table for half a hundred persons. She then opened the other; and I saw in one corner a pile of *doubloons*, on the other side heaps of dollars, and the intermediate space occupied with vessels of pure gold.

"Now," said the old lady, "put in your hands, and take as many of the *doubloons* as you can lift."

"No," said I, "you have treated me as your friend and guest; I cannot and will not rob you of your property."

She pressed me very much; but I continued firm, and we returned to the rooms above. The rest of that day I spent as usual with my friends, and retired at night to my own quarters; not without some serious misgivings as to the wisdom of the determination at which I had arrived touching the proffered alliance.

CHAPTER 11

Good Luck & Bad

I soon learned that the old lady had communicated to the priests the result of our visit to the cellar; and if I had been in favour with them before, I became now more a favourite than ever. To me, as often as I met them at table, all the conversation was addressed; nor did there seem to be any end to the questions relative to the English church, and the English army. Respecting the former, I gave the family all the information which I myself possessed; respecting the latter, I was much more reserved; for I did not know what use they might make of my statements, so I made them as vague and general as could be. Still they continued to treat me with a degree of kindness which became, at times, somewhat oppressive; and excited in me an apprehension lest my officers should suspect me of holding improper intercourse with the enemy. From Donna Maria, however, I never received aught except proofs of the most confiding tenderness. She too spoke to me about my religion; and I so far complied with her wishes as to accompany her every Sunday to church. But when she alluded to our marriage, I always treated the subject as a joke, even while I professed to hold her image in my heart. I remember one event, occurring about this time, which amused me at the moment, and has often caused me to smile since.

One of the first inquiries of my kind friends, after I made their acquaintance, was touching my name, which I gave them; and which they, according to the pronunciation of the country, called Norberto. *Signor* Norberto soon became every thing with them, especially with Maria, who appeared to find some positive pleasure in pronouncing the words. Now it came to pass one evening, that while I was strolling with her as usual in the garden, she said, with one of her most charming smiles, that I must grant her one request. I promised compliance, of course, provided compliance were possible, and she began.

"You know, Norberto, that the rainy season is at hand, and that it will be necessary very soon to accomplish our flight to Buenos Ayres, lest the rain stop us. One thing, however, must be done, ere we join our fates. You must make some present to the Virgin, and she will take us for ever under her protection."

I laughed, and expressed my perfect readiness to make the Virgin a present, provided she would tell me what was likely to prove acceptable; for the Virgin could not make use of money, and I had nothing else to give.

"Oh yes, you have," answered Maria, "there is the silver tassel on your cap; it will just do to form a fringe for the Virgin's petticoat."

It may be necessary to observe, that in a sort of sanctuary within the house, was an altar, on which stood various saints; and among others the Virgin, and a male saint who was nameless. The tassel, too, of which the Virgin had become covetous, had just so much of a history attached to it, as requires explanation. It was not a regimental tassel, but an ornament for my helmet, which I had recently purchased of the quarter-master at the cost of three pounds, and still held, because it was quite new, in high estimation. My gallantry was thus put to a severe test, for on the one hand I had no wish to part with my finery; on the other I did not know how to refuse my *enamorata*. As invariably happens in such cases, the lady's will prevailed. I put my helmet into her hand; she stripped it of its rich trimming, and carrying me along with her, hung it up, garland-wise, before the Virgin.

But this was not all. So delighted was the old lady with my pious offering, that she called her nameless saint after me; and there he probably stands, to this hour, with a perpetual lamp burning beside him, and a scroll beneath, on which are inscribed the words, "Saint Norberto."

Surrounded by such delights, and worked upon perpetually by such allurements, I should have been something more or less than human if I had not so far wavered in my duty, as to spend many a sleepless hour at night in weighing the advantages against the disadvantages of the course of proceeding which my Spanish friends suggested. As to the hazard of being retaken, that I well knew was a mere bugbear. Disguised in the dress of a Spanish gentleman, and attended by a skilful guide, I could have easily given my comrades the slip, and laughed at their efforts to follow, but there were other points to be considered as well as that. In the first place my own heart rebelled against the thought of committing an act of such treachery. A deserter is a character which we Germans hold in contempt; and I could not endure the idea of incurring even self-condemnation. In the next place, suppose I were to marry this girl,—if the English succeeded in conquering the country, where was I? if they failed, I must become an exile to the land of my birth for ever.

On the other hand, there was the sure prospect of at least an independence; and probably of promotion in the Spanish army; while Maria herself, though as I have already stated, by no means the queen of my soul, was just such a person as it was impossible to associate with, without becoming aware that she possessed strong claims upon your regard. When I acknowledge, therefore, that my firmness sometimes threatened to give way, I shall not, I trust, lay myself open to any very grave charge; for never has man prayed more earnestly than I did then, that Providence would in some way or another release me from my difficulties.

Such was my condition up to passion-week, in 1807, exposed every day to temptations which it required all my philosophy to resist, and sometimes tempted to quarrel with philosophy, because it refused to be overcome. The arrival of the bishop in our village, and the performance of all the ceremonies which in Roman Catholic countries give effect to the season, in no way relieved me. I was still a constant guest at Signora de Mendoza's table; and I acquired more favour both in her eyes and in the eyes of her ghostly counsellors, because I commanded the firing party, which our commanding officer lent them, to assist in the celebration of high mass. But that which bishops and priests could not effect, a movement in advance by the enemy's army promised to accomplish. Rumours began to be circulated that our post would soon be attacked, and the coming up from the rear of about three hundred infantry, gave to them a confirmation. Neither had we been misled. At an early hour one morning, about two thousand Spanish Horse showed themselves in front of the videttes, and driving them in, forced back the piquets also towards the village, in front of which we were drawn up, with our guns unlimbered and our infantry supporting us.

The skirmish which ensued is not worth describing, for it produced no results. As long as we were content to play at long bowls the enemy sustained their fire; but no sooner did we make a motion to charge either with cavalry or infantry, than they broke and fled in all directions. Thus, for about two hours we continued to annoy one another, they striving to outflank us, and we constantly driving them away, till at last they retreated, very little loss having been sustained on either side. They had, I believe, one or two killed, and perhaps half a dozen wounded; whereas our casualties amounted to no more than two men hurt. Nevertheless, the reconnaissance (for such it was) indicated among them a degree of activity which they had not heretofore displayed; and Sir Samuel Achmuty judged it expedient to make some changes in his dispositions.

We had resumed our old habits, and I was, as before, in constant communication with the Mendozas, when I found one night, on my return to my quarters, that the route was come, and that we were to proceed at dawn for St. Joseph, distant two full days' march from Canalon. Never was route better timed than this for me; for it left no leisure for discussion over night, and gave scarce a moment when daylight appeared to say farewell; indeed the promise of a speedy return was yet upon my lips when the trumpets sounded, and I tore myself from Maria's embrace. I never saw either her or her hospitable dwelling afterwards; but not till my dying day will her amiable qualities be forgotten; or the confidence which the whole family, herself included, reposed in my honour, cease to be remembered with gratitude. From Antonio, however, I was not yet destined to shake myself free. So strong was the youth's attachment, that he mounted his horse and accompanied me all the way to St. Joseph, introducing me, at each halting place, to the gentlemen of the country, and obtaining for me the kindest treatment.

We had been relieved at Canalon by a portion of the 17th, we relieved a portion of the 17th at St. Joseph; and passed our time, for several weeks, agreeably enough; having no enemy to harass us, and very little duty to perform. The confidence which is produced by the absence of danger is not, however, unapt to degenerate into carelessness; and by two of our officers a mistake was committed at St. Joseph, which caused some trouble to the whole detachment, and to me was the source of much suffering. These gentlemen, one of whom was the doctor, were in the habit of riding every day, to an *estantia*, or settlement, considerably in advance of our videttes, and amusing themselves in the society of the farmers' daughters. It happened on a certain occasion that they lingered too long with their *Dulcineas*; whose father had given notice to his countrymen of what was going forward; and that they found themselves, when about to depart, surrounded by an armed force, and made prisoners.

To march them off on the road to Buenos Ayres was of course the duty of the captors, while the farmer prudently resolved to guard against the danger of punishment, by reporting the accident at head-quarters, so soon the captives and their guards should have had a sufficient start. It was, therefore, profoundly dark when he arrived in St. Joseph, with intelligence of the misfortune that had occurred. The rain came down in torrents; nevertheless, the trumpets sounded to horse; and all the cavalry supported by a body of riflemen, were sent in pursuit.

I had the rear guard that night, and as you could not see your horse's head before you, I strove to preserve my communication with the main body by means of a file of men and a corporal. Neither did any accident befall for some time. There was no road of course—there are indeed very few roads in that, country—but we had guides who led us over the wet turf and through a rapid, but narrow river towards a farm-house, where our spies told us that the fugitives might be expected to pass the night. I followed with my rear-guard as far as the stream, safely enough, and crossed it; but somehow or other I there lost the track. Being ignorant of my mistake, I rode on, keeping a few paces ahead of my men, till, all at once, my horse's feet slipped from beneath him, and we went rolling one over another into a gravel-pit. It was well for me that the soil chanced to be a soft sand; for I fell flat to the ground, and my horse getting his hind and fore legs entangled in the bridle-rein, lay, heels upward, with the pommel of the saddle right across my chest. He could not move an inch, neither could I, so there was nothing for it but to cry aloud, and warn my comrades of their danger. They pulled up, threw themselves to the ground, moved about and about till they discovered a means of descending, and extricating the horse from his awkward position, get both him and his rider free. I shook myself, and found that no bones were broken, upon which I mounted again, and we resumed our march, as well as the pitchy darkness of the night, and an incessant fall of the heaviest rain, would permit. But I need scarcely add, we did not recover our officers—the enemy were by far too active for that—therefore, we halted at the house till the light of day came back, and retraced our steps, chopfallen and weary, to St Joseph's.

From the effects of my fall, and the severe wetting that accompanied it, I did not recover for months. I grew stiff and cramped—the sinews of my back and legs shrank, and I was in excruciating agony. It was, therefore, necessary to send me to the rear; and the medical attendants at Los Pedros being none of the best, no progress was made towards my recovery. Under such circumstances, the captain of my troop, to whose kindness I was at all times much indebted, advised me to return to Monte Video, and to put myself under the care of the staff-officers, by whom the business of the general hospital was carried on. I took his advice, but no good came of it. I was still bent double, and every effort to raise myself upright put me to the sharpest torture. There seemed, therefore, no other resource, than to pass muster among other invalids, and to embark for England. But the gentleman at the head of our medical department, though he gave me my choice, advised me not to take this step.

"Trust yourself to me," said he, after he had stripped and examined me somewhat roughly, "I'll cure you if any body can;" and he was as good as his word. By the use of hot baths, and bleeding, and starving, he reduced me to a shadow, but gave me back the use of my limbs, and as much vigour of mind and body as ever. He told me to thank him for a cure, which the neglect of ship-board would have rendered impossible; and as I did so at the moment, so I continue to do still.

I had no part in the fatal attack upon Buenos Ayres. While I lay in the hospital at Monte Video, General Whitelock arrived, and signalized his coming, by turning Sir Samuel Achmuty most unceremoniously out of his quarters. I was scarcely convalescent when he came back from the interior, a defeated and a humbled man. He was said to be a harsh officer,—he was unquestionably an unfortunate one, and the only time I saw him, his expression of face denoted that he was very unhappy. As far as I was concerned, however, his appearance on the stage had no other effect than to restore me sooner than might otherwise have taken place, to the delights of home. For, on the sixth of September, I being again fit for duty, the whole army embarked, and on the seventh our fleet weighed anchor to abandon the Plata. I need not dwell upon the homeward passage, with its varieties of calm and storm, cloud and sunshine. Enough is done when I state, that after separating from the convoy and being in imminent danger of foundering, the ship in which I sailed, together with a single consort, reached the Channel; that we, going round by the back of the Isle of Wight, arrived safely in Portsmouth harbour, whereas, our companions preferring the Needles, were wrecked; and that the two squadrons of the 20th, now reduced to a skeleton, proceeded for the purpose of being recruited and reorganized, to Guilford Barracks.

Before I pass from this subject to other and more stirring narrations, I may be permitted, perhaps, to say a few words concerning some of the habits and customs, to which, in South America, I was a witness.

The climate, in the provinces of the river Plata, is, perhaps, one of the most agreeable in the world. Not even in the dog-days are you oppressed by excessive heat, for there is always a breeze that blows from the eastward, or else, when the rain has allayed it for awhile, there comes a thunder-storm, of which the immediate effect is to clear the atmosphere and moderate the temperature. Moreover, there are no mountains to intercept the current of air, nor forests to condense and accumulate vapours. In winter, likewise, the cold is seldom so severe as to produce even a coat of the thinnest ice, and, as for rain, that falls from time to time heavily enough, but the proportion of moist to dry weather is quite inconsiderable. Indeed, it is one of the gravest grounds of complaint against the government of Old Spain, that by the excessive short-sightedness of its system, this, which might have been rendered one of the most fruitful regions of the earth, was, when I sojourned there, utterly barren, except in cattle.

I found upon inquiry, that not only were neither grapes nor olives cultivated there, but that there were public functionaries, whose business it was to prevent the growth of these useful plants, and to discourage the manufacture both of wine and oil. I learned, too, that for their very wheat the people of the Plata Provinces were indebted to Old Spain; that their fruit came chiefly from the same quarter, and that all their manufactured goods, if not of Spanish growth, paid an enormous tax on their transit through Cadiz. Had it not been for the extraordinary fertility of their cattle, indeed, their condition would have been deplorable enough. But these, wandering over the extensive pampas, increased so rapidly that nobody could guess from year to year of how many he might be possessed; while the abundance of food which was thereby at the command of all classes, tended not a little to foster and increase the constitutional indolence by which all seemed to be affected. A native of the district through which the Plata flows, would not on any account whatever, subject himself to personal labour or fatigue. If he has to pass from door to door, he always does so on horseback; and so admirable is the training of their active steeds, that some of them will stand for four-and-twenty hours on the same spot, provided the rider take the precaution to draw his bridle over the animal's head, and cast it on the ground.

The manner in which these South Americans catch the wild cattle by means of the lasso, is well known. There are, however, certain seasons of the year, when this process, which is pursued only when a bull or cow is wanted for a particular purpose, would not suffice, and then a different device is resorted to. When the period approaches at which their hides must be prepared for export, the Argentines (for so the people call themselves), drive enormous herds of cattle within *kraals* or enclosures, which, being surrounded by strong palisades, have an opening at one side of sufficient width to permit the passage of one beast, and only one at a time. This re palisaded in on both sides, and cut off from the rest of the *kraal* by a sort of portcullis, while above it is a stage, on which stands a man armed with a sharp knife, and well skilled by practice in the use of it. As soon as the *kraal* is filled, they raise the portcullis. One bullock passes into the covered way, and the portcullis falls behind him, while almost at the same moment the *toreador*, stationed above, thrusts his weapon into the animal's spine, and kills him on the spot. The carcass is immediately dragged off by horses, skinned, and left to cumber the earth, till perhaps some hundreds are disposed of, and the complement of hides procured; for of the carcasses no account is, on such occasions, taken. They become a prey to the birds of the air and the beasts of the field—creatures of almost every description, as well domestic as wild, scenting out the banquet, and repairing to it in troops.

The sheep in this country are not good, but the horses are excellent, particularly those of Chile, which the people very highly esteem. They are almost all jet-black, and very beautiful. As to the furniture, I need not describe it Long bridle-reins richly inlaid with silver, large silver stirrups, saddles with very high peaks and croups, and gorgeous bead-stalls—all these indicate both the wealth of the rider and the estimation in which he holds his steed; while enormous spurs and bits of the severest kind, imply that he is prepared, in case of a controversy, to support his own views, by arguments which few horses can resist.

The people of La Plata are, after their own fashion, prodigious gastronomists. Their favourite dish, and an exceedingly delicious one it is, consists of a portion of the rump of an ox, roasted, or rather baked, in the hide, which is fastened round the morsel with such excellent care, that not a drop of the gravy escapes. The beef of the country is, in general, excellent, far surpassing in flavour, if not in fatness, our stall-fed oxen. But the portions of it that are dressed in this manner would gladden the heart of the most conservative alderman, either in London or elsewhere.

There is not much smoking among the ladies of the Plata river, who, on the contrary, consume their leisure time in sipping a beverage called *Maté*, or the essence of the Paraguay herb. It resembles, when prepared for use, chopped hay, and they prepare it in little cups, made of cocoa-nut shells, mounted generally in silver, and covered by a lid, much as we do our tea, by pouring boiling water over it. Their mode of drinking it, is this:—A small silver pipe is introduced, something like a cigar-tube, through which they suck up as much as they may require, and then they pass it from hand to hand to be dealt with in the same manner by their friends. It is curious enough that the people, who are thus free with the pipe, which they use in consuming their *Maté*, should be particularly tenacious of your touching with your mouth an. other vessel out of which they drink in common. This is a glass decanter with a crooked pipe, which contains wine or lemonade, and out of which they pour the liquor into their mouths, holding the tube two or three inches above their lips. The stranger who unwittingly applies the tube to his mouth, is regarded as a boor, and the tube itself is immediately broken off.

CHAPTER 12

I Go to Portugal

There occurred nothing during our stay at Guilford, nor, indeed, for some time afterwards, of which it is worth while to take particular notice. Recruits came in rapidly; and in training these, and breaking young horses, and discharging the common duties of home-service, some months passed away. We changed our quarters, to be sure, more than once—moving from Guilford to Colchester, and from Colchester to Southampton; but neither our marches to and fro, nor our halts, whether of longer or shorter duration, produced one adventure of sufficient importance to remain upon my memory. At last, however, in the month of July, 1808, there came an order that we should hold ourselves in readiness for foreign service; and we soon afterwards marched to Portsmouth, where the two squadrons embarked, together with some infantry and artillery, on board of ships that lay ready to receive them.

We sailed with sealed orders, as far as the Cove of Cork, whence an expedition, under the command of Sir Arthur Wellesley, was preparing to set out, nobody knew whither. There we lay about a fortnight, at the termination of which period a magnificent squadron put to sea, amid the cheers of the troops, the playing of bands, and in a state of weather which held out every promise of an agreeable voyage. Neither did dame Fortune play us false in this respect, for no storms overtook us, nor were we compelled; either by negligence or accident, to separate, even for a moment, from our consorts. Still we were all in doubt as to our place of destination, till a signal from the commodore's ship directed us to steer for Mondego Bay, where in due time the fleet was assembled. Here, then, it was evident enough that our campaigning would begin; and never could men be in better heart to enter upon it, than we were at the moment.

The shores of Mondego Bay are open and shelving, so as to produce, when the winds blow fresh, a heavy surf; and it so happened that we brought with us to our anchorage just enough of a breeze to render the task of disembarkation a difficult one. Several boats were upset, and out of the infantry corps which landed first, some men were lost, though I believe that the casualties were not numerous. But for us, we suffered nothing. We were directed to stand upright in the boats, with bridle in hand, and prepared, in case of any accident, to spring into the saddle; a judicious precaution, which proved in two or three instances eminently useful. One punt capsized upon the surf; but no lives were lost, because the horses sometimes swimming, sometimes wading, carried their riders ashore. We then formed upon the beach, and carrying each man his three days' provisions, ready cooked, pushed forward to a village, the name of which I have forgotten, and there took up our quarters.

It is well known that the disembarkation of the army, with the arrangement of the commissariat and other measures requisite to put it in motion, occupied the space between the 1st of August and the evening of the 8th. On the 9th we marched to Lyria, where, on the 11th, the main body joined us; and on the 13th, the whole were as far on the road to Lisbon as Batalhah. There had been some firing in front more than once, though nothing to excite alarm; especially at a village called Brilos, where our riflemen sustained some loss. But it was not till we reached Obidos, if I recollect right, on the 15th, that we saw anything of the enemy; nor, indeed, had we any sharp controversy with them then. They were in possession of the town when we arrived in front of it, and presented a countenance so formidable, as to excite in us the expectation of a stout resistance; but they did not think fit to make a stand. As we drew on, they fell back, and we found ourselves, almost without the expenditure of a shot, masters of the place. Nevertheless, the struggle, though deferred for a few hours, was close at hand; and on the 17th, as every reader of history is aware, the battle of Roliça was fought.

Though it is not my business to detail the movements of the armies, nor to advert to subjects that have by better authorities been amply discussed already, yet I shall probably succeed in carrying the reader's attention along with me, if I endeavour to record such events as made the deepest impression upon my own mind at the moment, as well as to describe what passed under my own immediate eye, both in the enemy's presence and elsewhere. In the first place, then, it is necessary to state, that from a very early period after our landing, detachments of Portuguese cavalry came in, by fours and fives, to join us; some led on by an officer, others acting, as it seemed, under their own guidance. They were remarkably fine-looking men; Well clothed, well armed, and well mounted, and composed, as they informed us, a portion of the Lisbon Police—the most efficient cavalry force in the kingdom. These the general attached to our two squadrons; and so strong was the friendship which soon arose among us, that our officers were never without the company of the Portuguese officers, nor our men separated from their men, either at meals or during the hours of relaxation. On the morning of the 17th, we had about two troops, or one squadron, in the camp; and their appearance was such as to make us well pleased with the addition which they made to our otherwise feeble force. In the next place, I am compelled To admit, that we had no share whatever in the glories of Roliça. The enemy, occupying a position on the ridge of some steep heights, could not be approached, except by infantry, and we stood, in consequence, in a valley, watching the advance of our comrades, whose onset was as cool and determined as the most anxious could have wished. Forward they went, in long narrow columns, forcing their way among rocks and underwood, and suffering severely by a heavy fire, to which their order prevented them from making any effectual return; till, having won the crest of the hill, they wheeled into line and carried all before them. It was a magnificent spectacle, the general effect of which was much heightened by the peculiar beauty of the day—for the sun shone bright, and till the roar of cannon and musketry dispelled it, the silence was profound.

We had watched the progress of the battle for some time, without sustaining any injury, except from a single shell, which, bursting over our column, sent a fragment through the backbone of a troop-horse, and killed him on the spot—when a cry arose, "The cavalry to the front!" and we pushed up a sort of hollowed road towards the top of the ridge before us. Though driven from their first position, the enemy, it appeared, had rallied, and showing a line both of horse and foot, were preparing to renew the fight. Now, our cavalry were altogether incapable of coping with that of the French; and the fact became abundantly manifest, so soon as our leading files gained the brow of the hill—for the slope of a rising ground opposite was covered with them in such numbers, as to render any attempt to charge, on our parts, utterly ridiculous. Accordingly, we were directed to form up, file by file, as each emerged from the road—not in two ranks, as is usually done both on parade and in action—but in rank entire. Moreover, we were so placed, that the French officers could not possibly tell what was behind us; and thus made a show which appeared to startle them; for they soon began to change their dispositions, the infantry moving off first, the cavalry following: upon which we likewise broke again into column of threes, and rode slowly after them. But we had no desire to overtake them, They therefore pursued their march unmolested, except by a few discharges of cannon; and we, after seeing them fairly under way, halted on the field of battle.

We passed that night, the infantry in bivouac, the cavalry in the village of Zambugeira, without the occurrence of any adventure; and on the 18th marched to a place called Lourinha, where more of the Lisbon Police joined us. The 19th carried us into the position of Vimiero, and reinforced us by a division of infantry under Brigadier General Anstruther. As I have my own tale to tell of the operations at this place, it may be permitted me to preface it by such a description of the ground, as may assist the reader in comprehending the narrative which is about to be submitted to him.

The English army took up its ground upon two ranges of hills, between which was a valley, having the village of Vimiero close under a rising eminence, on the top of which was a windmill. A rivulet, called the Maceira, ran round one of these heights, and passing to the rear of our camp, fell into the sea. Our position was a good one, for it commanded a full view of every road by which an enemy could approach; and though extensive, seemed, at least to my unpractised eye, very capable of defence. Here, then, we lay, the infantry communicating, from brigade to brigade, along the banks and ridges—the artillery and cavalry in the valley—while the pickets, under General Fane, took post on the slope of the ascent, and faced the roads to Torres Vedras and Lisbon. It is worthy of remark that General Fane, by whom the advanced guard was commanded, pitched his tent in front of the cavalry outposts, so that between him and the enemy, should a sudden attack be made, there was no other force than the videttes.

I was ordered for picket on the evening of the 20th, and repairing to my post, found the general mounted, and ready to lead us forth on a reconnoitering expedition. His object was to make us thoroughly acquainted with the localities in our front; so that, in pushing our patrols at night from point to point, we should incur no risk of falling into error. Accordingly, he carried the whole of the picket along with him, including Lieutenant Burgoyne in command, and conducted us along the road for about two miles, till we reached a chapel, made of bright red brick, and thence called by us familiarly the Red Chapel. Here he halted us for a few minutes, and pointing out that we could thence command a full view of the sloping plain beneath, he told us that our patrols ought on no account to venture further. Nevertheless, as it was yet broad day, he determined to push on to a village about half a mile in advance, and ascertain from the inhabitants whether they had received any intelligence of the enemy's movements.

We followed General Fane, of course, and descending into the plain, moved on in a compact body, till we reached a point where three roads meet. We separated here, and passing, some by one flank, others by another, and a third party in the centre, we swept round the village, and ascertained that it was deserted. One man alone, indeed, continued to occupy his dwelling, and he was an innkeeper, from whom we received a slight refreshment of food and wine; after which we rode back again. The general now dismissed us to our duty, and retiring himself within his tent, we saw for awhile no more of him. Neither was any alarm given, nor the slightest stir made, till about ten o'clock, when the first patrol was ordered to mount, and go forth in quest of intelligence. It was my business, as senior sergeant, to take the command of this patrol—and I have never ceased to look back upon the circumstance as one of the most fortunate in my military life.

The patrol, consisting of twelve men and a corporal, besides myself, mounted and took the road as soon as I had received my instructions. These were, to move very slowly to the front, keeping every eye and ear on the alert, till we should reach the Red Chapel—not to engage an enemy's patrol, should we fall in with one—to hasten back to the picket on the first appearance of danger—and on no account to trust ourselves beyond the limits which General Fane had marked out. Thus instructed I ordered the men to march; and, as far as silence and an acute observation could go, we obeyed the officer's directions to the letter. Nor, indeed, would it have been easy, on such a night, and when so occupied, to indulge in idle or ribald conversation. The moon shone full and bright, millions of stars were abroad, and the silence was so profound, that the very ripple of the stream could be heard as it wound its tortuous way along the base of the hill down the slope of which we were riding. Moreover, the perfumes that hung upon the quiet night air were exquisite. Extensive groves of myrtle and orange trees, scattered here and there over the plain, loaded the atmosphere with fragrant scents, which we inhaled with a satisfaction that was certainly not diminished because of their novelty. In a word, I do not recollect having ever been abroad at a season more perfectly delicious, or of performing a duty which partook so much of the character of a pleasurable excursion; for nothing occurred even to startle us. The world seemed asleep; and we reached the Red Chapel, fully assured that no enemy was or could be within many miles of us.

At the Red Chapel we halted, quitted our horses, and, holding the bridles over our arms, applied ourselves to the contents of our haversacks and canteens. We entered, as was natural, into conversation; and seeing the village distinctly at our feet, I proposed that, in spite of the general's warning to the contrary, we should pay it a visit. I was the more ready to make this suggestion, from recollecting that on the other side flowed the stream, which must be crossed by a wooden bridge, ere any one from Torres Vedras could enter the place. My men, as I expected, cheerfully fell in with the proposition; so we again mounted, and taking every possible precaution, by sending forward a corporal and a file of troopers to feel the way, we pushed on. At the meeting of the roads the advanced file had pulled up, and once more we were all together; when I directed two men to pass to the right, two to the left, and, with the main body under my own command, I kept the centre. We were to meet in the square or open apace round which the village was built, and to communicate each to the other the results of our investigations.

Every thing was done with the most perfect regularity. My party, having the shortest distance to travel, was the first to reach the village square, though the detachments were not long after us; and we found, on comparing notes, that the same tranquillity had prevailed here which had prevailed elsewhere. Now, then, what should we do? I recollected the innkeeper, and thinking it not impossible that he might have acquired more information since General Fane had examined him, I rode to his house, and asked whether all was quiet?

"I am glad you have come," replied the *padrone*; "for I have some important news to tell you. My young man came home from Lisbon an hour ago, and passed the whole of the French army on its march; and so close are they by this time, that I expect them in the village in less than half an hour."

I questioned him very closely as to the degree of dependence that might be placed on this report, and he assured me that there could be no mistake in it; adding his advice that I would return to the English camp without delay, and put the general on his guard. I did not think that it would be prudent to neglect the recommendation, so I stated to my comrades how matters stood, and we evacuated the village.

It was not our policy, however, to return to the camp with a vague rumour. We were inclined to believe the innkeeper, certainly, yet we wished to have his tale confirmed; so I halted the patrol as soon as we regained the Red Chapel, and determined to wait the event. I knew that the advance of the enemy, if it did occur, would be made known to us clearly enough by the clatter of their horses' hoofs when crossing the wooden bridge, by which alone they could enter the village: and being now within my prescribed limits, and having a good half-mile start of all pursuers, the thought of danger never crossed my mind. Accordingly, after planting a couple of videttes somewhat lower on the slope, in such a situation that they could not be surprised, I directed the remainder to alight, and to keep their ears open. For awhile all was still. Not a breeze moved the branches; not a beast or bird uttered a cry; indeed, the only sound distinguishable was the running water, which came upon us most musically. But by and by "a change came over the spirit of our dream." Wheels began to rumble; there was a dead heavy noise, like the tread of many feet over a soft soil; and then, the wooden bridge rang again with the iron hoofs of horses. Immediately the videttes fell back, according to my orders, to report what they had heard, and to learn from us that we had heard it also; and then, after waiting a sufficient time, to leave no doubt upon our minds as to the formidable extent of the column that was moving, we vaulted into our saddles, and returned at a brisk trot towards the picket.

There was much challenging, of course, as we drew towards the videttes, and demanding and giving the countersign, for we rode briskly; and whether we came as friends or foes, our people knew that there must be something in the wind. Our protracted absence, too, had greatly alarmed them; and General Fane himself, irritated by the state of suspense in which he had been kept, was at hand to bid us welcome. He opened upon me with a volley of abuse, such as I had rarely listened to before; and charged me with all sorts of military crimes, not the least prominent of which was stupidity. I permitted him to exhaust both his breath and his anger, and then told my tale. The effect was magical—I was now every thing that was excellent; I was a true soldier, and deserved to be rewarded. It was necessary, moreover, that Sir Arthur should be informed of a discovery so important, and there was no person so well qualified to convey this information as myself. Accordingly, General Fane desired me to ride immediately to headquarter-house, with the situation of which I was well acquainted, and to tell my story as I had told it to him, circumstantially and fully.

Colonel Napier, in the first volume of his *History*, has stated, that, "About 12 o'clock, Sir Arthur was aroused by a German officer of dragoons, who galloped into the camp, and, with some consternation, reported that Junot, at the head of twenty thousand men, was coming on to the attack, and distant but one hour's march!" It was no German officer, but a German sergeant of dragoons, who made this, report; and, begging Colonel Napier's pardon, there was no consternation whatever in the manner of him who made it. The facts of the case, indeed, are these. I rode to the house where the general dwelt, and being admitted, I found him, with a large staff, all of them seated on a long table in the hall, back to back, and swinging their legs to and fro, like men on whose minds not the shadow of anxiety rested. Moreover, the general, himself not only saw no consternation in my manner, but closely examined me as to the details of my adventure, and told me that I had done my duty well. He then desired me to go below, and get something to eat and drink from his servant; which I did, though not till I had heard him give his orders, in a calm, clear, and cheerful voice. They were in substance these: "Now, gentlemen, go to your stations; but let there be no noise made—no sounding of bugles or beating of drums. Get your men quietly under arms, and desire all the outposts to be on the alert." This latter admonition, it is just to add, I had already conveyed to the outposts, warning each, as I passed it on my way home, of the enemy's approach; and the consequence was, that every man knew the ticklish nature of his position, and was prepared to do his duty, according as circumstances might require.

Chapter 13

The Battle of Vimiero

Having refreshed myself in Sir Arthur Wellesley's kitchen, I returned to my picket, to which nothing of a nature to excite alarm occurred during the night The enemy did not advance farther than the village, and for some time after sunrise next day, all was quiet. By and by, however, some heavy clouds of dust gave notice that the French were moving. Instantly drums beat and bugles brayed, to call in stragglers, of whom not a few had succeeded in quitting their arms, for various purposes; and in a short time regiments began to march, and guns to open their fire—the former in order to assume a fresh alignment, the latter to harass the heads of the enemy's columns as they showed themselves. With respect to ourselves, we were called in and joined to the rest of the regiment, which with the Portuguese cavalry, took post in the valley, having the village of Vimiero on our right front, and the Windmill-Hill covering us on the left.

In this position we stood for a considerable space of time, completely sheltered from the enemy's fire, and seeing very little either of their movements, or of the movements of our dismounted comrades. The regiments which occupied the hill near us, seemed, indeed, to be very hard pressed; for the shot came every instant more thick in that quarter, and if they advanced one moment a few paces, the next they fell back again. Colonel Taylor, who commanded us; repeatedly asked leave to charge, but was on each occasion held back, by the assurance that the proper moment was not yet come; till at last General Fane rode up and exclaimed, "Now, Twentieth! now we want you. At them, my lads, and let them see what you are made of."

Then came the word, "Threes about and forward;" and with the rapidity of thought we swept round the elbow of the hill, and the battle lay before us.

As we emerged up this slope, we were directed to form in half-squadrons, the 20th in the centre, the Portuguese cavalry on the flanks, and the brief space of time that was necessary to complete the formation enabled me to see over a wide extent of the field. The French were coming on in great force, and with the utmost show of confidence. A brigade of cavalry was in front, followed by a line of infantry, in rear of which again were some heavy columns and guns. On our side there were some infantry who had long and gallantly maintained the hill, but who were so over-matched, that our advance was ordered up for the purpose of relieving them; and never was purpose more effectually served. "Now, Twentieth! now!" shouted Sir Arthur, while his staff clapped their hands and gave us a cheer; the sound of which was still in our ears, when we put our horses to their speed. The Portuguese likewise pushed forward, but through the dust which entirely enveloped us, the enemy threw in a fire, which seemed to have the effect of paralysing altogether our handsome allies. Right and left they pulled up, as if by word of command, and we never saw more of them till the battle was over. But we went very differently to work. In an instant we were in the heart of the French cavalry, cutting and hacking, and upsetting men and horses in the most extraordinary manner possible, till they broke and fled in every direction, and then we fell upon the infantry. It was here that our gallant colonel met his fate. He rode that day a horse, which was so hot that not all his exertions would suffice to control it, and he was carried headlong upon the bayonets of the French infantry, a corporal of whom shot him through the heart. The corporal took, of course, his plunder, including the colonel's watch, seals, and a ring set with Mrs. Taylor's hair, as well as his horse; and though he sold the animal afterwards, he refused to part with the watch and its appendages, even when offered for them, at I have understood, more than their value.

We were entirely ignorant of the fall of our commanding-officer, and had the case been otherwise, we were too eager in following up the advantages which we had gained, to regard it at the moment Though scattered, as always happens, by the shock of a charge, we still kept laying about us, till our white-leather breeches, our hands, arms, and swords, were all besmeared with blood. Moreover, as the enemy gave way we continued to advance, amid a cloud of dust so thick, that to see beyond the distance of those immediately about yourself, was impossible. Thus it was till we reached a low fence, through which several gaps had been made by the French to facilitate the movements of their cavalry; and we instantly leaped it. The operation cost some valuable lives; for about twenty or thirty of the French grenadiers had laid themselves on their bellies beneath it, and now received us as well as they could upon their bayonets. Several of our men and horses were stabbed, but of the enemy not a soul survived to speak of his exploit—we literally slew them all—and then, while in pursuit of the horse, rushed into an enclosure, where to a man we had well-nigh perished. For the fold in which we were caught was fenced round to a great height, and had but a single aperture—the door of which, the enemy, who hastened to take advantage of our blunder, immediately closed. Then was our situation trying enough, for we could neither escape nor resist; while looking over the wall we beheld that the French had halted, and were returning in something like order to the front

While we were thus situated, vainly looking for an aperture through which to make a bolt, one of our men, the same Corporal Marshall of whom I have elsewhere spoken, was maintaining a most unequal combat outside the close, with four French dragoons that beset him together. An active and powerful man himself; he was particularly fortunate in the charger which he bestrode— a noble stallion which did his part in the *mêlée*, not less effectually than his master. The animal bit, kicked, lashed out with his fore-feet, and wheeled about and about like a piece of machinery, screaming all the time; while the rider, now catching a blow, now parrying a thrust, seemed invulnerable. At last he clove one enemy to the teeth, and with a back stroke took another across the face, and sent him from his saddle. The other two hung back, and made signs to some of their comrades, but these had no time to help them, for a hearty British cheer sounded above the battle, and the 50th regiment advanced in line with fixed bayonets. The consequence was, an immediate flight by the enemy, who had calculated on making every man of the 20th prisoners; and our release from a situation, of all others the most annoying to men who, like ourselves, had no taste for laying down their arms. Moreover, to that charge, supported as it was by the simultaneous advance of other portions of the line, the enemy did not venture to shew a front. They were beaten on all sides, and retreated in great disorder, leaving the field covered with their dead.

The 20th Dragoons had done their duty, as indeed was abundantly shown by their soiled and crimsoned, appearance; and the reception which they met with from the general staff as they rode back to their old ground in the ravine, was most gratifying. The Portuguese, on the contrary, were yet standing where they had deserted us, formed up like troops on parade, and quite bloodless. We had been good friends before this—we were never good friends after. We spit at them as we passed, and loaded them with execrations, while our officers turned away their heads, and refused to recognise their former acquaintances. Our next business was to call the roll, and ascertain who were missing. Strange to say, the whole of our officers, with the exception of Colonel Taylor, answered to their names; and among the men the slaughter was less terrible than might have been expected; yet we had lost some good soldiers, and we lamented them deeply. Then it was proposed by Colonel Blake, on whom the command had devolved, that a party should go out to seek for Colonel Taylor's body, and as he asked for volunteers I readily stood forth as one in a crowd, all of them equally willing.

We moved to the front, Captain Bingham Newland of my troop being along with us, and found the declivity of the hill and the plain below covered with the killed and wounded. There they lay, English and French thrown promiscuously together, while hordes of peasants, together with women from our own army, were already in full occupation as plunderers. Among other dead men, we passed a French officer of Voltigeurs, a tall, good-looking follow, who wore in his *chakot* a beautiful green feather, to which Colonel Blake took a fancy. "Landsheit," said he, "I should like to have that Frenchman's feather. He will have no further use for it himself—suppose you fetch it me." I dismounted immediately, and having taken the feather, I thought to myself why should not I look for something more? He is dead enough, that's certain, and neither money nor watch can avail him now. Accordingly I turned him over and took all that he had—a watch and three Spanish dollars. This done, I rode after the detachment, which was somewhat in front, and overtaking it, gave the feather to the colonel.

I was in the act of stooping forward, and he had reached out his hand for the prize, when a musket-shot came from behind a bush hard by, and the ball whistled between the colonel's head and mine. We looked about and saw whence the smoke ascended, upon which my officer directed that I would ride up to the spot, and desire the man, whoever he might be, to cease firing. I did so, and found a French grenadier wounded in the thigh, but who, leaning against a bank, was in the act of ramming home another cartridge, and persisted in doing so in spite of my remonstrance. "Throw away that musket,'" said I, "and I will give you quarter!"

"I want no quarter," replied the grenadier: "just stop a moment, and you shall see." There was no time to deliberate, for he was already returning his ramrod, and the next instant would have sent a ball through my body; So I gave him a rap over the head with my sword, which put a final stop to all his pugnacious propensities. As a wounded man I would have gladly spared him; but his blood be upon his own head; I could not allow him to live and be killed myself.

We found Colonel Taylor stripped to the drawers, lying where he had fallen, upon his face; and Colonel Blake, after cutting off a lock of his hair, gave directions that he should be buried. A hole was, in consequence, dug, in which we laid him; not without the hearty regrets of all who assisted at the funeral, after which we returned to the camp, and for a while all was quiet. I have nothing to say concerning the plans and counsels of my superiors, which led to the Convention of Cintra, and the evacuation of Portugal by the French. Of the first I know no more than I have since learned from history; and as to the last, I was not even a witness to it. My purpose will therefore be sufficiently served when I state that, marching with the rest of the army, I took up my quarters at Belem, of which, till Christmas eve, I continued to be an inmate. For with the movement of Sir John Moore into Spain, which began at the end of October, I was nowise concerned, and would therefore justly deserve to be censured were I to speak either of it or of the preparations that led to it. But there did occur, during our sojourn in Belem, a circumstance which seems to demand repetition, even though the story may appear to cast discredit on more than the individuals who took part in it.

The Palace of Belem is so situated that the royal stables abut upon the river—that is to say, that between them and the stony bank of the Tagus, which is somewhat steep, there intervenes a space of less than twenty yards. A portion of our squadron occupied these stables, and among others two men, remarkable for no single quality that becomes a soldier, not even for courage, which few soldiers lack. These men going into a wine house one evening, saw a Portuguese peasant imprudently tell over his money, and observing that the sum was considerable, a portion of it being gold, they determined to rob him. The one said to the other, "Stay you here, and keep the old rascal in view, while I run home for our cloaks and pistols—the money we want and the money we must have, let the consequences be what they may." Accordingly this man, whose name was Downes, hurried back to the Palace and provided himself with the cloaks and weapons, while the other, called Thorpe, managed to delay the peasant till his comrade returned.

At last the peasant mounted his ass and went forward, Downes and Thorpe following at a little distance, till they cleared the town, and emerged into a plain of considerable extent. "Now then," said Downes, "you go up and knock the rascal over. If he resists I will join you, but if you can rob him by yourself it will be so much the better." Thorpe did as he was desired, and being armed with a thick stick he struck the Portuguese a blow on the head and levelled him. But the old man's heart was resolute, or else he loved his money so much that Thorpe found it a more difficult matter than he had supposed to overcome him; and his comrade hearing the peasant's cries, ran forward and lent his aid in suppressing them. The poor countryman was plundered; but Downes was not content "He'll be at the barracks tomorrow, you may depend upon it We must despatch him on the spot, otherwise we'll have no good of the money." It was no sooner said than done. The rascal held a pistol to the old man's temple, and blew his brains out

The ruffians came back to barracks as if nothing extraordinary had happened, and exhibited no trace of the night's work in their countenances. They acted, likewise, with singular prudence; for they buried their ill-gotten hoard under a stone in the bank of the river, and took only such trifling sums as from time to, time they conceived that they should require. The consequence was, that while men wondered whence they had their funds for treating, nobody was able to say that they had more than a trifle about them, nor, of course, to charge them with unlawful proceedings. And as to the murdered man, no inquiry was ever made after him. Human life was too lightly esteemed at that time, and in that country, to make the absence of an aged peasant from his home a subject of wonder; and the miscreants, whose hands were red with his blood, ate and drank and were merry.

At length one of them, Thorpe, fell sick, and was removed to the hospital. He grew daily worse and worse, till his recovery began to be despaired of; and then conscience, which had slumbered so long, awoke, and he was a miserable man indeed. He raved about an old man's bloody corpse, and uttered such shocking and incoherent exclamations, that the nurses and patients around looked at him with horror, and asked him what he meant? He groaned and desired that the quarter-waster might be sent for, to whom he made a full confession; telling him both the name of his partner in the crime, and the spot where the booty lay concealed. Now it happened that Downes was on guard that day, and would not come off till the evening of the next—a circumstance which at once lessened the chances of his becoming acquainted with his comrade's confession, and encouraged the quarter-master to look for corroborative proof ere he brought so serious a charge against him. Instead, therefore, of giving Downes into custody and getting the evidence of the sick man taken down, he communicated to me and to others the substance of Thorpe's story, and requested us to assist him in his endeavour to find the money. We searched all night .but were not successful, and on the morrow Thorpe was dead.

It is not often that such a crime goes unpunished. There is a voice in the blood of a murdered man which neither earth nor water can stifle—and rare, indeed, are .the instances in which the hand that has taken away a brother's life grows cold by the operations of natural .disease. But in the case of the poor peasant, the avenger lagged in his pace, and Thorpe died miserable, and with him died the only evidence which could have brought Downes to the scaffold. For though the money was found where the wretched culprit represented it to be, Downes, when shown both it and the bag that contained it, denied all acquaintance with them. Moreover, there was nobody to make a complaint. The peasant had not been missed, or if missed, his family cared not to search for him; and to put a man on his trial for an offence, of which there was no proof; would have been madness. Downes continued to do his duty with the regiment; and is now, I believe, respectably settled, somewhere in the north of England.

With the exception of this affair, I am unable to recall to my recollection any occurrence during our four months' residence at Belem, which it would be worth while, at this distance of time, to commit to paper. At last an order reached us, to prepare for an immediate march into Spain, where Sir John Moore's army, though understood to be in a career of victory, stood in need of immediate reinforcements. It was Christmas eve when we began our advance; and during many days of incessant rain, we penetrated by Coimbra and Santarem to Abrantes. Here we halted, and the weather clearing up, spent some weeks with great satisfaction; especially to me, to whom my friendly stars gave a billet in the house of a singularly hospitable and obliging family. It consisted of an elderly gentleman and his three daughters, all excessively fond of music, whose friendship I secured for ever, by engaging some of our own band, and of the band of a regiment belonging to the German Legion, to play for their amusement. Accordingly, the sole hindrance to their favourite pastime being removed, they gave balls and suppers to their neighbours—all of whom they taught to regard me as the founder of the feasts. I enjoyed myself exceedingly under the roof of this wealthy Portuguese gentleman, and left, I have reason to believe, no bad name behind me.

CHAPTER 14

Adventures in Portugal & Sicily

Though there was not much to do, in a military sense, while the 20th occupied Abrantes, it cannot be said that we were wholly idle. We had guards to mount and patrols to send out as regularly as if the enemy had been near as, and, once at least, I had, while in charge of the former, well-nigh got into a serious scrape. The case was this:

There is a rivulet in front of Abrantes, which is spanned by a wooden bridge, at the further extremity of which one of our pickets was in the habit of establishing itself. It happened one evening that I was ordered with a corporal and twelve men to repair to this post; and that either through the negligence of the commissaries, or because our stores were exhausted, no supply was served out to us of food or forage, as in like cases is the custom. The men had but a mouthful of biscuit, the horses a half feed of barley ere they paraded, and we were marched off with an assurance, that in the course of the night or next day, an allowance would be forwarded to us. Well, we reached our ground, threw out our videttes, kindled our fire, and sat down; but eight, nine, ten o'clock came, without bringing a morsel for us or for our animals. And so it was throughout the night. No supplies reached us, and we felt as the dawn broke, both hungry and dissatisfied, having tasted hardly any thing since noon on the day preceding. As may be imagined, our good humour was not restored, when hour after hour passed by without bringing the wished-for rations; and at last, the general discontent became so great, that it seemed to me necessary to take some measures for its removal.

The horses had sought to allay their hunger by gnawing the bark from the trees under which they were picketed. We had looked in vain in our haversacks, for even a few crumbs; when about eleven o'clock I desired the corporal to take charge of the picket, while, with four men I went to the front in quest of *vivres*. There was an extensive plantation of olive trees before us, through which having passed, we found ourselves on a wide plain; at the farther extremity of which stood three houses, detached some way one from another, but all of them respectable. I determined to try whether in one or other of these, the articles of which we stood so much in need might be procured. The nearest at hand was, of course, the most convenient to us, and we trotted towards following grieved when we found that there were numerous outbuildings adjacent, and that it bore about it the air of a place of which the inhabitants could not possibly be paupers. Our first business was to examine the offices—if happily, we might discover a hen-roost, and our search was eminently successful. Fowls in abundance were at feed—-four or five of which were, after a tremendous cackling, deposited, with their necks considerably elongated, in a haversack. But we wanted bread, we wanted wine, we wanted corn for our horses; and these were to be had only by making requisition for them. I accordingly dismounted at the door of the mansion itself and giving my reins to one of the four men, I entered, attended by the other three, the great hall or *lumbre*.

The family were there, consisting of a gentleman and several ladies, to whom I stated my case, and the urgent necessity there was for supplying me with what I wanted. I told them that we did not come as plunderers, and pulling out some dollars, I desired them to name their own price and it should be paid. But they would not listen to me. The gentleman first said that he had nothing, and then peremptorily declared that whatever he might have, I should get no share of it High words followed of course, and probably we might have gone even farther, but that one of the ladies suddenly rose from her seat, and opening a door near the fire-place, ran up a stair that communicated with it I paid no regard to her movements, and was still arguing the point with the *Padrone*, when, to my horror, down came an English staff-officer, booted and spurred, and in full regimentals, to demand my business there. I told him exactly how we were situated, and showed him the money which I had tendered to the Portuguese, but my eloquence had no effect upon him. He abused me roundly, made me give him my name in writing, desired me to return forthwith to the picket, and assured me that I should hear of the matter afterwards. There was no disputing the will of my superior, so I obeyed; and my little party rode back to the bridge, the chagrin of all, but especially of myself, being increased fourfold by the issue of the excursion.

At last the relief came, and after a fast of more than four-and-twenty hours, we had rations served out to us. Something, too, was said by way of apology for the neglect which had occasioned us so much suffering; but I was not in a humour to understand it I felt that I was in a scrape, and I could not tell what might be the consequences. Providence, however, which has stood my friend on many occasions, did not desert me now. The men were at stables, littering up their horses for the night, when intelligence came in that the French were advancing; and that the whole of the troops, both cavalry and infantry, were directed to get under arms and move to the front. Immediately there was a sounding of trumpets and beating of drams in all directions. The infantry ran to their parades; we saddled, accoutred and mounted, and in half an hour were in full march along the road to Elvas. Nothing resulted from the alarm, which proved to be groundless; for the French discovering that Sir John Moore had taken the mountains of Gallicia, counter-marched upon him and left the Portuguese frontier unassailed; but to me, the movement brought deliverance from the most serious hazard that throughout may two-and-twenty years' service as a soldier ever threatened me. My friend, the staff-officer, forgot, amid the bustle of an opening campaign, that he and I had ever met; and it will not be doubted that I took especial care never to refresh his memory.

We advanced to Elvas, whence, after a sojourn of a few days, we returned again to Abrantes. Sir John Moore, it appeared, had abandoned the contest in Spain, and there was no need for us over the border; indeed it came out by and by that Abrantes itself was considered too far from the point of embarkation, and we were recalled, first to Santarem, and eventually to Coimbra. Here we spent the remainder of the winter and the whole of the spring, our lives being such as soldiers usually lead in quarters, without producing any incident which it would be worth my while to describe; or in the description of which the reader would be likely to take an interest But the early summer opened out for us brighter prospects. Sir Arthur Wellesley had returned to take the command of an army, which reposed in him unbounded confidence, and his arrival in the country gave an immediate impulse to the spirit of military preparation. There were reviews and musters, casting off broken-down horses, and supplying their places with better; and finally, in the month of May, we were in full march towards the Douro, for the purpose, as was given out, of rescuing Oporto from the dominion of Marshal Soult and his *corps d'armée*.

Sir Arthur had brought with him a large accession to our cavalry force; so that the 20th found itself brigaded, in this advance, with two other regiments, the 14th and 16th of Light Dragoons. General Cotton commanded us, and more than once we saw the enemy, but except a skirmish here and there between our scouts and their rear-guard, we never brought them to action. Once, indeed, at a place called Albergaria Nova, we drew up, after a severe night's march, in their front, and as the country was open before us, we anticipated a brush, notwithstanding that their horse was well supported by riflemen, but no charge was made. On the contrary, our own infantry got the start of us, I can't tell how, and we were but spectators of the excellent style in which they forced the French from their ground.

On the 11th there was a sharp encounter near the village of Grijon, where a considerable body of the enemy made a stand, and General Stewart, now Marquis of Londonderry, conducted a brilliant charge by the 14th, and took many prisoners. The 20th, however, had no share in that action, neither, indeed, did they proceed farther than the heights of Carvalhos; for the same night an order came which recalled us to Lisbon, there to be embarked for the purpose of joining our two right squadrons in Sicily. I need not say, that to abandon the theatre of war, just as a campaign of surpassing interest has opened, is not a very agreeable task to a soldier. Nevertheless, we were certain that no reproach could attach to us, whose first duty it was to obey the commands of our superiors; and if we were sorrowful as we turned our horses' heads to the rear, we experienced no feeling of shame. Our march was not attended by any circumstances worthy of record. We reached Lisbon in safety, and the next day went on board of ship at Belem, and dropped down the Tagus.

We had a tedious and uncomfortable passage to Sicily. Scarcely were we in the Bay of Biscay ere a storm arose, which scattered the fleet, and sent our ship for shelter into Carthagena—an admirable harbour, where we found the smoothest lying, and refreshments of every kind proportionate to our wants. There we waited till the gale ceased, when again putting to sea, we prosecuted the remainder of our voyage without any accident, and reached the Bay of Messina in safety. The appearance of Messina itself, and the noble scenery in rear of it, as beheld from the water in the clear light of a summer's day, is unusually striking. I thought, indeed, that amid all my wanderings, I had never looked upon a more attractive landscape, and I was scarcely satisfied with gating when the boats were lowered, and we made ready to disembark. Yet I was nowise displeased to find myself once more upon earth's solid surface. Moreover, the meeting with old comrades, the friendly shaking of hands, the anxious inquiries after those who would never come again—all this proved in its way inexpressibly delightful. Our squadrons marched into the quarters which their fellow-soldiers occupied, and for some days it was among us an unceasing routine of mirth and jollity.

It is not necessary for me to give a detailed account of the condition of Sicily, both political and military, when we arrived to do duty over its degenerate court, and to protect its inhabitants from French domination. Charles VII., driven from his continental provinces, had long found an asylum in the island, and, supported by the English, contrived to enact there the part of a sovereign prince. His consort, however, was, for more reasons than one, suspected of holding the English alliance in disfavour, and hence, though treated with the utmost deference, her movements were watched with a degree of vigilance of which she was quite unconscious. Yet no circumstance, for many months after our arrival, occurred to justify this circumspection, by confirming the suspicions in which it originated; so that the ordinary affairs of the country went on as if there had not been a party among its supreme governors to whom the existing order of things was detestable.

With respect, again, to the military situation of the island, that may be described in a few words. The battle of Maida had been fought, and the impossibility of maintaining a footing on the continent of Italy was not only demonstrated, but, for the safety of Sicily itself; strong and just fears were entertained. Along the opposite shores of Calabria a numerous army, under Murat, lay encamped, for the conveyance of which across the channel, scarce three miles in width, a numerous flotilla of gun-boats and open launches crowded the bays and harbours. On our side again, in addition to the naval force, which was formidable, every preparation was made to resist and repel the invasion. From Faro Point all the way round to Skeleta, that is to say, to the suburbs of Messina itself, was one continued line of troops; pickets, and detachments, occupying the beach at short intervals, while the main body lay in the towns and villages near. Moreover, on the hill above St. Stephano, a telegraph station was erected, whence, on the first appearance of danger, an alarm, it was supposed, could be given; while patrols passing perpetually from one station to another, rendered it next to impossible that a hostile foot should be planted, unobserved, upon the strand.

Our first quarters in Sicily were at Messina, a large and handsome town, remarkable for the splendour of its cathedral, and at once protected and overawed by a strong citadel. We were here when the conspiracy came to light, which the Queen, as appeared afterwards, had long been hatching, and, with the rest of the garrison, were kept for some nights under arms, in expectation of a tumult, if not of something more serious. How the movement began, or by what means it was detected, I am unable to say. All that I can relate, in reference to it, is this: that we received one night a sudden order to saddle and equip; and that going forth next morning, we found the house of Sir James Craig, the commander-in-chief, guarded by detachments both of horse and foot, and a couple of field pieces at the door. Then followed arrests beyond number, of noblemen and gentlemen, and officers of various ranks, some of whom died under the hands of the common executioner; while others were sent into exile. I believe that it was from one of these condemned conspirators that the share which the Queen had in the projected rising was discovered. A Sicilian colonel, having been condemned to suffer, was already at the foot of the gallows, when he produced a bundle of papers which told a curious tale; while the consequences were, his own reprieve, or ultimate pardon, as well as the hasty flight of the Queen from Messina. She was pursued and overtaken; and being sent back to Germany, she there ended her days, leaving us free from the annoyance which her intrigues had constantly occasioned.

Besides this, there befell, while we occupied our quarters in the city, two events, of which, as they made a very deep impression upon me at the moment, I am bound to speak. The first of these was an eruption of Mount Etna; the most remarkable that had occurred in the memory of the existing generation: the second, the appearance of the great comet, which showed itself in 1811 to all the nations of Europe. I recollect that on the morning of the day when Etna burst forth, I was busy upon the parade-ground, drilling a batch of recruits. There had been for some time previously an extraordinary closeness of atmosphere, but that day the heat was so intense that no one could breathe, except with difficulty, and, as it seemed, in opposition to a positive weight upon his chest; yet there was no sunshine. On the contrary, the heavens were covered by a dense fog, which grew every moment darker, till by and by some large drops of rain fell with a heavy splash upon the pavement. I felt them strike me; and on looking to my white trousers, observed that each left a stain behind as black as ink. The natives, dreadfully alarmed by the aspect which nature had put on, began to flee from their houses, anticipating, as they took care to tell us, an earthquake; but they were deceived. About ten o'clock a noise was heard as of distant thunder; and immediately afterwards the thick clouds were illuminated to a degree which no language could adequately represent. Mount Etna had burst his bounds; and volumes of flame ascended up to heaven, loaning upon their bosons stones of a prodigious size, and colouring the whole face of the surrounding country with a dark palpable powder, of which portions were wafted as far as the island of Malta. Meanwhile old Stromboli, though he emitted no fire, began to smoke tremendously, while rivers of lava were pouring down the sides of Etna, involving whole tracts of cultivated land in irretrievable ruin.

 I need not pause to relate how strongly the curiosity of all classes, natives as well as foreigners, was excited, or how they hastened to ascend the mountain, in order that they might observe near at hand the whole process of the eruption. For myself, the nature of my duties confined me to the city, over which, not long afterwards, the great comet made its appearance. I know not how this memorable visitor may have shown himself in England, or the nature of the feelings which his arrival excited among such as beheld him; but in Sicily, the light which he shed around rivalled that of day—at least it much surpassed in brilliancy the brightest moonshine. It will much surprise me if I ever cease to look back without wonder on the effect produced by his coming; or to treasure up the sensations of astonishment, not unmixed with awe, of which I was conscious, while night after night I watched his eccentric progress.

The comet had disappeared and Etna was once more at rest, when the 20th Dragoons received instructions to furnish a sergeant's party for duty at Faro Point I was employed upon this service, and for many weeks commanded a detachment of twelve men; out of which two orderlies were each day at the disposal of the general, whose business it was to observe that part of the coast. During the whole of that period the common routine of our existence was this. By day all except the orderlies occupied quarters in a house not far removed from the batteries and entrenchments with which the nook of the point was covered. By night some patrolled in the direction of St. Stephano; while the remainder, scraping holes for themselves in the sand, slept in their cloaks, fully armed and accoutred, with the bridles of their horses fastened to their wrists. Neither were these precautions unnecessary. Immediately opposite, along a range of commanding heights stood hundreds of white tents, around which we could distinguish, even with the naked eye, crowds of soldiers collected. It was their custom to descend every night, and to embark on board of the vast flotilla which lay at anchor near the shores, from which, as the morning dawned, they as regularly withdrew, and returned to the camp. Now our chiefs wisely concluded that a manoeuvre, so often practised for the purpose of deceiving, might, sooner or later, be converted into a real attack; and they were determined, let it come when it might, not to be caught napping. The consequence was that the whole extent of sea-shore, from the Point of Faro to Messina, was nightly covered with armed men, not indeed sufficiently numerous to oppose a landing, if attempted in force, but adequate to all the purposes both of offering a temporary resistance, and giving an alarm to the main body.

It must not be imagined, however, that the armies thus opposed to one another abstained from other and more serious methods of mutual annoyance, than by parades and demonstrations. The enemy's gun-boats would, from time to time, put to sea, and ours meeting them about mid-channel, various sharp encounters took place. As often as this occurred, we landsmen watched the issue with an intensity of interest, such as must be felt to be understood; a feeling which was indulged in to its utmost extent by the enemy as well as by our own soldiers. For we could see them clustering on the brow of the opposite hill, and waving their caps, while their shouts, which the wind blew towards us, were heard by us as distinctly as the roar of the combatant's artillery. It was not, for the most part, Murat's wish that these contests should be waged to an extremity, but occasionally both sides fought as if they were in earnest; and once at least our gallant seamen, though they won the battle, did not prevail till after their courage and endurance had been both tried to the uttermost.

Chapter 15

More Adventures in Sicily

While the naval forces of England and France thus came occasionally into collision, the soldiers on both sides gazed upon one another as two angry dogs are apt to do, whose chains will not permit them to meet. I cannot tell exactly what space there may be between Faro Point and the Calabrian coast; but that the one lies within long cannon-shot of the other we had the best means of determining; as well from the practice of the enemy's gunners as from that of our own. The French had on the slope of the opposite hill a lofty flag-staff with a long six-and-thirty pounder beside it, mounted on a traversing carriage. From this, which we were accustomed to call Long Tom, it was their "constant habit of an afternoon" to give us a salute, to which we invariably replied from a battery of four-and-twenty pounders planted not far above the high-water mark. That our shot were admirably thrown we could perceive, because more than once they cut down the French flag-staff, a hit which never failed to call forth from us the loudest cheering. Neither were the French gunners less skilful in their vocation. On both sides a great elevation was used, so that the balls fell in many instances almost perpendicularly, yet they never went very wide of their mark on either side, and the escapes among us were well-nigh miraculous. Take the following examples:

I was myself reclining, one day, upon a sort of couch—a stretcher which I had placed in one corner of my room—with a cigar in my month and a cap of wine beside me, when down came a cannon-ball through the roof and struck the stone floor within a yard of me. Being a good deal spent it rolled towards the partition, through which, as it was made of deal, it burst, and then running over the foot of another man, who lay on a blanket in an adjoining apartment, it lamed him for life. Not yet exhausted, it passed thorough a second partition and tumbled into the kitchen, beneath the grate of which, to the astonishment of several persons who witnessed its evolutions, it made a final lodgement. There was of course a search made in the house for the purpose of ascertaining the extent of damage done, and though all pitied the poor wounded trooper, all at the same time admitted that matters might have been worse.

On another occasion, an officer being about to shave in his tent, had suspended his looking-glass against the tent pole, and called repeatedly to his servant to fetch hot water. The man was out of the way, so the officer ran himself to the kitchen, which chanced to be near at hand, for the purpose of supplying his own necessities. He was scarcely gone when Long Tom struck his looking-glass, shivered it to pieces, cut the tent pole in two, and levelled the tent with the ground. Without doubt the gentleman owed his life to the temporary negligence of his servant.

Another occurrence, though not less remarkable, was more unfortunate in its results. General Henebere, commanding at this station, occupied a house close to the beach, in front of which a sentinel was always mounted, It happened on a certain day that the enemy directed more than the usual quantity of fire at this house, insomuch that the sentinel observing the balls throw up the sand around him, became impatient. He therefore retired into a court, outside of which he had heretofore been pacing, and shut the gates. He was yet in the act of fastening the latch, when a ball came, shivered the staple to pieces, and killed him on the spot. So much for getting out of the way to avoid a fate which is reserved for us.

On a fourth occasion I saw a ball strike the ground near a battery, at which some men were working. It seemed to be quite spent, for it was travelling along the beach like a cricket ball when the force which has sent it from the bowler's hand is exhausted; and an artificer, being, I presume, of this opinion, ran up and clapped his spade before it. It snapped the spade asunder as if it had been a thread and bounded forward; but it inflicted no damage on any one—as another did, not long afterwards.

Two artillery officers happened to meet at a mortar battery, and were giving directions for settling the bed, when a ball came with such precision of aim, that it slew them both. It will be seen, therefore, that though the sea was between us, neither we nor the French troops were absolutely out of danger, and the progress of a short time sufficed to prove that dangers greater and more urgent were continually impending.

The summer of 1811 had passed away without any effort on the part of the enemy to invade us, and though we relaxed in no degree from our vigilance, a conviction began naturally to gain ground, that Murat would never embark on an enterprise so pregnant with danger. Our patrols, therefore, while they went their rounds night after night, did so with a sort of moral conviction on their minds that they should meet with nothing to alarm or molest them.

It was in this spirit that two dragoons passed, one night in the month of September, from Skeleta to St. Stephano, and reported at the latter place, as others had done before them, that all was well. They then faced about, and having paused only to tighten their girths and give their horses an opportunity to shake themselves, they rode back in the direction from which they had come. It was now drawing towards daybreak, and in the eastern sky a brighter and brighter glow was continually appealing.

At last the dawn came in, by the glimmering of which they beheld, just under the hill on which the telegraph stood, groups of men collected on the shore and a number of boats rocking upon the water.

The dragoons, taking it for granted that they were fishermen returned from plying their trade, approached them; and their astonishment may be conceived when they ascertained that it was a party of the enemy. The fact, indeed, was this. Murat, finding the breeze set fair from the Calabrian shore, had ordered his flotilla to put to sea, and to pass, by its three divisions, to Messina, St. Stephano, and Faro Point; one of which, destined to act upon the centre of our line, succeeded in gaining its haven. It is probable, too, that had the French been more perfect masters of their business, a serious affair would have taken place; for the flotilla of boats was very numerous, and appeared crowded with soldiers, so that all that was needed to give the invader at least a chance of success, was, that his opponents should receive no alarm ere he had effected his landing. But when our men, on discovering their mistake, wheeled about, some French soldiers, in order to stop them, fired—a most unwise proceeding, which had the immediate effect of putting all the pickets within hearing on the alert. The consequence was, that while the greater portion of Murat's musquito fleet was yet at sea, brigade after brigade was in full march to oppose him, and to the farthest extremity of our line we were all under arms waiting for orders. Murat was very brave, but he was not then insane. He therefore drew off with as many of his people as he could re-embark, while the remainder, left to themselves, dispersed and fled like hunted robbers to the mountains. There the peasantry tracked them out and would have put them all to death, but for the intervention of our troops, by whom about eight hundred prisoners were made, including several officers of rank, and among others an *aide-de-camp* of the intrusive King himself!

I was still on duty at Faro Point when the alarm of an invasion was given, consequently, except by standing for some hours beside my horse fully accoutred, I took no part in the business. Not long afterwards, however, my party was relieved, and we marched back to our quarters at Messina. I do not recollect that there happened during my second sojourn there any thing deserving of record, assess an extraordinary display of credulity among the people, and an act of remarkable knavery by a priest, deserve to be so accounted. I have not forgotten that both affected me very strongly at the moment, though I much question whether they will bear to be described; nevertheless, here they are.

In a certain part of Messina remarkable for the low profligacy of its inhabitants, and fronting a street which was not frequented except by the most abandoned characters, stood a convent of Benedictine monks—one of the gates of which was surmounted by a picture of the Virgin, before which a lamp was kept perpetually burning. The picture, being painted on copper, was covered by a glass, and, with a gilt frame, faced the south-west, so as to be exposed to the influence of a burning sun, at the very hours when his power is the greatest. One morning, the monk whose business it was to provide that the lamp should never go out, announced to the pious inhabitants of "Black Dog Street," that the Virgin had wept. The intelligence spread like wildfire through the city; and from all its quarters flocked the high and the law, the rich and the poor, to witness this great miracle. Now, the monks were not disposed to let the miracle pass unprofitably for themselves;—they encouraged the people to come forward, but they laid in their way baskets, wine-casks, and boxes, with small orifices in the lids, all of them empty. Into these the pious were invited to cast money, wine, oil, bread, fruit, fowls, and valuables of every description; and, to do them justice, the liberality of the Messineans could scarcely be surpassed. In gratitude to the holy fathers, who erected a temporary staircase for their accommodation, by means of which they might ascend and view the weeping Virgin face to face, they filled, over and over again, the vessels that were laid in their way; while, the more to encourage them in so pious a proceeding, a grand procession of all the clergy took place. With the bishop at their head, and carrying the Host in great state, a whole regiment of priests and monks walked two and two from the convent steps to the cathedral, while his lordship took care to exhort his deck to walk worthy of the high distinction with which they had been honoured. Nor is this all. There appeared, the morning of the second day, a legend beside the picture, which accounted for this extraordinary display of sorrow on the part of the Virgin: she wept because a country so pre-eminently Christian as Sicily should have passed under the dominion of heretics.

All this was very well—that is to say, it served the purposes of the monks to admiration; but the English authorities were scarcely pleased with it. They, therefore, commanded the artist by whom the painting had been executed to be brought to the spot, and proved, through him, that the miracle was not so portentous as the good bishop had described it. The heat of the sun, it appeared, had melted the lead, and caused the paint to run. Still the offerings were presented—they could not be restrained; and though the written account of the Virgin's sorrows was taken away, I never heard that the bishop or his clergy exerted themselves to persuade the people that she had not wept at all.

The second circumstance to which I have alluded may to the reader seem still more trivial, though to me it was affecting enough when it occurred.

There was a Sicilian nobleman, the Prince Salvestro Gustavellio de St Stephano, who did me the honour to notice me a good deal, and to make me his companion more than once, upon a shooting expedition. He had a chaplain—Don Titto—whose vicarage adjoined the Prince's chapel, where, as the house was a large one, the Sergeant-Major of the 20th, with some others, myself among the number, had their quarters, Don Titto kept a horse, and being very desirous of getting it into good condition, he conceived that his purpose would be best served by feeding it—not on his own straw and barley— but upon the beans and oats that were served out for our chargers. Now, stores of this description are always committed to the charge of the sergeant-major—and ours, being surprised at the havoc that was made in the sacks, desired the man who waited upon him to keep a sharp watch. The man did so, and in an evil moment for poor Don Titto, caught him in the very act of filling an enormous nose-bag out of a sack of beans. He seized the thief immediately, gave the alarm, and assisted the sergeant-major to tie the nose-bag round the *Padre's* neck, and drag him into the Prince's presence. I never heard a human being being beg for mercy in language more abject than that which Don Titto employed. He fell upon his knees, and entreated that they would spare him. The sergeant-major, however, was inexorable; and Don Titto, being sent about his business, was never heard of more.

The period of the occupation of Sicily was remarkable for the prevalence of crime among that portion of the British army which was employed in the service. How to account for the circumstance I do not pretend; but it is certain that a greater quantity of murders were perpetrated, and more acts of depredation committed by the English troops, while they held Sicily in their hands, than by the whole of the Duke of Wellington's forces in Spain, though surpassing them at least four to one in point of numbers. On one occasion, for example, a soldier belonging to an infantry regiment came off guard at night, and feeling fatigued, lay down upon his bed, in order to sleep—but was hindered from sleeping by the sergeant of his squad—who, sitting in the same room, entered into an animated conversation with those about him. The weary man looked up, and begged the sergeant to be silent; a request with which the speaker did not think fit to comply. Again the man raised himself on his elbow, and declared with an oath, that if the sergeant would not hold his tongue, and permit him to sleep, he would blew his brains out The sergeant paid no ether regard to his threat than to laugh at it; but he little knew the sort of person with whom he was trifling. The man sprang from his bed, deliberately took down his musket from the arms-rack, and shot the non-commissioned officer dead on the spot. He was, of course, tried —found guilty—condemned—and executed; a poor compensation for the life which in his anger he had taken away.

On another occasion a soldier was caught by a *pisano*, plundering his vineyard. The countryman either wished to seize the robber, or in some way or another excited his fury, for a struggle took place, and the Sicilian was killed. The court which tried the murderer found him guilty on the clearest evidence, and he was sentenced to be hanged. In order to give to the execution as much solemnity as possible, all the troops in garrison were ordered to attend; while a proclamation went forth, in the Sicilian language, which called upon the people to come and witness the zeal with which the English authorities were prepared to protect their lives and properties. Large crowds of men, women, and children, came together where the scaffold was erected, and three cannon-shot were fired to warn them of the approach of the hour which was to close the marauder's eyes upon the world for ever. The first gun gave notice that the prisoner had quitted his dungeon; the booming of the second told that he had reached the fatal platform; and when the third sent its echoes among the roots of Mount Etna, the drop fell. It was a hideous spectacle—for the rope being weak, and the man heavy, the former gave way, and the wretched creature was taken up, bruised from the ground, but quite sensible. A pause necessarily occurred ere a fresh rope could be procured, and then he ceased to live.

Strange to say, the effect of this example was so slight, that the very same day a man of De Rolle's, a foreign regiment in the English service, was put in confinement for murdering his wife. He had gone home from the mention, quarrelled with the poor woman about some trifle, and stabbed her to the heart. He, too, suffered the penalty which the laws both of God and man have awarded to the homicide. Yet the practice continued occasionally, amid such aggravations of horror, as to chill the blood of those who listened to the tale at the moment, and effectually to hinder me from adverting to it now.

CHAPTER 16

To Minorca & Spain

Such was the order of my existence in Sicily for a period of many months, during which the 20th Dragoons may be said to have been constantly on duty; till in the summer of 1812, an order reached us to prepare for more active employment somewhere on the continent. Our preparations were soon completed, and on a beautiful day in June we embarked on board of transports at Messina, whence we passed round to Melazzo, where the rest of the convoy joined us. We never cast anchor in the latter roadstead, but kept beating on and off, while those at the head of affairs were adjusting their plans; after which the fleet put to sea with a light but favourable breeze.

An agreeable voyage of a few days' duration carried us to Port Mahon, where, in an excellent harbour, the ships cast anchor, and a signal was made to land the troops. Minorca, it appeared, was the appointed rendezvous for the entire expedition of which the Sicilian army formed but a part; and till the expected reinforcements should come up, it was judged expedient to refresh both men and horses. Accordingly, on a small island, divided from the main by a narrow channel or ferry, we disembarked with all our equipments; and here for several weeks we amused ourselves eating and drinking, and exercising the animals, which even a brief confinement on board of ship had cramped and stiffened. Neither were we hindered from crossing over in our turns to Port Mahon, and spending a day among its shops and *caravansaries,* so that upon, the whole the season of inactivity passed agreeably enough; and we almost lamented when it came to a conclusion.

While we lay in this situation, there occurred to me an adventure, of which, because of certain events that befell at a subsequent period, it is necessary that I should give an account. Like the rest of the sergeants I took frequent advantage of my position to visit Port Mahon; and, as soldiers are apt to do, found out a good house of entertainment, and frequented it regularly. I found that it was the resort of a young countryman of my own, a remarkably handsome and intelligent youth, by name Conrad Hettendorff between whom and myself an acquaintance was soon struck up, which ripened by degrees into friendship, Conrad had received an excellent education, and was possessed of some property. He had been brought up to the mercantile profession, and was a clerk in one of the chief houses in Gibraltar, where a young lady, the daughter of an officer of rank, belonging to the garrison, won his heart, and gave him her own in return. The attachment could not, of course, be revealed; but the lovers met frequently, and something was talked about an elopement; when the father of the young lady discovered how matters stood, and put a stop to the courtship. Poor Conrad, in short, was obliged to quit the rock, and had in consequence repaired to Minorca, where, being an excellent Spaniard, he soon found employment in a counting-house. But his mind was unsettled. The routine of a mercantile life grew odious to him, and he longed for a more active occupation. He told me his tale, and then proposed to enlist in a corps, of which I shall have occasion to speak more at large by-and-by, and accompany us to Spain. As may be imagined, I did not oppose myself to an arrangement which at once assured to the army an excellent recruit, and gave me the promise of the society of a man for whom I had formed a sincere attachment .Conrad accompanied me back to my quarters, was gladly accepted by the commanding officer, and took his place among the Foreign Hussars.

Meanwhile a large force of Spaniards arrived day by day to strengthen us, and a fleet of the most formidable appearance crowded the harbour; on board of which, so soon as an adequate supply of stores had been laid in, we took our stations. The weather was beautiful, though intensely hot, and the breezes fair, so that we held our course in admirable order, and free from every accident, till the bay of Blanes opened out before us. The scenery, as we swept over the quiet waters of the gulf, became interesting in the extreme. A shelving beach, covered with low underwood, and studded in all directions with villages, hamlets, and country-houses, gave place by degrees to a fine open country, far away in the background of which uprose the Pyrenean Mountains, leaning like dark clouds against the horizon. On our right, and within point-blank range of the sea, stood the castle of Tosa, from the battlements of which the French flag was waving; while sweeping round from it we could detect, with the aid of our telescopes, large bodies of troops in position.

There could be no doubt whatever as to the standard under which they served. The whole of the district was known to be in the enemy's possession; and we gathered from the spectacle before us, that a disembarkation effected here would soon bring us into practical acquaintance with their system of warfare.

We steered into the bay slowly and majestically; for the number of vessels, great and small, that composed our fleet was prodigious; and having approached as near to the shore as the admiral considered to be prudent, we let go our anchors. Neither was any thing farther attempted that day. We lay perfectly still; and as we were just out of gunshot of the French batteries, and no orders were issued of any kind, our sole employment consisted in making surveys of the beach. It seemed as if the enemy had long been jealous of this spot; for they had a formidable army collected when we arrived; and each new hour brought some accession to its strength: indeed we could perceive columns of horse and foot marching from every point of the compass towards the rising ground, on which our original acquaintances stood. Now, though willing to give our chiefs credit for as much of foresight as attaches to men in general, we were not without our misgivings when we beheld that all the activity manifested was on the side of the French. Why this delay in landing? Why wait till such a force should be collected in our front, as must render the very opening of the campaign a service of extreme hazard? Such were the observations that passed from man to man, when that sun set, and another, and another, without bringing the expected order to disembark; till by-and-by the hearts of the bravest began to fail them, and we suspected that the whole affair would be mismanaged.

At last, after occupying our anchorage four whole days, during which many vessels, which had lagged behind, joined us, a signal was hung out from the admiral's ship, that three days' provisions should be cooked and issued to the troops. This was followed by a second order for the boats of the fleet to be hoisted out, and the landing to be begun as soon after dawn on the morrow as circumstances would allow.

There was some bustle and much rejoicing on board our transport, when the signals being interpreted to them, the men received instructions to prepare. Pork was boiled, biscuit measured out, arms inspected, pouches stored with ammunition. After which, the horses being dressed as carefully as their straightened berths would allow, we lay down in our cloaks. Among us, who knew what war was, there was comparatively little excitement. We understood the importance of going fresh into action, and therefore slept soundly. Among the young hands it was different; but upon both classes the dawn came with its accustomed regularity, and the trumpets sounded. We sprang to our feet, got up our horses, saddled and equipped them for field-service, and lowered them into the flat boats that were already alongside to receive them. Finally, about six o'clock, the flotilla moved off and a line was formed with armed barges in front, that seemed to stretch well nigh across the bay.

The sun had by this time risen, and the day being calm and bright, we could observe with great exactness the preparations which the enemy had made to give us a welcome. Along the face of the rising ground, in rear of the hamlets, four or five dense columns of infantry stood fast, at such distances, the one from the other, that they needed but to wheel up, and a perfect line would be formed. In rear of these was a strong force of cavalry, the men as yet standing beside their horses; while field-pieces were run forward, and guns of a heavier metal showed their muzzles here and there from behind a wall or embankment. As yet, however, all was quiet. We lay considerably beyond cannon shot, though in momentary expectation of an order to push on; and the enemy appeared too much at home in the business in which they were going to be engaged, to put themselves out of the way unnecessarily.

At length the signal gun was fired, and the flotilla began to advance. It was a magnificent spectacle; and the absolute silence which prevailed, broken only by the splashing of the oars in the water, produced upon me a very powerful effect. Yet the excitement, if such it may be called, of which I was conscious, never unmanned me for a moment. I continued to sweep the French position with my glass, from which, by and by, the uprising of a column of smoke gave testimony that they were not indifferent to our proceedings. They had thrown a shell, which dropped short by so wide a space as to call forth a laugh from our rowers; and we pushed on, still preserving our line with an accuracy that was very remarkable.

We had got within the range of their heavy guns, the shot from several of which passed over us, when a signal from the fleet commanded the flotilla to halt It was obeyed, of course; and we lay on our oars while the man-of-war's barges and galleys crept on towards the shore and began with great diligence to take soundings. They were saluted both from the beach and from the castle with frequent discharges, but paid no regard to them, continuing to ply their task not only with diligence, but as it seemed, very slowly. Our men, therefore, once more betook themselves to the office of speculating—"How can this be accounted for?—What's the matter now?" These were the questions which became more and more urgent in proportion as the day stole on, till, in the end, it was pronounced by many, and by myself among the number, that no landing would take place that day. Neither were we deceived in this opinion. After we had lain till a good portion of our *prog* was consumed, and the intense heat had affected us rather painfully, a signal of recall was hung out, and the troops returned about five in the afternoon to their respective ships. Immediately horses and men were taken on hoard, and all things resumed the appearance which had been worn two days previously.

The plan upon which our admiral and general had acted was excellent. By making a demonstration in the gulf of Blanes, they drew thither every squadron and battalion of French troops that was disposable, and placed them on a plateau, whence it was impossible for them to act against the real landing, which had been resolved on at a point that was far more accessible. Moreover, they had managed matters so well, that not till the wind set fair for their true destination, was this show of disembarkation made; and the very same night, as soon as darkness had set in, the whole fleet got under way. An eighteen, hours' passage carried us, by this means, into the bay of Alicant, and the few French troops that lay there, hastily evacuating the place, we were all on shore, and organized as a movable army, without having sustained the slightest annoyance.

Alicant, as is well known, used to be a place of considerable trade, and is commanded by a citadel, of which, though they occupied the town, the French had never obtained possession. The town is separated from the suburbs by a double wall, built at a time when artillery could have been little used in sieges, and, therefore, incapable of sustaining the attack of a regular army. Nevertheless, it formed no bad *appui* for the operations which we were appointed to conduct, because it supplied us with good quarters, and was accessible by the fleet; and our chief, General Maitland, lost no time in availing himself of the advantages that were secured to him. The French, to be sure, being few in number, and taken completely by surprise, did not venture to face us. They fell back, on the contrary, towards Elda and Vincente, two villages about six miles distant from the town; while we, establishing our pickets a little way in advance of the walls, underwent that species of organization which is in all cases necessary to fit an army for active operations in the field.

There had been raised in Sicily a corps called the Foreign Hussars, an independent squadron, which mustered about a hundred and twenty men, the natives of almost every country under heaven. To the command of that body Captain Jacks, of the 20th, had been appointed; and while we lay in Alicant, I saw my name in orders, as serjeant-major under him. These foreigners, with the 20th, and a regiment of Brunswick Hussars, constituted the advanced guard of the army, and were supported by three regiments of the line of the King's German Legion, a regiment of German Rifles, and a strong and most intelligent battalion called the Calabrian Free Corps. It was our business, of course, to furnish the pickets, and to go abroad whenever a reconnaissance might be necessary; and I do not think that I deal unfairly by any other troops, when I say that none could have performed these duties more accurately. The enemy could not make a move, either in advance or retreat, without our observing it. We stole in upon them day and night, so as to see with our own eyes all that they were doing; and the country people being friendly, we were never at a loss for intelligence, which rarely failed to be confirmed by the event. We ascertained, for example, after we had been about a fortnight in possession of Alicant, that the enemy were not at their ease in Vincente. We pushed them there, though delicately, and they retreated; upon which our outposts took possession of the ground as they abandoned it, and those in rear felt more secure by reason of the wider space that was before them.

We had been thus circumstanced about a week, when intelligence reached us that the enemy were advancing in great strength. Crowds of peasants pouring in with bundles on their backs, confirmed the rumour; and the outposts received orders to fall back skirmishing, to a position outside the walls of Alicant.

Our informants had not deceived us; for about noon on the 18th August, the French appeared in front of the pickets, which, acting up to the instructions communicated in the morning, retired skirmishing upon the line. By and by the heads of the French columns showed themselves in front of the main body, which stood to their arms; and after a short time spent in manoeuvring, a cannonade opened, and the battle began.

The nature of the ground on which we stood was such as to prevent cavalry from acting, consequently I was little more than a spectator of this affair, which lasted from two o'clock in the afternoon till dark. The French came on with great boldness, and served their guns well, but they made no impression. On the contrary, the British line kept advancing, as it seemed, quite unconsciously —so that by degrees the whole of the field of battle came into our possession. It was not, however, General Maitland's policy to hazard any desperate movement. He, therefore, held his people in hand—and when the sun west down, and darkness gathered round us, he caused the firing gradually to cease. But we never laid aside our arms. We lay the whole of that night upon the ground, among the dead and the dying; the latter of whom shocked our ears with their piteous moans, and their wild cries for water;—while a storm, which had for some time previously been collecting, burst upon us with a degree of violence, which reminded me of the rains and thunder and lightning that I had witnessed in St. Domingo. Now, as we were not permitted to kindle fires, and had no covering at all, our plight soon became such as few persons need envy, for cloaks and great coats proved quite unequal to resist the rain, which came upon us as if it had been poured out of buckets.

It was cheerless enough, crouching under our horses' bellies, and seeking by that means to shelter ourselves a little; but I must do my fellow-soldiers the justice to state, that I heard no grumbling among them. The only symptom indeed of dissatisfaction which they exhibited, was when they thought of tomorrow's probable employment, and they looked at their carbines, saturated with wet, and so rendered quite useless. "Never mind," said one, "the French are just as badly off as we; and we have still our swords."

"True," replied another; "but the French know the country, and we don't; they are under cover somewhere, depend upon it." Yet when the morrow came, the perfect inutility of all this speculation was demonstrated. Not a Frenchman could be seen; they were all gone we knew not whither, and we remained masters of the field.

There had been a good many men killed and wounded on both sides, and the hospitals became in consequence a little crowded; but the circumstance which we lamented the most, was the effect of exposure to the storm on General Maitland's health, who was taken so ill that he found it necessary to return to England. He was a kind man, and much liked by the soldiers, to whom he had ordered double rations of every description, in order to console them for the ducking which they had sustained; and we lamented his departure as well on private grounds as on public. Nevertheless, soldiers are not much given to the melting mood: our usual good spirits soon came back, and we made ready, under our new chiefs, whosoever they might be, to do our duty, amid new scenes, and to play our parts in new adventures.

Chapter 17

A Skirmish With the Enemy

The retreat of the French not only gave us back all the ground which we had occupied with our outposts, previous to the attack, but put us in possession of the whole of that tract of country which they had before held about Elda and Monforte. For finding that they had left no pickets about Vincente, we pushed on, without seeing anything to alarm, far less to stop us, till we gained the villages, from which recent events had removed them. The consequence of this forward movement on our part was to give something of a novel character to our plan of operations. The main body no longer crowded in upon Alicant; but, leaving a sufficient garrison to do the duty of the place, a new position was taken up in front of the ground which hitherto our light troops, or, as they were termed, our corps of observation, had occupied.

We remained thus for some time; no event of consequence befalling to disturb us, while fresh regiments of Spaniards poured in from all quarters to swell our numbers. Of these troops it is but just to state that they were well-armed, well-clothed, and singularly patient of fatigue and hardships; and that when supported by British soldiers, they did their duty gallantly. Doubtless the officers were very inferior to ours. They seemed, in. deed, to possess little intelligence; and as to courage, in that respect they fell short of the privates. Yet the regiments, as every body that served with them will freely attest, exhibited a good deal of fortitude, under circumstances which might have shaken the endurance even of an Englishman.

At all events, the arrival of nine thousand armed men, to enlarge the amount of a force so inconsiderable as ours, was not without its moral influence. We derived from it an accession of confidence, while, as the event showed, it was productive in the enemy of an effect diametrically the reverse. We were all aware that between our leader and the Duke of Wellington a constant communication was maintained, and that as long as Suchet should act as a covering party to the left of that French army to which the Duke was immediately opposed, so long it would be our business to keep him in play, and hinder him from detaching largely to the northern coast. We were not, therefore, surprised at the state of inactivity in which, during the greater part of the autumn, we were kept; nor, our quarters being upon the whole good and our, supplies ample, did we greatly murmur at it. Yet I do not recollect, apart from the ordinary incidents of patrolling, more than one occurrence during this pause in our warlike operations which seems to demand notice. The incident in question, was as follows:

There were sixteen of our men quartered under my orders at a *quinta* in the neighbourhood of Monforte, where our horses were put up in what had originally been a couple of apartments on the basement of the mansion. The floor of these rooms had once been paved with flat stones; but at the date of our arrival the stones were all dug up, and lay in an enormous heap in a corner of the stable. Nothing could exceed the kindness and hospitality of the *Padrone*. He had always bread and cheese, and wine, at the service of the troopers; and so partial did he appear to their society, that even during stable-hours he was seldom absent from them. On these occasions the old man would bring a chair into the stable, sit down upon it, and converse on all manner of topics; always taking care to have a pig-skin of liquor beside him, out of which he supplied his new companions with the greatest liberality.

The men were much struck with the generous temper of the landlord, and still more with the regularity of his attendance in the stable, which, however, first one and then another began to suspect could not originate entirely in the disinterested love of their society. For they observed that he had no favourite among their number. No matter which of them proposed to dress his horse, the *Padrone* was sure to accompany him; and even at night nobody could go down-stairs without rousing the old man from his bed. At last it occurred to them, that perhaps he might have some money buried in the stable, and they resolved to search for it. Accordingly a spade and pickaxe were smuggled in one night, and hidden beneath the heap of stones in the corner, while a sharp look-out was kept for the first opportunity that might offer of bringing them into play.

The opportunity came at length: the old man, after sitting some time in the stable, was called out one day while the men were feeding—and his back was scarcely turned, when they set to work with might and main, to pull down the heap of stones. They were sure that the prize, if any there was, would be found beneath them; and the appearance of the earth, which seemed to have been recently turned up, satisfied them that their surmise was correct Instantly the spade and pickaxe were called into play, and so zealous, as well as able, were the workmen, that a hole of considerable depth was dug ere the *Padrone* returned to make his remarks on their proceedings — but they discovered nothing. Neither could they make a secret of what they had been about, for the old fellow's eyesight was a great deal too acute for the awkward attempts which they made to deceive him.

"Aha!" cried the *Padrone*, exultingly; "is that your game? You are all wrong; all upon a false scent Come hither, and I will show you where it lies."

So saying, he took the spade; and leading from its stall the horse which stood nearest to the door, he cleared away the litter from the spot on which its off fore-foot must have rested. Then with two strokes of the implement he uncovered a flat stone, which he rolled aside, and drew from beneath it a watering-bucket, filled to the brim with dollars. "This is what you wanted, gentlemen," said he; "but you did not know where to search for it. Now I did, and I mean to keep it to myself?" So saying, the old rascal laughed heartily, heaved up the bucket on his shoulder, and walked away. Moreover, he not only took especial care that the bucket should never again run the risk of detection by us, but he intermitted from that hour all the little acts of munificence in which he had heretofore indulged. We saw no more of his bread, nor cheese, nor wine, during the remainder of our sojourn; and though we could not help being amused with the result of the whole adventure, there were those among us who never ceased to regret that it had not taken a somewhat different turn.

The affair of the bucket had occurred about a week, when one day a crowd of peasants came in with intelligence that the French were advancing. Immediately the outposts stood to their arms, and while an orderly proceeded to the rear to warn the general of his danger, dispositions were made to keep the assailants at bay for as long a time as possible. The line of skirmishers was, formed on this occasion of German riflemen on the right, to whom succeeded a party of the 20th Light Dragoons; next came the pickets of the Calabrian Free Corps, with a detachment from the Foreign Hussars; then another picket of Calabrians, and, supporting them, a half troop of Brunswickers. The supports again consisted both of horse and foot, under their proper leaders, each of whom was of course expected to keep an eye in an especial manner on the detachment that belonged to his party, and to take care that it was not overpowered.

I was in command that day of the skirmishers from the Foreign Hussars, amounting in all to some twenty mounted men; and a captain, whose name it is not worth while to mention, had charge of the support. We were all in high spirits, for we had full confidence both in ourselves and in those beside us; and we knew that the main body was prepared to give battle, so soon as we should be driven back upon it. The country, too, chanced to be particularly favourable for cavalry operations. It was a fine open plain, overrun with long grass, and only here and there intersected by the fences which enclosed a vine-yard, or by some open grove of myrtle or other low-growing underwood. The weather too was most propitious, hot, to be sure, but dry, and both men and horses were in the best condition. Though the French came on therefore in dense columns, we waited for them nothing doubting, and we met the skirmishers, which they threw out in clouds, with all the alacrity that could have been desired.

There was in the service of the French on this side of the Peninsula, a regiment of hussars, called the 4th, which consisted almost entirely of Germans, the natives of many different states, and far surpassed all their competitors in gallantry and intelligence. In the course of the war we were often opposed to them, and I do not hesitate to say that we held them in greater respect than all the rest of Suchet's cavalry besides; so perfectly were they masters of the various arts in which cavalry ought to excel, and so ready at all times to meet us in fight or in skirmish.

Today, for the first time, we came in contact with them, and it was impossible to refuse, to their intrepidity and skill, the tribute of our highest admiration. They came on at first, each man sustaining an infantry soldier in his stirrup, whom they deposited in his proper place, fresh and ready for work, and then directing their attention exclusively to us, they soon put our mettle to the test.

Not content to fire their carbines at long shots, they would ride fearlessly up to our line of skirmishers, and either discharge their fire-arms at a few yards' distance, or close upon us with their swords.

More than once their skirmishers and ours met hand to hand, and it did not always follow that from the encounter our troopers came off victorious.

Where all were brave it may appear invidious to particularize an individual; but the circumstances of the case must plead for me if I err, more especially as the gallant fellow of whom I am going to speak, did not survive to receive the plaudits which otherwise must have been heaped upon him. He was a sergeant, and so confident did he appear to be in his own prowess and horsemanship, that without once pausing to ascertain whether his comrades might be at hand to support him, he rode directly into the heart of our advanced line. He then spurred about from man to man, firing at one and cutting at another, and calling aloud in excellent German for our best swordsman to come forward and engage him in single combat. It was impossible not to admire the bravery of the man, but it was necessary to put an extinguisher on it.

An Irishman, called Mackan, who waited upon me as a servant had the merit of doing so.

"Do you see that fellow, Sergeant-Major?" said he to me.

"To be sure I do, Mackan, and what then?"

"Just wait a bit till he comes again, and the devil's in it if you and I don't stop his capering anyhow. You ride at him in front and my name's not Phil Mackan if I fail to give him a crack on the sconce, before or behind, when he least looks for it."

I was amused with Phil's manner of expressing himself, but approved of his arrangements, and accordingly dashed at my countryman as soon as I conceived that he was in such a position as to be at once removed beyond the reach of immediate support in his rear, and incapable of escaping me. He made no attempt to fly, but met me like a man, and we exchanged a cut or two without advantage to either, when Mackan, true to his pledge, joined in the fray, and with one blow sent the gallant fellow's head from his shoulders. I never saw such a stroke struck in battle. The horse instantly bounded forward, and passing within our line, was seized by a German rifleman, between whom and us who slew the rider, the produce of its sale (sixty dollars) was afterwards divided.

But our triumph was not of long continuance; the French came on in such numbers that it was impossible for us to hold our ground, more especially when forming up they made ready to charge.

I had heard several bugle-calls from the rear, but not detecting the sound of our own trumpets, had paid no regard to them. I now looked round for the support, and my astonishment may be conceived when I discovered, that right and left of us the skirmishers had been called in, and that all, including the party which was in some degree answerable for our safety, were gone. The officer commanding, it appeared, became so convinced of the impossibility of maintaining the combat any longer, that without so much as pausing to warn us of his intentions, he had trotted to the rear. What was to be done? It was in vain that we fell back by files, loading, and firing, and practised all the ordinary manoeuvres to withstand the enemy's approach. They saw and despised our weakness, for they put their horses to their speed, and a whole regiment in line bore down upon us. There was nothing for it but to turn tail, so away we went helter-skelter to the rear; such as were well mounted getting clear of their pursuers; such as were otherwise being cut off and taken prisoners. We lost in that flight about sixteen men, most of whom were wounded, while the remainder came to the ground, which the army occupied, burning with rage, and utterly exhausted. For myself I was quite furious.

I rode up to the officer who had commanded in my rear, and told him that it was his handiwork—adding, that I would report him to the commander-in-chief, if other means failed of obtaining satisfaction. He was excessively angry, and threatened to cut me down; but I was not to be intimidated. Captain Jacks, however, to whom I made the circumstance known, was too humane to press the charge; and my own indignation moderating after the first burst had escaped me, I, too, was prevailed upon to keep quiet, and the thing was forgotten.

By this time the enemy had approached our position in force, and the line being formed, we made ready to receive them, our cannon opening with excellent effect so soon as the heads of the columns showed themselves. But it soon appeared that Suchet had no intention of bringing on a general engagement: his sole object was to ascertain how we had disposed of ourselves, and what strength we might seem to have in his front; and this, after exchanging a few volleys, he seemed to have effected, for his people drew gradually out of the field, and melted away. Nor did we quit our ground to pursue, so the enemy retired unmolested.

For some time after the occurrence of this affair all remained comparatively quiet in our immediate front. As the enemy gave ground, we, according to custom, moved forward, till our pickets were again established at Elda and Monforte. As they advanced we fell back again, and resumed our old position in front of Alicant.

I believe, indeed, that an attempt was made to surprise the castle of Denia, of which, as I was not engaged in it, I can give no farther account than that it failed—till the season for active operations wore itself out, and we retired into Alicant for winter-quarters.

Chapter 18

The Campaign Opens

I do not recollect that there happened during our winter sojourn in Alicant any event of which it would be worth while to give an account

We had our pickets out, of course, and we reconnoitred occasionally along all the roads, and went through the routine of garrison duty within the walls—but of the enemy we saw nothing; and among the inhabitants I was not fortunate enough to form any acquaintances of whom I at this moment retain a particular recollection. Our provisions were good, and served out in great abundance. We received pay from time to time, though kept for the most part a good deal in arrears; and we mixed in the ordinary amusements of the place, such as the theatres and other public shows. But above all, we continued astonishingly free from sickness; and the best spirit prevailed both among men and officers. So passed the winter, till the return of spring brought with it, as is usual, preparations for a more active life; and, though the weather was unsettled, the army took the field.

Our first movement was in the direction of Alcoy, a populous village, or rather town, beautifully situated behind some low woody hills, and surrounded by streams of water. The French, it appeared, had a detachment there, which it was, I have been told, our object to surprise, and in the attempt to surprise which, a good deal of adventure took place. We moved from Alicant late one day (if my memory serves me right) in the month of February, and arriving at the village of Beira, we halted for the night

The men and horses were put into such quarters as could be found, and the outposts were stationed; after which I was just going to lie down when Captain Jacks sent for me. I repaired to his room, and found with him Lord Frederick Bentinck, who said that he had occasion for an intelligent non-commissioned officer to be employed upon a particular service. I made, of course, no objection to the compliment which it was his pleasure to pay me, but followed him to the house of the *alcalde*, where I was, it appeared, to receive my final instructions.

We found in the house two Spanish gentlemen, well dressed and very good-looking fellows; they were sitting by the fire, talking to the *alcalde*, who rose to salute Lord Frederick when we entered. He made some remark to them, which I could not exactly catch, and, then turning to me, said, "I wish you to go with these Spaniards in disguise to the front. You are not to pass the French videttes—neither are they aware why I send you with them; but you must keep your eyes wide open and observe all that they do, and make a faithful report to me in the morning. Your ostensible business will be to look after the mules."

I answered, that I would attend carefully to his instructions, and turned round—when I saw that my friends were in the act of casting aside their own garments, and putting on others, such as the peasantry wear, of which a bundle lay in a niche hard by. A third suit I soon found had been prepared for me, and I followed their example by assuming it. No disguise could be more perfect. Our huge hats, brown jackets, breeches open at the knee, and leather leggings, gave us all the appearance of peasants; and when our short cloaks were wrapped round us, it would have puzzled the most prying to detect that we were other than what we seemed to be.

"Remember," said Lord Frederick to me, "you are never to open your lips;—your speech would at once betray you. But play the dummy. Only take good care that nothing escapes you."

I again promised to keep his orders strictly in view, and I and my companions went forward.

We did not make straight for Alcoy by following the main

road, but struck into a by-path, which led by our left round some low hills, and began to penetrate through the wood with which they were flanked. It was dusk when we mounted our mules, and the darkness had closed in when about a couple of hours afterwards we pulled up beside a lonely cottage. We entered and found there only one old man, who rose from his seat to bid us welcome, and produced bread and cheese and wine in abundance, with which we refreshed ourselves.

My companions conversed with him as with an old acquaintance. I, bearing Lord Frederick's admonition in mind, never spoke a word; and the peasant, either because he was acquainted with our secret, or that he did not choose to pry into matters that concerned others, took no notice of my taciturnity. He was, however, just as attentive to our animals as to ourselves. They were all put up under a shed, and got fed with water and barley in abundance.

We sat by the fireside till ten o'clock, when my companions rose, and each loading himself with a fagot, of which about a hundred were packed up against the cottage wall outside, threw it over his shoulder upon a stick, and walked out. I looked after them, and saw that they took the direction of a line of fires, which I was at no loss to surmise were those of the French pickets. They were absent about an hour and a half before they returned; and again thrusting their sticks each into a fagot, they again, departed. This time, however, I observed that they did not make directly to the front—they diverged considerably to the left, and were soon lost to my observation amidst the darkness.

I walked about a little while, gazing on the half-circles of fires which were burning, as it appeared to me, scarce a musket-shot before me, when the trampling of horses' hoofs caught my ear, and I hastened back to the house. It was, of course, my policy, if I wished to avoid detection, to feign sleep; so I wrapped my brown cloak round the lower part of my face, drew my broad-brimmed hat over my eyes, and lay down upon a bench in front of the fire. I had scarcely done so, when a French cavalry patrol entered. They demanded bread and wine, and forage for their horses; but the peasant had nothing of the sort to give. He was a poor plundered man—the English troops, and his own countrymen, had alike robbed him in their turns, and now he had nothing left in the house to supply his own wants. They cursed and swore, as was natural, and rummaged about to satisfy themselves, but found nothing. At last one of them approached me, and seizing my head, gave it a shake, as if to awaken me. I cannot deny that I felt a strange chill come over me when the Frenchman's hand first grasped my hat: but I never lost my presence of mind for a moment; and giving a loud grunt, I rolled heavily round, as if too much overcome by fatigue to be easily awakened. The French soldiers laughed, and uttered a few oaths, after which they went away, and I had, by-and-by, the indescribable satisfaction of hearing the trampling of their horses, which grew every instant less audible, till in the end it died away.

So passed the night, to me a somewhat weary one, though the issue of the adventure with the French dragoons tended greatly to encourage me; and towards morning, but long before dawn, my Spanish friends made their appearance. Our mules were immediately saddled, and away we went at a brisk trot towards Beira.

We reached it some time after daybreak, and repairing to the *alcalde's* house gave an account of all that we had heard and seen since our departure; from whom I learned that my companions had been employed as spies, and that their business was to ascertain exactly the position and strength of the French outposts. For this purpose, having nothing else to bring, they had conveyed the fagots to several of the pickets, and thereby made themselves masters of the necessary information, which they now communicated. The consequence was, that about two o'clock in the afternoon, the troops got under arms, and orders having been issued that no man should speak a word, we all moved forward.

It was a cold frosty day, the snow fell in large flakes, and the whole face of the country was covered with it; indeed there needed but a biting wind in our faces to render the discomfort of our situation complete. But, happily for us, that was altogether wanting.

On the contrary, the air was so still that each particular snowflake retained its round shape as it came to the ground, while the effect of the storm was to hinder the transmission of sound beyond the narrowest conceivable distance. All this was in our favour. Neither did the general seem disposed to throw away the advantage through any misplaced attention to the immediate comforts of the men.

We moved on, therefore, silent as the grave, till we reached the wood of which I have spoken, as covering the low hills behind which Alcoy is situated, and there the word was passed to halt, the cavalry to dismount, and the infantry to lie upon their arms. I had been up all the preceding night, and therefore, in spite of the excessive cold, experienced such a desire to sleep that I could not resist I therefore hung my horse's bridle over my waist, and wrapping my cloak about me, lay down. My sleep was sound and refreshing, but when I awoke my helmet and cloak were both so completely frozen to the ground that I was obliged to draw my head out of the first and my arms from beneath the last, and to leave them in their places. Nor was mine a singular case—every individual who slept under that frost, found himself on awakening in a similar plight, and we were forced to let the cloaks lie till the sun had attained sufficient power to melt the icy cords that bound them to the earth.

I know not how it happened, but if our project really included the surprise of the French troops in Alcoy, from some cause or other it went wrong. The outposts being fully on the alert retreated on the main body skirmishing, and the whole evacuated the town, almost at the moment our advanced parties entered it. On the other hand, our arrival among them seemed to occasion the greatest satisfaction to the Spaniards. Food, wine, and corn for the horses—every thing, in short, of which we stood in need, was distributed with a liberal hand, and many and bitter were the execrations which they poured out against the French invaders.

But it was not our purpose to keep Alcoy. Having delayed, therefore, only long enough to perceive, that it was a remarkably nice place, well-watered, well-wooded, and famous for its manufacture of paper, we marched back to Alicant, and returned once more to our ordinary winter's employment

It was the month of April, 1813, ere the business of the campaign can be said to have begun, or an attempt was made on either side, seriously to molest the other. Then, however, having received considerable reinforcements, General Murray took the field, and the army advanced about twelve miles inland to an admirable position, in front of the town of Castella. Castella itself is an old Moorish town, with a castle, which at the period of our arrival was in ruins—large breaches having been effected in the walls, and the interior entirely dismantled. It stands upon the ridge of a low hill, which, stretching away both to the right and left, becomes connected with other ranges of greater attitude and ruggedness. Those on the right, though scarcely to be called mountains, are very precipitous and rocky, while through them runs a stream, by damming up which you can inundate a large portion of the plain, just in front of what would otherwise be the most assailable point in the position. On the left, again, the hills are of a different character; though steep they are not rocky, and in their faces are cut a series of platforms, on which grow extensive vineyards. To be sure, when you go beyond the distance of half a mile from the town, the country becomes much more rugged, but that part on which our left rested was such as I have described—a succession rather of abrupt undulations than hills. Moreover, there was a pass through the heart of these perfectly level and accessible to wheel carriages, which, in the event of a battle, it was obvious would become an object of very serious attack.

Here then we halted, and for about ten days or a fortnight working-parties were abroad continually repairing the defences of the old castle, and throwing up breast. works and batteries wherever they appeared to be required. Meanwhile, some strong parties of Spaniards joined us, some of which, and especially the brigades of Sarsfield and Rodil, were really magnificent-looking fellows—their clothing being entirely new, their arms and appointments complete, and the cavalry horses of the very best description that the country affords. Nor must I omit to mention that both they and their artillery, of which half a brigade served with Sir John Murray's army, did excellent service when they were brought into collision, with the enemy, though, acting as they did on a theatre apart from ours, we had few opportunities of witnessing their valour. But the few which were presented left behind an impression the reverse of unfavourable to Spanish courage: they might not possess the chivalrous daring of the French; they were certainly behind the English in obstinate endurance, but they were spirited and enterprising, and if judiciously commanded might be rendered as good troops as any in the world.

In this manner we employed ourselves till the second week in April, no enemy appearing in our front, nor any certain intelligence respecting either their positions or designs being received. The general then determined to push forward a reconnoitring party, of which the command was given to a brilliant officer, Colonel Adam. The party in question consisted of detachments from the Foreign Hussars, the Brunswick Hussars, and the 20th Light Dragoons, amounting in all to some four hundred sabres. There were, besides, the German Riflemen, the Calabrian Free Corps, and two mountain guns, the whole of which began their march in the highest possible spirits: for nothing could exceed the beauty of the scene, and men and horses were in high health, and fit for almost any act of exertion. The sun shone bright, and the face of the country, refreshed by the winter's rains, was one sheet of brilliant green. The vines were putting out their new shoots, and the olive-trees were in full leaf. It was altogether one of the most agreeable excursions in which I had ever taken part, so that to the present hour the image of it is fresh in my memory.

Our march that day was very short, for it was late ere we quitted the position, and we passed the night in the village of Beira, among the avenues and folds adjacent Next morning we resumed our route, and arriving by-and-by in the town of Vallena, we found it filled with Spanish troops, both cavalry and infantry; and, as it seemed, recently put into a posture of defence. For Vallena, like most of the towns in this province of Spain, was surrounded by a lofty wall, which bore marks of having been newly repaired, banqueted and battlemented; while the old gates turned upon their hinges to give us the admission which they were designed to refuse to an enemy.

We halted here for a brief space, merely to refresh the men, and to strengthen ourselves with the addition of a battalion of Spanish infantry, and then resuming our progress, we soon reached the brow of an eminence, from which on all sides the panorama was magnificent.

Before us lay the great plain of Vallena, stretching far to the north, and covered wherever the eye could reach, with the most luxuriant herbage. On the left, though removed to a considerable distance, was a range of lofty mountains, which came down gradually into the level; and lost themselves in a succession of gentle undulations. Northward, too, was another range, but so remote that only the broad outlines could be discerned; while on the right there seemed no termination to the level, which a slight rise here and there served only to diversify, by no means to interrupt. Yet extensive as was the range given to the eye, not a trace of the French army could be discerned in any direction. Our leader, it was said, had heard of their moving; and certain fugitives from Yecla brought in a rumour of their having cut to pieces a division of General Elio's Spanish corps, which had been imprudently left there.

Yet though Yecla was but six leagues from Vallena, and the action, if fought at all, must have been fought all the night, there was no symptom of a desire on Suchet's part to push his advantage farther. Nevertheless, the purpose of our expedition was to obtain information, and Colonel Adam was determined not to go back without it; so, after a brief pause upon the brow of the last hill, the word was given to march, and we descended into the plain.

On we went, using all the precautions customary among people that are placed in our situation. The cavalry were in front, preceded by scouts and skirmishers; while both flanks were covered by riflemen. Then came the mountain guns, slung across the mules; next, the Calabrian Free Corps; then the Spaniards; and, last of all, the German riflemen, who likewise furnished a rear-guard. On, then, we went—no enemy showing himself—no dust rising—nor any peasant meeting us by the way from whom we might obtain information.

At last, as we drew towards the line of the low hills of which I have spoken, as closing in this prodigious plain on the left, Colonel Adam gave orders to halt; while parties of horse and foot should advance to examine with care the valleys that in great numbers intersected then. Accordingly, the cavalry demounted, the infantry piled their arms, and we addressed ourselves with good will (for it was about ten o'clock in the forenoon) to each supplies of food and wine as our canteens and haversacks could furnish.

We had scarcely begun to make ourselves comfortable, when bang came the report of a pistol from the scouts. We looked round, and saw the cavalry, who were farthest in advance, firing their carbines, and retreating upon the infantry, which in like manner began to give ground. In an instant the word was passed—"Stand to your arms!"—and the column was formed again in almost less time than it may take the reader to follow my description of the movement.

Still, as the cause of this alarm was not yet manifest, Colonel Adam would not abandon his ground. "We must see what they look like," said he. "It's no use going back with a cock-and-a-bull story: it will be time enough to retire when we have ascertained the amount of force that threatens us." And in this respect we were not long left in the dark. The scouts, which had at first fallen back slowly, now began to gallop towards us. The infantry, happily for themselves, had a good start—when, all at once, the rising grounds, which it had been their business to examine, became covered with French troops. Dense columns, both of horse and foot, were moving, from which detached parties were thrown out—with the design, as it appeared, of preserving the communication between the head of one and that of another. Now, then, it was indeed high time for us to be off. "We shall fall back, my lads," said Colonel Adam, with all the coolness in the world; "but we shall do so at our leisure. We were not sent here to fight—but the rascals shan't have it to say that we ran away from them. So, keep your ranks, and move steadily: no fear but that we shall keep them from pressing us." Our men perfectly understood, and acted up to these instructions; so that the whole of the retreat, as far as Vallena, was as orderly as a movement at a field-day.

Chapter 19

Some Adventures

The French came on with great boldness. Their numbers were so superior to ours, that to have waited for them would have convicted our leader of insanity. Indeed it is not going too far to assert, that almost any other troops would have been hurried by their fears into irretrievable confusion; so that the retreat must have been converted almost immediately into a flight It was not so, however, with us. Our column marched rapidly, doubtless, but it never once broke into a run; and as to stragglers, not one was left behind. For our rear-guard did their duty gallantly. There was no end to the skirmishing as well with infantry as with cavalry, nor any limits to the devoted heroism which individuals displayed; while slowly, and keeping our faces constantly towards them, we gave ground, till the walls of Vallena were before us.

It was late in the evening when we came in sight of the town, which was so situated, that to pass it both to the right and left would have been the easiest thing in the world. Colonel Adam, however, willing to engage the French in such a struggle as would afford to his jaded troops leisure for breathing, marched into the town; while the Spaniards, manning the battlements, opened upon the pursuers such a fire as effectually arrested their progress.

In Vallena, however, we made no halt. It was our business, having ascertained exactly how the enemy were situated, to return as soon as possible, and with as little loss as might be, to the main body: consequently, taking with us the mass of the Spanish division, and leaving in the place only men enough to hold it, we marched out in the direction of Castella, carrying all our wounded along with us. But the night was by this time closing fast, and the face of the heavens became obscured by quantities of black clouds. By and by, a few drops of rain fell, which were followed soon afterwards by a furious thunder-storm, and the showers which succeeded were of such a nature as to penetrate through cloaks, coats—I had almost said skins—in a moment. Under these circumstances, and finding his people begin to fall out, Colonel Adam did not consider it wise to proceed too far, so he halted about Beira, the head-quarters and general staff occupying the village—the troops, and especially the rear-guard to which I was attached, bivouacking in the open fields, or finding what shelter they could in such huts and cabins as might be scattered near the ground which they were directed to maintain.

The Foreign Hussars, among their other admirable qualities as soldiers, were famous for discovering for themselves and their horses quarters somehow or other, wherever they might chance to serve.

Tonight the prospect at first halting seemed gloomy enough; for there was neither cottage nor farm-house near, and the olive plantations, though they might have done very well in a calm night, presented few attractions under the peltings of such a pitiless storm. At last, after looking hither and thither for some time to no purpose, one of the men discovered a lonely chapel, planted at the skirt of a wood, and at the bottom of a ravine, a little way removed from the road. Thither in a moment the whole squadron moved, and bursting open the door, we soon found ourselves under the shelter of a roof, sufficiently umbrageous to shield us all from the violence of the rain. There was a lamp burning, a perpetual lamp, which was suspended from the ceiling, the feeble light of which sufficed to make us aware that quantities of wax candles stood on the four altars, which in different parts of the building were erected. No time was lost in applying to each of these a match, so that in five seconds the chapel was lighted up as if for some high festival.

And then followed a scene abundantly characteristic of the ravages of war, and the manners of those that wage them. The chapel was full of chairs, set there, of course, for the accommodation of the worshippers. We had no use for these, so they were cast out without the smallest ceremony into the open air; while men and horses entered without hesitation, and all found room to bestow themselves.

This done, we began, as was natural, to look round us; and the first thought being about money, a sharp eye was cast into every corner where we supposed it possible that treasure or plate might be secreted. The poor's-box, I blush to confess, was broken open in an instant, and its contents, be they abundant or otherwise, were soon divided among the spoilers. Then came a hunt far and near for the cupboard, in which the church plate might be concealed. Yet,—let justice be done to the Foreign Hussars—no violence was offered either to the decorations of the altars, or the priests' vestments; though the latter, being found, were turned over and over with great care, ere they were restored to the place from which the first discoverers had drawn them.

The chapel of which we had thus taken possession, was dedicated to St. Eustatius, of whom an enormous wooden statue, about six feet three in height, surmounted the principal altar. It was curiously carved, in long flowing robes; but it was the countenance of the image that most powerfully arrested our attention, and drew towards it the wondering gaze of every individual within the walls.

The hair of the image—for it had a wig—was black. There was a black beard and *moustachios*; the cheeks were coloured with vermilion, and, above all, the eyes were dark, brilliant, and most expressive. Go where you would, indeed, the eye of the Saint seemed to be upon you; so that there were not wanting those among us over whom, as they gazed upon his countenance, a feeling of superstitious awe gained an ascendency. The majority, however, after cracking their jokes upon his reverence, resumed their search, which introduced them into the vestry, exactly in rear of the Saint, and of the altar upon which he was planted. We examined that little apartment carefully; but having discovered nothing of which we were in search, we were about to return to the chapel, when a shout from one of the party caused me to look round: he beckoned us to join him, in doing which we ascertained that he had just detected a door, is the wall adjoining the altar, of very small size, and so artfully constructed, that by other eyes than our own, it would have escaped detection. We directed all our attention forthwith to ascertain by what means the door was to be opened, but we failed. There was neither lock nor handle, so we adopted the approved method of allaying curiosity in such cases, and burst it open. We hoped to find some hidden treasure, but we found only the source of it; for the aperture introduced us to the hollow interior of the statue, down which two strings were dangling. These, of course, we began to pull, when the Saint rolled his eyes about in the most extraordinary manner, to the great astonishment, at first, and eventually amid the laughter of those who from the chapel-side watched the proceeding. Nor did our researches end here: one after another we insinuated ourselves into the Saint's interior—and the cause of many a miracle, with the fame of which the whole valley of Vallena rung, was made manifest to us. Following the course of these strings, each of which we ascertained was attached to one of the Saint's eyes, we became aware that the eyes themselves were made of glass, and that, in the very centre where the pupils lay, both were slightly perforated. Moreover, the eye was so constructed that it could contain a small quantity of water, which, by pulling the strings, was forced through the aperture—a mighty source of wealth to the priests who performed mass in this chapel, and the cause of no slight honour to the Saint himself. For, once in every year, as we learned that night, pilgrims from all quarters, not only near at hand, but far distant, were accustomed to repair to his shrine; and, bringing with them offerings of money, wine, oil, and merchandise of all sorts, to ask his intercession for the pardon of their sins, and their reconciliation to their Maker. It did not always follow that the Saint would listen to their prayer. If the offering happened to be of small value, or they were known to be rich, and likely to come again, the Saint would give no proof that he heard them, for the first and second, and sometimes the third time. But, sooner or later, provided they were sufficiently liberal, he was sure to deal liberally by them, when, as their reward, he shed tears, on the falling of which the bells rang, the host was elevated, and there was as much rejoicing as if some great national victory had been achieved.

We were assured by our informants, that at times as many as a thousand votaries would be on their knees, at the same instant, some in the chapel itself, others in the field beside it; and such was the reputation of the Saint, that in all that quarter of Spain, none had so many worshippers, or such liberal offerings presented to him.

The movements of the Saint's eyes, so soon as the cause same to be known, produced, as may be imagined, extraordinary merriment among the soldiers, in which the officers joined heartily, and we played at Punchinello with the wooden holiness till the strings broke. Then were our hands employed to produce the effect which machinery had heretofore brought about; when all at once there arose a cry, "Here come the priests!" and we, who had hitherto acted as showmen, made all the haste we could to escape detection. We leaped the altar, and closed the secret door; but having broken the lock, we could not, of course, fasten it, so we ran out of the vestry to watch among the crowd what consequences would follow.

We had scarcely taken our stations when the chapel-door new open, and half-a-dozen priests, followed by a crowd of old men, women, and children, entered. Among us the most profound silence prevailed; we squeezed our lips with our fingers, to suppress the titter that rose to them, while, with hands upraised, and every other demonstration of horror, the procession moved forward. As to the priests, their care was directed immediately towards their tutelar saint They ran into the vestry, and ascertaining in a trice that their secret had been found out, they burst into the wildest exclamations of grief and anger. But their cunning was not even now at fault. The church-bier was brought hastily forward. In the twinkling of an eye the image was taken down from the altar, and, laying him upon the bier, and covering him with a white doth, they raised a cry that might have awaked the dead. The Saint, the altar, the chapel, and every thing pertaining to it, had been profaned by the presence of these heretics. What could they do—what was to become of the country? But one thing was quite certain—it was necessary, if they hoped to escape the vengeance of Heaven, that the Saint himself should be removed elsewhere. Accordingly, the bier was lifted from the ground, and, amid weeping and howling, the priests bore him off; followed by their blinded dupes, all of them in tears. It was from some of these persons my friend Conrad Hettendorff obtained all the information which I have given above; and, as the poor people spoke in the very bitterness of their hearts, I see no reason to doubt that they spoke truth.

The Saint being gone, and our curiosity in other matters satisfied, we lay down upon the floor, and, in spite of our wet clothes, obtained a few hours' sleep, which refreshed us exceedingly. We were mounted, and in our stations, of course, an hour before dawn, which, indeed, was the more necessary; for in the course of the night the French got possession of Vallena, and our position lay distant from the town scarcely two miles. We could hear their drums and trumpets calling them to arms, almost at the same moment that we threw ourselves into our saddles. It was broad daylight, however, before they advanced, and our position, on the rise of a well-wooded eminence, covered on both flanks by ravines of a considerable depth, prompted Colonel Adam, in the spirit of the instructions which he had received at the commencement of his expedition, to wait for them. They came on with the utmost resolution. Their skirmishers, thrown out in clouds, bore hard upon our light troops, and forced them to give ground; and then the opposing lines came into play.

For ourselves (I speak of the handful of cavalry), we were riding about continually; now making a movement, as if to meet the enemy when threatening a charge; now scattered into detached files; till our horses, having fared badly throughout the previous night, began to manifest such symptoms of fatigue, that it became necessary to spare them as much as possible. It was at this juncture that Colonel Adam received a musket-ball through the fleshy part of his arm, and withdrew for a brief space to the rear. But he was soon at his station again, having his coat cut open, and carrying the wounded limb in a sling; in which plight he continued to issue his orders, and show himself, wherever his presence appeared most requisite, with as much composure as if he had been directing the movements of a brigade on some parade. ground in England.

We made a stout resistance; but the odds were fearfully against us, and we lost ground continually, multitudes dropping both from our ranks, and the ranks of the French, never to rise again. At length they won the crest of the hill, upon which our two mountain guns, after having been fought with incredible courage to the last, were abandoned. When the enemy saw that they had taken our cannon, they raised a shout of triumph; and pouring down the slope made as if they would have destroyed us at a single rush. But we met them, as we had hitherto done, with a well-directed fire, which checked their ardour, so much as to afford time for the formation of a new line on the ridge of another eminence that lay beyond the valley. By this time, however, the main body of our army was discovered drawn up in the best order, as it seemed waiting for the attack. The French, therefore, abated from pressing us farther; and we were permitted to march back at an easy pace, and to assume our proper stations in the line without being molested.

It was something past noon, when, spent with toil, and covered with dust and sweat, the Foreign Hussars drew up in the rear of a couple of guns which crowned a height in the centre of the position.

If it had been the general's design to plant us where we might obtain a distinct view of the arrangements of both parties, he could not have selected a more convenient spot, for from the brow of the hill I was enabled to see to the extremities which flanked our position, as well as to observe all the enemy's manoeuvres, which were neither few nor little varied. For a space of two hours or something more, they closely reconnoitred us. Halting just out of cannon-shot, they brought up a heavy column of infantry to oppose our centre; their cavalry, which was numerous, swept away in one mass towards the right, seeking for some open space through which to approach us, and expecting to find it where the heights of Castella dropped down into the plain. On that side, however, the waters of the river had been damned up, and now the entire surface of the level, being covered by the inundation, presented the appearance of a vast lake. By-and-by, therefore, as if satisfied that nothing was to be done there, the larger portion of the French horse returned, and again, doubtless with a view to intimidate us, rode leisurely along our front in a solid and yet deep column. Then followed masses of infantry with guns, which, filing to our left, showed in some measure on what point the storm would burst, and warned our general that in heaping hie strength upon the centre he had somewhat miscalculated the chances. But this error, if such it may be called, was not of so serious a nature but that It could be rectified at almost any given moment, for the gorge on our left was well blocked up with cannon, and several battalions of tried infantry were at hand to support them.

It was now two o'clock, and as yet not a shot had been fired, when suddenly a swarm of French Tirailleurs, whom we had observed spreading themselves among the underwood in front of our centre, began to move forward. Two heavy columns moved slowly as if to support them, and a battery of six or eight pieces being brought within range, opened upon us first with round, and by-and-by with grape-shot.

The Tirailleurs were met in gallant style by our riflemen and light infantry, and a sharp skirmish ensued, but there was nothing more than a skirmish. The columns shifted their ground, indeed, more than once, but they did not deploy, and the officers took good care not to bring them under the fire of our line. It was different on the extreme left. There, a furious discharge of cannon and musketry gave notice that a formidable attack was in progress, and the length of time during which it was sustained, left no room to doubt that it was pushed with all imaginable vigour.

Thrice, and on each occasion, with numbers largely increased, the enemy charged the position, and thrice the admirable practice of the artillery, with the obstinate courage of the infantry, drove them back. But now a fourth assault was menaced, and an order arrived for the hussars to move to the support of their comrades, who had been so long and so obstinately engaged.

We left the two guns which we had hitherto guarded to the protection of some of the 20th, and riding along the rear of the position, were moved up into a hollow between two heights, so as to be as much as possible protected from the fire of the enemy's guns. For their artillery no sooner saw us in motion than they opened upon us, and keeping the range with tolerable accuracy, they ceased not to throw both shot and shell about us, even when we were partially covered by the elbow of the hill.

All, however, with a single exception, either fell short or flew over, and that a ball from an eight-pounder took effect only on a horse. It struck him full in the chest, upon which the poor animal reared up, sprang into the air, and fell dead upon his side. Captain Jacks observing this, directed us to move a little farther to the left, where the ground was broken; remarking, that if they did observe our change of position, they would at least be obliged to take a new elevation with their guns, and to find out the right one. And well it was for me that this flank movement was made. I was on the right of the troop, a few yards detached from the men, and so sharp was my horse's appetite, that he gnawed the bark from off a young olive-tree that stood in my front. I had not taken three paces from the tree when a round shot struck it, and shivered it to atoms. But the moment was close at hand when even this escape, narrow as it unquestionably was, ceased to be thought of. The enemy had charged again, they were again repulsed, and now the word passed for the cavalry to dash forward, and do as much mischief as possible to the disordered and flying columns.

I have already described the nature of the heights on which our left rested. They were steep downs, out out into platform or terrace, on each of which grew a plantation. of vines, with here and these a few olive-trees.

It was our business, of course, to keep as much as possible under cover—not only because by so doing we should escape a portion of the enemy's fire, but because by breaking out upon them in a moment when they were not prepared for us, our opportunities of doing them damage would be increased.

In order to accomplish these two ends, Captain Jacks led us along the edge of the hill on our left, from which we were forced to descend gradually into the plain below, by leaping our horses from one terrace to another. The effect of these jumps upon, animals, already worked well-nigh beyond their strength, was to exhaust them thoroughly; while upon us the nature of our position soon brought a terrible salutation. Though some of the French infantry were in the plain and in great disorder, a still larger number continued still to crown the hills, which they were obliged to cross for the purpose of escaping from the fire of our artillery. These no sooner beheld us below them, than they opened such a fusillade as to make the most practised among us ask himself the question, whether he had ever stood under a musketry fire before. Men dropped from their horses—horses fell beneath their riders; and some who held their course received impressions which were never effaced to their dying day. Of these there was near me one, through whose lower jaw a musket-ball passed, carrying away some of the teeth, and coming out at his throat. He kept his seat, and was induced to quit the field only by perceiving that he ran the risk of being suffocated in his own blood.

We gained the level at length, and then, though our horses were cruelly spent, we rushed forward sword in hand, determined to take vengeance for the loss which we had sustained.

Our charge was completely successful. The broken enemy could make but little resistance, and we secured about a hundred prisoners; with whom, finding the fire grow more and more hot, we endeavoured to make our way back to the line. But ere we could reach it the French brought some cannon to bear, and threw upon us such a shower of cannister as to shake us greatly; while our wearied horses refused to go beyond a walk, and we saw a regiment of cavalry hurrying forward to charge. So circumstanced, we felt that in order to take care of ourselves, it would be necessary to abandon our prisoners; and these being allowed to steal away by fives and sixes at a time, soon left us nothing to provide for except our own safety. Conrad and I, however, had secured two fellows whom we were exceedingly reluctant to abandon. One was a sergeant who wore a silver chain. across his shoulder, and produced a watch, which, I regret to say, we had no time to take from him; the other was a drummer, who carried on his back two drums. These we compelled to accompany us, till the storm grew so furious that we could not carry them further.

We told them to shift for themselves, and the mode in which they showed their gratitude was, to snatch a couple of muskets from the ground and discharge them after us.

"What fools we were," said I to Conrad, "not to stop these rascals firing!"

"We'll be wiser next time," replied he; after which, having happily escaped without a wound, we rejoined the squadron, and took up our old position.

Our horses were yet panting with their recent exertions, and ourselves leaning on the pommels of our saddles, when Sir John Murray rode up, and praising us for our gallantry, called aloud, "You must be at them again, Hussars. They must not escape in this way. See, here comes the 20th. Show them that, though you have had all the toil of the day, they shan't leave you behind."

We answered with a cheer, and bearing our horses up as well as we could, in five minutes we were once more in the heart of the French infantry; upon whom, the officer commanding, led us and the 20th straight down the ravine. The carnage was dreadful, and the prisoners taken amounted to more than double the number which on a previous occasion we had secured. As Providence would have it, our friends, the sergeant and the drummer, fell again into Conrad's hands and mine. Our blood was hot; we remembered their treacherous and cruel act, and we slew them where they stood. I thought at the moment they richly merited their fate, and I think so still.

At the same time a hearty cheer caused us to look about, and we beheld the whole line of British infantry advancing with levelled bayonets down the slope, before whom the enemy were fleeing in the utmost confusion, while over their heads our own cannon continued to fire. This was the last that I could distinguish of the battle, for it was already dark when we made our charge, and night set in so rapidly that we were compelled, in order to secure the prisoners already taken, to check the pursuit In like manner the fire both of cannon and musketry ceased, and the troops were directed to lie upon their arms, each squadron and company on the exact spot which it occupied when the battle ended.

Chapter 20

We Lay Siege to Tarragona

Never has an order to halt arrived either to man or beast more seasonably than this, for I may say with truth, that during two whole days, we had been continually marching, without being allowed as much of time or leisure as would suffice to allay the common wants of nature.

Fortunately, too, there were issued out both provisions for the men and forage for the animals; the latter being to the full as much needed as the former; after consuming which we threw ourselves on the ground in our cloaks and closed our eyes. But in spite of the fatigue of which I was conscious, I could not for some time compose myself to sleep. Around me on every side lay numbers, not only of dead but of wounded men, whose cries, heard distinctly in the stillness of a calm night, were very shocking. It was to no purpose that I turned first on one side and then on the other, or burying my head in my cloak strove to shut out the sound; it was still in my ears, and coming upon the back of the excitement occasioned by so desperate a struggle, it was more than a match for weariness. At last, however, one of the parties whom our medical staff employed to search the field for such as might be exposed upon it, drew towards me, and I pointed out a little group of wounded men whom they removed. I was greatly relieved when I saw them depart, and then looking up towards the clear blue sky, I thanked my Creator for having preserved me, lay down beside my jaded horse and slept soundly.

We lay down that night in the confident expectation that the morrow would witness a renewal of the combat for the enemy though repulsed on all points were both numerous and daring, and we believed that if they failed to attack us, we should be the assailants.

But the dawn of day gave proof that we had erred in our calculations. Not a Frenchman was to be seen; and the patrols which were immediately pushed forward reported that the line of their retreat was marked by the dead and dying, which they had left by the roadside. Immediately there came an order to mount and follow. We obeyed it of course, but we never overtook the fugitives, and after a sojourn of some days in the neighbourhood of Alcoy, we retraced our steps and took up our old position in Castella.

We remained here in a state of apparent inactivity, till the month of May was far advanced, when the camp was suddenly broken up and the whole army marched back to Alicant.

A secret expedition, it appeared, against some point nearer to the frontier had been a good while in contemplation, and as it would have been unsafe to march by land in the face of so great a superiority of strength as the enemy were understood to possess, a movement by sea was resolved upon.

Neither were we long kept in the dark as to the precise object of our intended expedition. The troops being removed on board of ship with a large train of artillery both for siege and field operations, the fleet put to sea for the avowed purpose of attacking Tarragona, one of the strongest if not the strongest place along the whole of the western coast of Spain.

A pleasant passage of some hours' continuance carried as round the coast of Catalonia, till we entered the mouth of the noble harbour of Tarragona, and beheld the city and castle, both of prodigious strength, rising above it. Built upon a rock and fortified with all the skill and care of which the site appears to have been capable, it presented a very formidable front; and at the period when we made our appearance in the bay, was occupied by a French garrison, perfectly capable, both from numbers and discipline, to maintain it to the last extremity. Moreover, the whole of the surrounding country may be said to have been in the enemy's possession. It is true that bands of armed Spaniards prowled about among the hills, cutting off convoys and harassing the march of weak detachments. But Marshal Suchet was, to the utmost extent of the phrase, in military occupation of the province, and had under his orders an army far surpassing that with which it was purposed, on our side, to undertake the siege of this second Gibraltar.

Under such circumstances, it seemed the obvious policy of our leaders not to land a greater amount of stores and ammunition than might be required for daily consumption, because the anchorage was a safe one, and the space between it and the beach not so extensive as to render our communication insecure at any moment; yet our chiefs were of a different opinion, and the consequences, as I shall have occasion by-and-by to point out, proved unusually disastrous.

Besides the heavy sea batteries that covered Tarragona itself, there was a small fort on the left of the bay, of which it was considered necessary to obtain possession, for the purpose of rendering the communication between the shipping and the camp at once safe and commodious. The task of reducing it was undertaken by Admiral Hallowell and his seamen and marines; and so gallant was their bearing, that in the course of a single night, after some bombarding from the ships of war, it was carried by assault Meanwhile the troops with a huge train of battering-guns, and an enormous quantity of shot, shell, powder, beef, biscuit, and hospital stores were conveyed, as rapidly as the means of transport would allow, to the shore. No opposition was offered by the French, neither indeed could such have availed them; for the beach was open, and the guns of our lighter craft swept it far and near, so that without the occurrence of any casualty, the whole force reached the land, and the investment of Tarragona was effected. Then came in the usual routine of digging trenches, fabricating fascines, throwing up batteries, and laying down platforms; after which the guns were run in and a heavy firing began.

But so superior was that of the defenders to anything which we could bring against them, that it generally ended in the dismantling of our artillery. One by one our guns were dismounted, and the siege made but tardy progress.

In the labour of such operations the cavalry have no share. It is their business to observe the rear of the camp, to take the patrol duty, and otherwise guard their comrades against surprise; and there was occupation enough of this sort presented to us day by day to hinder a complaint of the absence of employment from being heard any where.

We pushed our reconnaissances on in all directions, to a wide extent, and for a time nothing appeared to create alarm. Moreover, our intelligence was excellent; for the country people were all on our side, and General Donkin, the quarter-master general, appeared indefatigable. At last, however, the bubble, which we had long and anxiously fostered, was destined to burst After reconnoitring the roads that led to Reuss and Valls, we proceeded one day in the direction of Arbos, and entering the village with General Donkin at our head, we talked of commencing our inquiries; but there was no occasion for that; the inhabitants anticipated us by reporting that the French were on the move with thirty thousand men, and that nothing could prevent them from arriving in front of Tarragona within the space of eight-and-forty hours. Now General Donkin knew the characters of his informants, and felt that he might depend upon them. He therefore commanded us to mount as soon as we had baited our horses, and we returned at a brisk trot towards the camp.

It so happened that we found Sir John Murray walking with Admiral Hallowell upon the sands, and the information which we had picked up was immediately communicated to them. General Murray credited the report at once, but Admiral Hallowell scouted it as ridiculous. It was to no purpose that General Donkin assured him of the reliance which he placed in his spies; the admiral insisted that the whole story was a fabrication; and that it originated in treachery. Instead, therefore, of assenting to the general's proposal of getting the guns and stores off with as little delay as possible, he contended that it would, not be requisite to remove even the men till the latter should have fallen; for nobody seemed to take into account the impossibility of resisting an attack from Suchet's troops on one side, and the garrison of Tarragona, on the other. The only question between them was, as to the probable approach of a French army; and this the admiral persisted in rejecting as a fable. I am the more forward to state all this, because a different account of the transaction has, I believe, gone abroad; and having myself overheard the conversation of the chiefs, I am able to speak of it from my own personal observation. The result, accordingly, was, that throughout the whole of that night and the next day, our batteries continued to fire; and that not a movement was made calculated to create a suspicion that the siege would be raised.

Time passed, and every new hour brought in a fresh rumour of the approach of Suchet. Patrols were again sent out, which falling in with the scouts from the French advanced guard, skirmished with them for awhile, and then returned to report what had befallen.

Now then at last the admiral, as well as the general, received a conviction that the enemy were coming on, and guns, stores, ammunition, and entrenching tools, were all abandoned. The provisions and powder, of which quantities had been brought on shore, were rolled into the sea. The guns were spiked, the shot and shell buried in the trenches; yet so inadequately was all this done, that the booty left behind must have greatly delighted the captors, and given them means to recruit the exhausted magazines of Tarragona. Finally, just as the enemy began to show themselves on the high grounds at a distance, the last of our detachments entered the boats, and the whole were brought off without disaster, and lodged on board of ship.

It it not my province to criticise the behaviour of my superiors, far less to pass judgement on the wisdom or folly of this attempt; but the results were as mortifying both to us and to the Spaniards, as they must have been satisfactory to the French. The fact, indeed, is, that except by the bomb-vessels and boats of the fleet, no useful service was performed. These harassed the town, it is true, by approaching close under the batteries by night, and showering shells and rockets into the streets; yet even their services were productive of perhaps more inconvenience to the inhabitants than mischief to the garrison, which kept them in a state of unwilling subjection. But however this may be, the enterprise terminated as I have described. We went off like a dog that has lost a battle, and were welcomed back to Alicant by the jibes of our own comrades, and the well-deserved ridicule of our allies.

CHAPTER 21

New Leaders & New Operations

The account which I have given of the expedition to Tarragona, is, I am aware, very imperfect There were some movements made, previous to the final embarkation, of which I cannot speak at all, and others, concerning which my memory serves me so little, that I am unwilling to touch upon them. It strikes me, for example, that though the British force was all taken on board at Tarragona, some Spanish corps that served along with us, retreated by land as far as the Col de Balaguer, and that preparations were at one moment made for a second debarkation at the latter spot. Moreover, if I do not deceive myself, a large portion of our infantry did disembark, and for a single day faced the enemy. But not having myself had any share in the operations, I am unwilling to hazard statements which may be quite erroneous, and can amount only to conjecture. One thing, however, is quite certain, that while we lingered at this part of the Catalonian coast, new commanders-in-chief both for our land and sea forces arrived; and that the troops had at their head, when we renewed our old quarters in Alicant, Lieutenant-General Lord William Bentinck.

We re-entered the harbour of Alicant towards the latter end of June, and remained perfectly quiet till the 8th of Jury. The interval was doubtless spent by the heads of departments in making preparations for a move; for on the morning of the 9th, the army took the field. No enemy appeared to harass us; none were reported by the peasantry to be near, so we pushed forward leisurely, and in excellent order, towards Valencia. It was not so with our Spanish allies, the brigades of Sarsfield and Rodil. These, moving upon our flanks, were engaged in constant affairs with detached bodies of French troops which gave way before them, and acquitted themselves, as far as we could learn, with great gallantry. But to us no opposition was offered, so that our progress resembled more the passage of an army through a country which is at peace, than the opening of a campaign in the free of an enemy, whose activity and numerical strength were alike formidable.

When we broke up our camp, we were given to understand that Valencia was in possession of the French: as we drew towards it, which was done by slow marches, intelligence came in that they had retreated. Our faces were immediately turned in the direction of the town, and we entered it in triumph. Neither would it be possible to exceed the joy with which the inhabitants received us, or the marks of respect with which, on all hands, we were greeted.

As we approached the city, the walls were observed to be hang with pieces of silk of all colours, and here and there with tapestry. Across the streets triumphal arches were erected; green boughs strewed the pavements; While, in the balconies stood ladies and gentlemen, who waved their handkerchiefs, and showered down flowers upon our heads. As to Lord William Bentinck, I thought he would have been smothered with their nosegays. They heaped them upon him, not from their hands, but out of baskets, and made the air resound with cries of *"Viva los Angleses!" "Viva le Général Liberante!"*

In this manner we marched through Valencia, our colours flying and bands playing, and sure I am that if the prayers of the poor people could have availed, not a man of us would have sustained hurt from that moment to the close of his life. Yet they mixed up their congratulations with statements to the effect that the enemy were not far distant, and that without doubt we should be called upon, ere many days elapsed, to give them battle. The Foreign Hussars were soon made to understand that the general had not been careless of this intelligence. We halted in Valencia only one day, when, together with our old friends the Calabrian and German rifles, we were sent out to do the duty of patrolling and advanced posts.

It was not our policy by lingering long in this place, to give an opportunity to the French of maturing their plans at leisure. After a brief halt, therefore, the columns once more pushed forward, following the road by the sea-shore which leads to Tortosa on the Ebro. There was nothing worthy of record in all this march. No hostile bodies opposed us, no patrols encountered ours, and we reached the bank of the river, at a place called Amposa, without having occasion to fire a shot. There is a ferry here, across which Lord William made haste to throw us, supporting his cavalry as soon as possible with infantry and guns. But we did not land at Tortosa: that was still in possession of the enemy, and being strongly fortified, it was not judged expedient to waste our valuable time in front of it.

While the rest of the army was crossing the Ebro, the advanced guard went out in all directions to reconnoitre; we of the Foreign Hussars following a road which seemed to conduct towards Tortosa. We were riding along expecting no adventure, of any sort, when all at once we observed in a valley below us a caravan of sixty bullocks, carts, and a large train of mules marching under an escort of French infantry. To charge them was the work of a moment. Forward we rode down the slope of the descent, without drawing either carbine or pistol, and threw ourselves upon them, sword in hand, with such rapidity that they never thought of attempting to make resistance. They flung away their muskets, called for quarter, and to a man were made prisoners. This was the first opportunity that we had had of coming into collision with the French since the arrival of Lord William Bentinck to command us, and it was hailed as a favourable omen of what might follow. Moreover, it was the source of mock rejoicing, both to us and to our comrades the Calabrese; all of whom helped themselves without scruple to the wine and food, with which in great quantities the cars were loaded. We had taken a convoy of provisions on its way to Tortosa, of which the governor was anticipating the blockade; and besides being publicly thanked in orders, each man got his canteen filled with excellent wine, and as much bread and salt fish as he chese to carry along with him.

From the period of our crossing the Ebro, we began to feel that we were engaged in something more than a mere game of warfare. The enemy seemed reluctant to abandon the ground between Tortosa and Tarragona, and were not removed from it without frequent encounters between our advanced parties and their rear-guard. But they did fall back leisurely, permitting us to occupy at Cabrils a position which they had taken up in order to cover the town; and eventually when threatened at Arbos, Valls, and Reuss, retiring still farther towards the frontier. The consequence of these successes was, that Lord William Bentinck invested Tarragona, and pushing back the enemy to Villa Franca, established his line of observation in and around Arbos.

With the general movements of the army I am too little acquainted to hazard an opinion concerning them. I do not even know where our headquarters were at this time established; but for myself, my station was with the corps to which I belonged, the Calabrese, the riflemen, and a battalion of the 27th on the right of the line, so as to touch the sea between the villages of Torre del Borra and Altafalla. Here, being far in advance of the main body, we were required to exercise the utmost vigilance; and never, for one moment, either by night or day, was our vigilance relaxed.

At first, our pickets were stationed in front of Torre del Borra, the main body itself being posted in the village; but such an arrangement was considered too dangerous, and another took place. Torre del Borra was held as a post only during the day, and regularly as ten o'clock at night came round, it was evacuated. We then left a picket in its rear, fell back about a mile to Altafalla; and keeping saddled and accoutred, were ready for action so soon as the alarm should be given.

We were thus situated—that is to say, Torre del Borra was still kept as a prominent station, when Colonel Adam one day directed a party of the hussars; with some of the riflemen and light infantry, to attend him on a reconnaissance to the front.

He expressed a wish that I should take command of the hussars; and about six o'clock in the evening, or perhaps somewhat later, we moved from the village towards some low woods that skirted the base of a rising-ground, a little to the left.

A guide, of course, attended us; indeed, in a strange country, guides are essential to all military operations, and we were instructed to preserve a perfect silence, and to be greatly on the alert. In this manner we traversed the wood, at the farther extremity of which the escort was halted, while Colonel Adam handing his portfolio and writing-materials to me, desired me to attend him. "We must go very cautiously to work, Sergeant-Major," said he, "for we are close upon them—they are at the opposite side of the hill." And cautious we undeniably were: moving at the slowest possible walk, we crept up the face of the ascent till the colonel reached a point whence he could make his observations.

Immediately the telescope was at his eye, and he swept the enemy's position; after which he took his portfolio from me, and throwing his right foot on the pommel of the saddle, noted down what he had seen. This was repeated several times; and we had kept our ground about ten minutes, when bang came a musket-ball from a neighbouring copse, which just grazed the side of the colonel's hat.

"This won't do," said he, looking up and handing me the portfolio, "I must preserve my life for another occasion. It's no use sitting here, for we are discovered." Accordingly we wheeled about and rode towards our escort, just as a picket of the enemy, both horse and foot, crowned the ridge. They gave us a volley to no purpose, but they did not venture to pursue, for it was already getting dark, and they saw that we had support at hand; so we retraced our steps leisurely through the wood, and returned to Torre del Borra uninjured.

I do not know whether this little reconnaissance had any influence in producing the movement, but we shortly afterwards withdrew from Torre del Borra, and left only a picket in front of the village, which fell back every night as darkness set in, to a station in the rear. Meanwhile our division, if such it deserves to be called, was quartered in Altafalla. Not that Altafalla was our rallying post; on the contrary, it was our nightly custom to march about three miles backwards on the road to Tarragona, where, in certain vineyards and among some broken ground that flanked the highway to the left, we formed line; after which, both men and horses bivouacking in order of battle, we stayed there till daybreak came in, and then marched back to the village.

Moreover, it soon became apparent to us, that the enemy, besides having some great object in view, were perfectly aware of our numerical inferiority.

Scarcely a day passed, without their pushing forward some attack upon our pickets, which sometimes succeeded in forcing them from their ground, and sometimes ended in the repulse of the assailants.

The French had a strong force of cavalry opposed to our single squadron. These were the 21st Dragoons, a regiment of Grenadiers à Cheval, and though last not least, our old friends the 4th Hussars, whose courage and dexterity put us to infinitely more trouble than that of the other two regiments combined.

These fellows seemed, indeed, to have no sense of danger. They would ride close to our videttes, fire their pistols in their faces, or exchange a few passes with their swords, as if for exercise; and as to their vigilance, no cat, when watching at the hole of a mouse, could be compared with them. A rat might not stir without their detecting it; and they were never shy to let us know that their eyes were open. It was impossible not to respect enemies, who occasioned to us so much trouble; and as we were not inferior to them in any of the qualifications that make up the soldier's character, I have reason to believe that the feeling was mutual.

Thus it fared with us for the space of about a fortnight, when there arrived from another part of our line such a reinforcement, both of men and guns, as put us pretty much at our ease. Besides the Brunswick Hussars—a very acceptable addition to our small cavalry force—there came several battalions of infantry, together with four pieces of cannon of small calibre, but still worth mentioning. The addition of this new corps seemed to produce the same effect upon Colonel Adam that it did upon us. It encouraged him to hold his ground more resolutely: and as we had a couple of gun-boats in a creek, just in front of Torre del Borra, we felt tolerably secure. The result was, that, instead of retiring, as we had previously done, immediately after dark to Altafalla, we pushed forward about half a mile in front of it, and threw up a couple of batteries in a sort of échelon line, one on each side of the high road. It became our custom henceforth to form there night after night; though indeed not many nights elapsed ere the value of our new position, in a military point of view, was put to a severe test.

It was somewhere about the 14th of August, just as the village clock had struck two, that, being in line, as usual, on each side of the road before Altafalla, we heard one morning a more than common bustle in the street of Torre del Borra. I regret to say that the piquet stationed there consisted of a Serjeant's party of the Foreign Hussars, who were so little attentive to the important nature of their trust, that they all lay down and slept. It is true that they had their videttes out, to whose vigilance they were justified in trusting a little; but the commandant of an outpost who trusts to anything except his own eyes and ears, is not worthy to hold even the meanest rank in the army. Well, the piquet slept—while the French, advancing in profound silence and perfect, order, rushed upon the videttes, who had barely time to fire their carbines, wheel about, and gallop off.

The horse of one man stumbled and fell, and he was instantly made prisoner; the other effected his escape, but he was the only individual belonging to the entire party that did so. For the French, pursuing at speed, entered Torre del Borra close at his heels, and coming upon the piquet ere they had time to mount, made the whole of them prisoners. In Torre del Borra, however, their advance made some pause, so as to permit the main body to come up with them, by which means our solitary scout succeeded in reaching the position unharmed, and prepared us for the sort of visit that we were about to receive.

Silent as the grave we all stood to our arms. The batteries of which I have just spoken were already armed, each with a couple of guns; and heir situation was such, that while both could fire at once, the one being a short space in advance of the other, it was competent to them to rake an enemy who should have penetrated beyond the more forward of the two.

Behind their parapets, as well as among the fields beside them, there was the most perfect stillness. Moreover, no lights were shown; for the very slow matches were concealed under cover of the banquet; and as to the rest, the night was sufficiently dark to cover all that. Silent as the grave, therefore, and with all our senses wide awake, we stood ready for the contest; neither were we kept long in suspense. There came up upon the quiet night air the tramp of many feet, regular, firmly set, and nowise hurried; denoting the approach of a strong column, which entertained no suspicion that it was in the immediate vicinity of danger. It was in vain that we strained our eyes, in the hope of discovering the outlines of the men from whom the sound proceeded.

There was no moon in the heavens; and though the stars were out, yet their brilliancy had at this hour begun to fade; or if it were not so, it sufficed not to give effect to our powers of vision. Therefore, we could only guess at the probable numbers of our assailants from the long, hollow, and unceasing noise occasioned by their march; and that to ears that were accustomed to pay regard to similar annunciations, afforded a tolerably distinct proof that their force was very great.

On they came, no drums beating, nor any word of command being pronounced in a tone more audible than a whisper, till the head of the column had arrived within pistol-shot of our more advanced battery. Bang, bang, went the guns at this instant, both loaded to the muzzle with grape and cannister, while a volley of musketry from each side of the way shed a bright but momentary glare over the darkness of the night I have no words in which to describe the effect of this unlooked-for salutation. The guns were admirably served; the musketry, though fired more at random, told; and the enemy's column halted, wavered, and recoiled, and then broke into a confused mass among the fields on either hand.

Now could be heard the voices of officers calling to the men to follow—now a sort of yell or shout gave notice of a second attack; and, by and by, a rush, at double-quick or charging pace, carried a large body of men clear beyond the advanced battery. But they came only into a situation where a twofold slaughter overtook them. The second battery opened, while the infantry in support of it poured in such a close and well-sustained fire, that no man could face it and live. Again the enemy were driven back, and again our people cheered triumphantly, as daring them to a renewed encounter.

In this manner, the French made repeated attempts to burst through us, while a lesser body made an oblique movement to the left, in the hope of turning our position; but in this direction, as well as on the main road, we were prepared for them. They were met, roughly handled, and driven back, leaving upon the field many killed and wounded, among the former of which was an officer on Marshal Suchet's staff, and the bearer, as was ascertained on examining his body, of important despatches. This man seemed resolute, at all hazards, to penetrate as far as Tarragona, and met his death in attempting it. He was a very gallant fellow, and died as became a good soldier.

The affair at Altafalla, though very sharp while it lasted, was not of long continuance. Foiled in three attempts to force our position, the enemy ceased by degrees to molest us, and long before dawn had retired in some disorder to their position in front of Villa Franca. For us, we did not attempt to follow them. It was enough to have maintained ourselves against such fearful odds; it would have been madness to have aimed at more; so we held our ground, and congratulated one another when daylight came in, on the success which had attended our efforts. To the Foreign Hussars, indeed, the sense of this victory was not without its alloy. We were heartily ashamed of the negligence of our comrades, and blushed when we read in general orders next day a rebuke which we felt to be merited. It is only surprising that Lord William did not extend his censure to the commanders of the two gun-boats which lay in Torre del Borra creek. Though thrown into that situation for the express purpose of enfilading a large space of the high-road, they never fired a shot, but permitted the enemy's column to pass them, both in the advance and in the retreat, without the slightest molestation.

Chapter 22

Amusements in War

So far we had triumphed; but it soon appeared that to maintain the forward position, and carry on the siege of Tarragona at the same time, was more than our feeble army could accomplish. Suchet, we learned from our spies, had received large reinforcements, and was making every preparation to relieve the place. It is not in my power to tell either how the French general manoeuvred, or what measures Lord William Bentinck took to oppose him, for I only know that in a day or two after our fight at Altafalla, we were commanded to retreat. We fell back, in consequence, immediately after nightfall, and never came to a halt till we reached a position which we had formerly occupied between Tarragona and Cabrils. Here the whole army halted, leaving Suchet free to deal with Tarragona and its garrison as might to himself appear most expedient.

We took up our ground at Cabrils, either on the 16th or 17th of August, and kept a sharp lookout to our front; when, on the night of the 18th, an explosion took place that shook the very earth beneath our feet The sound was louder than the loudest thunder; and the effect open all living and dead substances, within reach of its influence, resembled that of an earthquake. We were utterly at a loss to conjecture to what cause the event ought to be attributed, and put to one another a thousand questions which nobody could answer; till, with the morrow's dawn, came intelligence that the enemy had evacuated Tarragona, after blowing up its powder magazines, and ruining its defences.

Immediately the word was given to march to the front. The French, our spies informed us, were in full retreat: they had left not so much as a post of observation behind them; and such of the stores as they found it impracticable to carry away, they had committed to the flames, or cast into the sea.

We pushed on, after receiving this intelligence, in the highest possible spirits; and, arriving at the site of the encampment which our investing force had occupied, we there halted. I applied for, and obtained, permission on the following day to visit the city, and found it, as to both defences and buildings, in a state of cruel dilapidation. The solid walls, torn by the force of the gunpowder, presented here and there enormous breaches, at the base of which lay fragments of masonry resembling rocks that had been cast down from the summit of a mountain, rather than portions of a work fabricated by the hand of man. In other places, where the quantity of powder applied had been less, there were mere rents and fissures in the ramparts, through some of which a man might have squeezed his body, and that only with difficulty. But the most re-markable effect of the explosion was exhibited in the condition of the houses. Many were, of course, a heap of ruins; but many more, though they stood for a day or two after the concussion took place, had received such a shake, that the walls gradually crumbled, or the stone work clave asunder, and the roofs fell in, burying beneath them all that chanced to be within doors. There was one occurrence of this kind, so remarkable, that I must be permitted to describe it in detail.

Tarragona being now in our possession, was immediately converted into a sort of general depôt, in which not only the magazines for the army might be established, but the sick and wounded taken care of. The best houses in the place were appropriated, as is usual in like cases, to the service of the hospital; and into these our invalids, now a very numerous body, were removed. It happened one day that a wounded man, as he lay awake and uneasy upon his bed, cast his eyes towards the wall of the room which was opposite to him and adjoined the street To his inexpressible dismay he beheld the stones begin to rend asunder, and the plaster to fall down upon the floor in a shower. At first he distrusted the evidence of his own senses; but when the crevice yawned again, and became wider, he shouted for one of the attendants, and, pointing out the state of the building, explained what had happened. The medical gentleman, being made aware of the fact, lost no time in clearing out the hospital. The sick were removed as fast as an abundant command of means would allow; and, in less than a quarter of an hour the house was empty. Had the measure been less prompt, it would have been attempted in vain; for scarcely was the last litter conveyed beyond the threshold, when the front wall gave way, and of that once stately mansion nothing remained but a heap of ruins.

Having seen, in the course of this day's ramble, as much of Tarragona as I desired to see, it was with infinite satisfaction that I heard not long afterwards that we were going to move upon Arcos, and ultimately as far as Reuss.

Of the beauty of the latter town we had heard much, and we longed greatly to see it; neither did the reality, as sometimes happens, fall short of our expectations. Of Arcos I cannot say so much; it was very dirty, with few houses from which almost all the inhabitants had not fled —circumstances which effectually barred us from experiencing the smallest regret at leaving it But Reuss was in every respect the reverse of this. The suburbs, consisting of villas rather than of houses, clustered together, exhibited a profusion of groves, pleasure-grounds, flower-gardens, and water-courses, while inside the walls, streets, clean and regular, conducted you, on all sides, towards a great square, within which a daily market was held. There might be seen exposed for sale, poultry, eggs, fruits, vegetables—every thing, in short which the surrounding districts could supply, or the most determined lover of the table desire to possess: and round that open space were houses on one side, consisting entirely of hotels; on another of excellent shops; on a third, of private dwellings; while on the fourth was what may be termed the high street To complete the picture, I may add, that in front of these habitations, at least on two sides, ran a piazza, beneath the shade of which it was customary for the citizens to lounge, either smoking their cigars, or transacting such business as might, from time to time, make demands on their attention.

I must now return to my friend Conrad Hettendorff, of the Foreign Hussars. He had become, in every sense of the term, an excellent soldier; and his knowledge of the Spanish language, as well as his general intelligence, soon gained for him promotion to the rank of sergeant. In this capacity it became his duty to superintend the billeting of his men; for while the 20th were put into barracks, our squadron, as being the weaker corps of the two, had quarters assigned to it in the town. I cannot say that either to Conrad or myself this arrangement proved disagreeable; for in the town we were more our own masters than in barracks; and as we had plenty of money in our purses, the prospect of spending a short space in the heart of a civilized city was regarded as no trivial ground of mutual congratulation. Accordingly, after well providing for the comforts of the men, Conrad applied to the alcalde for a billet in some house where both he and I could be accommodated; and the magistrate, who favoured a man that was capable of conversing freely with him in his own dialect, apportioned us quarters in one of the best hotels in the city, which stood at the corner of the market square.

We proceeded to the house appointed for us, and finding that it answered, in every respect, to the description which the alcalde had given, we experienced some reluctance to enter, for several officers had taken up their abode there, and we had no wish to come into collision with them. But the host and hostess, a young couple, had recently set up in business for themselves, were so pressing, and so kind, that we did not like to turn our backs upon them. They conducted us upstairs, and ushered us into an apartment which, in point of size and furniture, and the air of comfort that attached to it, might have sufficed for a general of brigade. Not content with this, they gave us our choice, either of bed-rooms adjoining, or of camp-beds in the chamber itself; for Conrad's excellent Spanish found a passport to their affections; and a Spaniard, when his affections are won, does not know how to behave to you with too much generosity. We were not so unreasonable as to require further accommodation than this one spacious room afforded. We therefore thanked them for their kindness, and expressed ourselves willing to put up with even a single bed, should the providing of two prove at all inconvenient to them.

Having arranged these preliminaries, we sallied out, and spent the rest of the day in perambulating the town, at one of the busiest taverns in which we dined among a crowd of Spanish officers; for, besides our cavalry, some battalions of Spanish infantry were here, between whom and us the best understanding prevailed. We sat a reasonable time, smoked our cigars, drank coffee and noyau, and such other liqueurs as were brought to us, and returned at night, as men ought to do, cheerful and sober to our lodgings. Our sleep, too, was most refreshing, and when we awoke in the morning, we again congratulated one another in having steered our boat into so commodious a harbour. Curiosity, however, soon began to exercise itself as to the sort of neighbourhood into which we had been thrown, and we went to the window for the purpose of ascertaining what the objects might be on which we could look out We found that ours was an apartment at the back of the house, and that the view from it was very circumscribed. A high dead wall stood opposite, between which and our house ran a lane—while within that wall was a large gloomy mansion, only one window in which, and that obscured outside by a wooden grating, looked towards our apartment. Moreover, there was nothing either to the right or left calculated to arrest attention. Ours was a corner room, which neither commanded a view of the square, nor was itself overlooked; indeed the single aperture that bore upon us at all was, as I have just said, the grated window opposite.

I had picked up an excellent telescope on the field of Vimiero, and carried it ever afterwards about with me whither soever I went. Today, partly in the wantonness of our mirth, partly to assist our powers of vision, we made use of it, directing its focus, among other objects, on the grated window in the mansion that stood within the dead wall. It was Conrad who first turned his gaze in that direction, and immediately exclaimed that a nun was watching us from behind the grating. "We'll have a little fun, anyhow," added he; "so hold you the telescope, Norbert, that I may open at once a course of telegraphic communication with the fair religiosa."

I took the glass as he desired, while he, seizing a pen, tore out a leaf from his orderly-book, and wrote upon it in large characters some Spanish words. He showed them to me, and they ran thus: "I am grieved to see you shut up in that prison, and would gladly be your deliverer, Señora, if I could." He then drew back a pace from the window, and held up the scrawl towards the nun, who showed that she understood the writer's meaning, by laughing heartily and clapping her hands.

Encouraged by this first essay, Conrad wrote again—"Why don't you show yourself more distinctly? It is impossible to see through those envious bars."

This signal, like the last, was answered by laughter; and not long afterwards a writing appeared at one of the apertures, saying, "How can I remove the bars?"

In a moment Conrad's reply was prepared. "Take a knife, and cut out as large a space as will permit me to see you as plainly as you see me. But be careful to cut, so that you may be able to replace it at will, without running the risk of being detected." The nun clapped her hands again, and laughed more heartily than before; after which for a while all was quiet.

Quiet, however, it was not, within the lady's cell, for we were yet speculating on the probable result of this last hint, when, to our great joy, an aperture was effected in the framework sufficiently capacious to gratify all our wishes. Still the lady, though she presented herself before it and clapped her hands, wore a veil over her face, which, being superadded to the other garments of a nun—large wide sleeves and plaited bodice—altogether disguised her. Conrad accordingly set to work, and wrote—"Withdraw that horrid veil, and permit me to sun myself in thy bright eyes." But the nun, though she laughed heartily, met this request by asking in her turn from what part of Spain we came? Here was a puzzler: what ought we to say?

I was not slow in giving my advice, nor Conrad backward in adopting it "Say that we are Irishmen," said I, "or Englishmen; at all events, don't let her suppose that we are Spaniards." Conrad wrote accordingly, and the effect was magical. The veil was thrown aside in a trice, and a countenance beamed upon us, of which it is candid to admit, that, though I have beheld some more beautiful, I have seen a much greater number that were less so.

We saluted the nun by bowing and kissing our hands, after which Conrad wrote—"What is your name?"

The answer was—"I will find a more convenient opportunity of telling you, but for the present we are interrupted."

"When shall we meet again?" wrote Conrad, hastily.

"This evening or tomorrow morning early," was the reply; immediately after which the grating was put up.

We took this as a signal that our fair friend had been called away, and ceased to watch her window; but we did not cease to speculate on the whole adventure. To us it was a mere pastime. We never dreamed that anything serious could arise out of it, nor indeed had we a wish that such should be the case. But our curiosity was excited, and we determined to go forward with the correspondence on every favourable opportunity. We then sallied forth, and having visited the stables, and seen that all was right among the men, we adjourned to a hotel and dined.

Being anxious to renew our correspondence with the recluse, we did not sit long over the meal, but hurrying back to our quarters, desired the landlady to send up wine and fruit, and other requisites for a dessert, to our apartment Our wishes were promptly attended to, and drawing our table near to the window, we fixed our eyes on the grated aperture across the way. Not many minutes elapsed ere the framework was taken down, and our telegraphs went to work. We pledged our fair friend in bumpers of wine; and then Conrad, who was always the scribe, demanded her name and place of birth. There was a pause of some little duration, at the conclusion of which a paper was shown, so well filled, that it took us some time fully to decipher the writing. The substance of the communication was this, that the lady's name was Matilda Elienora Gustavava; that she was a native of Reuse; that her father kept a haberdasher's shop in the same square of which our hotel formed a part; and that we could not fail to find him out, provided we followed such directions as she gave us. Scarcely had we clapped our hands, however, in token that we understood the communication, than she hastily waved hers as a signal of farewell; and closing up the aperture, we saw no more of her for the rest of the evening.

We were, as may be imagined, in the highest possible spirits. Our adventure, if such it might be called, appeared to assume every hour a more interesting character; and, like hunters that draw upon their game, the feeling of excitement became with us more acute, in proportion as our questions were answered with increasing confidence. We were, therefore, not a little mortified at the abrupt termination of the interview. Nevertheless, being aware that the evil was beyond remedy, we resolved to lighten its pressure as much as possible; and with this view, after finishing our bottle of wine, sallied forth in quest of adventures.

The town, as I have already hinted, was full of troops, English and Spanish. Every hotel, therefore, or other place of public resort, was crowded; yet there was no brawling, no confusion, no apparent disposition to riot in any quarter. Our cruise, therefore, for such it was, proved exceedingly pleasant, and we retired to our mattresses about twelve o'clock, just sufficiently wearied to ensure a sound sleep.

Our last thought, when we laid our heads on the pillows, was about Señora Gustavava; our first, when we raised them again, was directed towards her, and as soon as we were dressed, we repaired to the window in order to watch for her coming. She was beforehand with us; indeed, we never once succeeded in getting the start of her; and the grating being down, our telegraphing commenced with inquiries on both sides, as to the manner in which the night had been spent. Then came a fresh batch of questions:

Conrad asked "How old are you?"

She laughed, and made answer, "Two-and-twenty."

"Are you not tired of your imprisonment?"

Answer. "Yes, heartily tired, and mean to escape from it whenever I can."

"Will you accept of me as your deliverer?"

"Will you be true to me after I am delivered?"

"As the needle to the pole; but how can we get you out?"

"That may be managed if you are to be trusted."

"What is your history?"

There was a pause after this, and then came another well-filled slip of paper, which contained the following statement:

Matilda was one of twin sisters, and the elder of the two. Her mother had devoted her to a nunnery from her birth; and having been educated in a convent, she took the veil without reluctance. But she had since discovered that it was one thing to be a pupil, and another to be a nun. She deeply repented the step she had taken, and only waited for a favourable opportunity of escaping from her prison. That we might assure ourselves of the truth of this statement, and of more which she yet had to communicate, she begged that we would go to her father's shop, behind the counter of which we would find her sister, and the strong resemblance which they bore to one another would satisfy us that we were not deceived. Finally, she must leave us for the present. But when we saw the grating down we might be sure she was within hail, and ready to receive our communications, and to answer them. As soon as we had finished reading this, her screen was put up, and we were left to meditate on what had been told us.

Our first determination of course was to seek out Señor Gustavava's shop, and to ascertain whether the description which Matilda had given of it corresponded with the reality. As soon therefore as we had been to stables, and breakfasted, and gone through the duties of the morning, we set out, and were at no loss, from the accuracy of the directions which we had received, in discovering the place of which we were in quest. It stood among other shops on the opposite side of the square, and seemed to be well stored with goods, though, like Spanish shops in general, there was no sign over the door, nor the owner's name any where about it. We walked by, and looking in, saw an elderly gentleman, two young men, and a young lady standing at different positions behind the square counter, and supplying their customers, who were very numerous, with whatever they might chance to require.

"I never saw such a likeness in my life," said Conrad, after we had once or twice crossed the threshold. "She is the very image of Matilda!—only look!" I did so, and certainly the resemblance was very striking.

"Now, then," said I, "let us enter. We will purchase a silk handkerchief apiece, and in doing so we will find an opportunity of making the young lady smile, and so of comparing the expression, as well as the features of the one with that of the other." Conrad readily agreed, and we moved towards the shop door.

The rush of customers seemed by this time to have passed away, and there were only two or three ladies beside the counter when we entered; but as these had engaged the attention of the fair shop-woman, we were compelled to have some dealings with her father, who offered his services. "Well," said I, "we must purchase something. I want a new pair of overalls, such as I may wear when off duty, and I cannot do better than provide myself here." Conrad expressed a wish to equip himself in the same manner, and, as our purses were well filled, we bought each cloth and trimmings enough to render our lower extremities as smart as those of our officers.

We contrived, moreover, to keep the chaffering in progress a sufficient time to allow the Spanish ladies to finish their business, and then passing round, to the further counter, we requested the Señorita to show us some pocket-handkerchiefs. Here, too, we were wonderfully fastidious in our tastes; while Conrad drew the young lady into an interesting conversation, which she, finding that he spoke excellent Spanish, appeared very much to relish. In particular, he put a great many questions to her respecting the French—whether they had behaved well in the place; whether they were favourites with the ladies, or had carried any away with them; and after a good deal of laughing, and some serious remarks, we learned that they had proved quite irresistible.

Heavy contributions the authorities had levied on the town, but there was no plundering; and as to the women, they had almost all fallen in love with the invaders, and not a few had followed them when they departed. We were by this time quite satisfied respecting the truth of Matilda's story, and experienced a strong desire to tell her so; therefore, having selected a couple of handkerchiefs, and a silk nightcap apiece, we paid the amount, and withdrew.

We got home about five in the afternoon, and found, as we expected, that the grating was down. Immediately we showed ourselves, and holding up the silk handkerchiefs and nightcaps, made the nun aware that we had visited her father's shop. Then followed all sorts of questions and answers, as to whether we saw any resemblance? whether we still desired to set her free? as well as the warmest protestations of regard on both our parts, and love on the part of Conrad. And now came the last announcement of all. She had well considered the steps that would be necessary in order to insure her deliverance, and if we would be at our posts next morning, she would communicate her plans. We promised, of course, and spent that night as we had done the night previous, the first portion of it in rambling from place to place—the last portion in our beds.

Chapter 23

The Consummation

I need scarcely pause to state that we were true to the hour of appointment on the morrow. Matilda likewise was at her post; and it was very evident that she had written down her principal budget over-night, for scarcely were the compliments of the morning paid ere it was held up for our inspection. I must give only the substance of it, for it was very long, and contained some extraneous matter, which it is not worth while to repeat

After telling over again the tale of her early devotion to a life of seclusion, and describing her disappointment and disgust with all that occurred within the nunnery, Matilda proceeded to inform us that, independently of what might come to her from her father, she was entitled to a considerable property at the death of an aunt, which, if she continued in the convent, would, of course, be taken possession of by the society; but which, in the event of her deliverance, she would be in a condition to receive. With respect again to the means of securing this most desired end, these were to be as follows:—She had already applied to a friend who would afford her an asylum in which she could lie concealed till the British troops quitted Reuse, when she would immediately join Conrad, and go with him wherever he went. In the meanwhile, he was to procure a rope-ladder, of sufficient length to reach across the garden wall, and hire a carriage in which she might be conveyed to her hiding-place; to bribe the coachman largely, so as to insure his silence; and to engage to be her protector through life. Let him consent to all this, and she would cheerfully throw herself upon his honour.

Conrad read and explained the long epistle to me— after which we stared at one another, and observing that matters were beginning to grow serious, put the important question, what was to be done? We had no wish to get the poor girl into trouble, and were very unwilling to burden ourselves with her company; yet it was clear that we had excited hopes which must either be realized, or we should have the comfort of reflecting by-and-by that we had trifled with the peace of one whom we had no right to injure. At last I said to Conrad, "Tell her that you would gladly fall in with her schemes, but that you have not the means of supporting her in the style to which she has been accustomed. This may help us out of our difficulties." Conrad wrote accordingly; but the result was not such as we had hoped for.

The answer was; "I have money enough: but come at seven o'clock this evening, when the sisters will be at vespers, to that side of the garden which adjoins an open field, and when you see an orange thrown over, know that I am there. This will be the spot whence I am to make my escape. Throw another orange back, to assure me that mine has reached your hands; and take care of what you get, for it will contain more than juice or pulp." As we had some obscure idea of the field to which she alluded, I did not doubt that we should somehow or other find it. Conrad replied that he would be there at the time appointed, and the grating being put up, our communications for that morning were ended.

I cannot say that we spent this day altogether so light of heart as we had done some others, for there was an apprehension on our minds that we were pushing matters beyond the limits of generosity; and we were neither of us inclined to abuse the poor girl, and then leave her to her fate. Still, having gone so far, we felt that retreat was impossible; and accordingly, as the hands of our watches pointed to half-past six, we wrapped our cloaks about us, and sallied forth. With difficulty we made out the trysting place; and had not reached it many minutes when over came an orange: we took it up and threw ours in reply. There was a cut in the rind, which we soon made wider, and, lo! within was a piece of paper rolled, which we immediately drew forth. It contained a massive gold ring, on which was a portrait of Matilda in ivory, set round with brilliants, and a letter, the important part of which ran thus:—We had spoken of our lack of money. No consideration of that sort was to weigh with us for a moment. The rope-ladder must be got, the carriage hired, the coachman bribed; and, to render all perfect, we were to be prodigal of our resources. We had only to provide ourselves with a ball of stout twine, and to fasten a bag to the end of it, and if by putting a stone into the bag we could manage to throw it over the garden wall, we should find, when it was drawn up again, that the necessary funds were forthcoming: only let no time be lost in getting our arrangements into a state of forwardness.

Conrad put his ring on his finger, and both he and I gazed at it in astonishment—the painting was well executed, and the gold and the brilliants evidently of great value; while the girl's proposal was altogether so generous, that we began to treat the affair more gravely than we had yet done, and to agree that she deserved to be set free, and protected for life by her deliverer. I do not mean to deny that the prospect of obtaining a bag full of coins may have had some effect in producing this change of sentiment, but I declare that admiration of Matilda's confiding disposition, and unfeigned pity for her case, were motives much more influential with both of us. On the whole, therefore, we made our way back to the town, full of romantic determinations and generous sentiment; and wandered from coffee-house to coffee-house, in a state of more than common excitation. But we were neither of us given to drinking; we took as much, perhaps a little more than could do us any good, and returned to dream of what the morrow or the next day might bring forth.

With the morrow came reflection, and the difficulties of the case which overnight had well-nigh disappeared, presented themselves again before our eyes in their full magnitude. What could be done with the girl after we got her out? To desert her would be to disgrace ourselves in our own eyes for ever; to think of carrying her about with an army so much harassed as ours was madness. "Had we not better give the thing up at once?" said Conrad.

"Yes," replied I, "and restore the ring; it won't do to keep that when you reject the donor."

"I esteem the ring," answered Conrad, "much more for her sake than because of its intrinsic value; but I believe you are right, we must try and send it back to her."

"Stop," cried I, "the grating is down, let us ascertain what she has to say this morning."

We moved forward to the open window, upon which a paper was instantly held up containing this question, "Did you get the contents of the orange?" Conrad replied by holding out his hand with the ring on his fore finger and kissing it. Matilda clapped her hands and immediately produced another scroll, which demanded, "Is the ladder of ropes in preparation?"

"Now, what are we to say to that?" asked Conrad. "It will never do to answer no—what shall I say?"

"If you don't choose to say no, say yes, to be sure," said I,— "but, remember, that you must either go through with this affair at all hazards, or bring it to a close at once."

"Well, then, I'll go through with it," replied Conrad, and forthwith stooping down, he wrote "Yes."

A long pause followed, at the close of which the lady's signal appeared to the following effect:—"I am afraid that you may be hampered for want of means—bring your bag and string round to the old corner this evening at seven, and your wants shall be supplied." It was impossible now to do otherwise than promise a compliance with her wishes— so, after a few more remarks on both sides, our morning's telegraphic communication came to an end.

"Norbert," said Conrad, as soon as the grating resumed its place, "I am but half satisfied with the position into which I have cast myself. I cannot think of marrying this girl—and, as to taking advantage of her confiding disposition, that is not to my mind. What a pity it had not been you that she fell in love with! You are not withheld by any previous tie from making her your wife. Suppose I were to make over my interest in her regards to you?"

"In the first place," answered I, "that may not be altogether in your power; and in the next, I am not, perhaps, so free as you imagine. Besides, I might have had my *señorita* long ago, and under far more favourable circumstances, had I been inclined to such matrimony. Therefore, friend, you must deal with her as you see most fitting, but you must not look to me to take her off your hands."

"Well, then, we must make the most of it," replied Conrad. After which we walked abroad attending to the duties of our station, and spent the remainder of the day, when these were accomplished, pretty much as we had spent other days.

At last the hour of assignation drew nigh. We had already provided ourselves with a ball of stout twine, and caused one of our men to fabricate such a bag as we judged would serve the purpose required. It was not too large, and being drawn with a string at the mouth, we fastened it to the end of the line. A stone was then put in to insure its passage through the air, and a loose knot tied above it. Thus equipped, but carrying no weapons with us, we repaired to the well-known spot It was still broad daylight, nevertheless we threw our orange over the wall, and the immediate return of another, assured us that Matilda had been faithful to her tryst. Upon this the bag was launched on its journey, and it flew direct into the garden beyond. We paused, in order to afford time for Matilda to make use of it, and having guessed by the slight tug that she gave that all was right, we were just beginning to pull it back again, when three huge Spaniards, not soldiers, but dressed in the ordinary garb of civil life, rushed upon us from behind, and an immediate scuffle began. We had no arms; fortunately for us they too were without weapons of any kind; so the battle was waged with fists, and head, and feet, and no trivial discharge of oaths and execrations. Our assailants seized the twine and began dragging it towards them. We struggled to repel them, when blood began to flow profusely from all our faces—but, three to two are great odds, when the only weapons used are those with which nature supplies us. They were gaining somewhat the superiority, when Conrad called aloud to me in English, "Have you no penknife with which to cut the cord?" In an instant my hand was in my pocket, and before any thing could be done to stop me, I had drawn my knife, and severed the line. The bag fell back with a crash into the garden, and we felt, in some measure, safe.

Our next object was to make the best of our way back to the house, and this without stopping to seek for the ball of twine, we endeavoured to do; but the Spaniards continued to press upon us—there was a sort of walking-fight, indeed, all the way to the market-place—the Spaniards abusing us as sacrilegious heretics, and we replying to them with all manner of opprobrious epithets, as well as with blows. But we could not shake them off— neither indeed did we get rid of them till we entered the hotel, and escaped to our own apartment And then what figures we were!—from our noses the blood had flowed in such quantities, that not our faces only, but our very apparel was soiled. Our cheeks were bruised and scratched, and altogether we beheld such apparitions in the mirror that we were glad to turn away from it. But this was the least of the evil. We were washing off the blood from our faces and looking about for sticking-plaster to apply to the wounds, when first the hostess and then the host made their appearance, both full of anxiety on our account, and anxious to be informed of the circumstances which had led to so dire a catastrophe. On this latter head, however, we refused to gratify their curiosity in the least We only begged them to send up some supper and wine, and having patched up our wounds as well as we could, sat down to consider how the affair was likely to terminate.

We had gathered from the language of our assailants, when mutually belabouring one another, that our detection had been a thing of pure accident; they happened to be passing near the spot, and being struck with the progress of two oranges that crossed one another in the air, they had approached and watched us. So far, there was ground to hope, that though the general purpose of our proceeding could not be concealed, the particular object to whom our addresses had been paid, might escape detection; and we were much more anxious on her account than on our own. For ourselves we never doubted that we should get out of the scrape, no matter to whom it might be reported; but we knew that for Matilda there would be no pardon in the event of her design being discovered. We passed the night, therefore, gloomily enough, and our load was not lightened, when on going to the window the first thing in the morning, we found that the grating was up.

"Poor Matilda!" said we, "what will become of her? that which was a good joke to us may be fatal to her." Nor did we stir from the apartment throughout the whole of the day. I, indeed, as Sergeant-Major, had no stable-duty to attend to, and our officers were too considerate to harass the men with dress, parades, during the brief interval of repose in the middle of a campaign. I therefore kept the house tenaciously while Conrad made his excursions as unfrequent as he could, and took care to hurry back again as seen as duty would allow. Still the whole of that day passed without bringing Matilda to the window, and we spent another night in a state of anxious suspense, which dwells to this hour on my memory.

In the evening we were again on the alert, and had not watched long ere the grating was taken down. Matilda was there, but her communication was brief and hurried. "It is all over—we are discovered—farewell." The grating was closed again immediately and never opened again. What became of her I do not know. Within the walls of these horrid prisons, whatever atrocities may be committed, the world is never made acquainted with them; and of Matilda's fate a whisper was not breathed, out of which it would be possible to draw a conjecture. Hope, however, seems to suggest that probably her crime was not brought home to her. She was too clever to leave any traces of her intrigue about, unless, indeed, the bag might contain a letter, and both fall into the hands of her superior. But even that I am willing to believe is improbable; for if she stood, as she doubtless did, on the other side of the wall, she could not fail to learn, from the tumult on our side, that we had been surprised. All this, however, is mere conjecture; and the fact amounts to nothing more than that we never saw her grating removed again, nor had with her the slightest communication.

Our apprehensions on Matilda's account were by far too lively, and well-grounded, to leave us much leisure for thinking about ourselves, yet we were taught ere many days went by, that ours was not a situation of safety. One evening the landlady came to us, and in a mysterious manner said, that she wished to hold a minute's confidential conversation with us. We begged her to take a seat, and as there was wine on the table, we poured her out a glass, which she drank. "Gentlemen," said she, "you have committed an offence which a Spaniard does not know how to forgive. You have been trying to steal a nun, and the object of my present visit is to warn you, that your lives are not worth an hour's purchase. Take my advice and shift your lodgings. I shall be very sorry to lose you, for you have conducted yourselves excellently since you became my guests; but I should be still more sorry to have you brought in some night stabbed to the heart. Go and provide accommodation for yourselves nearer to the quarters of your own men, and never show yourselves in this part of the town again."

The landlady's advice was sound, and we determined to act upon it. Hitherto our bruises had confined us a good deal to the house, for we were not willing to exhibit countenances either swollen or scratched; but they were now getting well again, and as we did not choose either, to throw away our lives, or to preserve them at the expense of perpetual imprisonment, we thanked the kind hostess, and told her that we would do as she recommended.

Accordingly, next day Conrad repaired to the *alcalde*, who had heard nothing about our adventure, and making the great distance of our hotel from the men's quarters his excuse, requested to be furnished with another billet. The *alcalde* was very civil, and told us that we should not find ourselves so comfortable in any hotel in the place as in that to which he had originally sent us; but finding that we were bent on a change he complied with our wishes. We availed ourselves of the hour at midday when the generality of the Spaniards are asleep, and sending our baggage to a house in the very centre of the street where the squadron lay, we there established ourselves. We took care not to enter the market-place again during the remainder of our halt in Reuss.

CHAPTER 24

We Take the Field Again

From this time forth till the army quitted the town, there occurred little of which it would be worth while to give a detailed account. Hettendorff and I spent our days and evenings together as usual, but an indescribable anxiety respecting the fate of the nun, not less than the dread of assassination, put a damp upon our enjoyments, each as we found it impossible to set aside. Our great desire, indeed, soon came to be that we might be moved to some other quarter, where, amid new scenes and fresh adventures, the past might be forgotten. And though, to men who suffer from "hope deferred," every minute seems an hour, and each hour a day,—our wishes were accomplished at last Early in September intelligence came in that the enemy had fallen back behind the Labrigat, and the long-looked-for directions were issued at last, that our troops should prepare to push forward.

The Foreign Hussars had received orders to march on the morrow, when Hettendorff and I, with two other sergeants belonging to the corps, determined to spend our last evening comfortably together. With this view we ordered dinner at a tavern, in a quarter of the town as far as possible removed from the market-place, and at five o'clock sat down to an entertainment, which would have done no discredit to the best eating-house in London. The wines, too, were excellent, and the liqueurs of the richest flavour, which with cigars and coffee took just so much effect upon our spirits as to render us proof against care. We were not drunk—it was not our habit to make beasts of ourselves—but we were exceedingly merry, and rejoiced in the prospects which tomorrow held out. The consequence was that we sat late, and saw the house emptied of all other guests: after which we paid our reckoning and proposed to return home.

But there was one of our party, a Sergeant Knoll, on whom the liquor had produced a greater effect than upon the rest of us. He was at all times a humorous fellow, and now being heated with wine, he declared with an oath, that he would not lay his head upon the pillow till he had his spree. "See if I don't frighten somebody out of his wits," cried he, "and rob him with a candlestick." As he said this he seized one of the candlesticks that stood upon the table, both of which were made of brass, and both so fabricated that you could push the candle up by raising a sort of socket, the clash of which when it touched the bore, sounded not unlike the cocking of a pistol. We all laughed at his whim, without supposing that he would carry it into effect; but he was as good as his word. He clapped the candlestick under his left arm unnoticed by the waiter, and forth we sallied arm-in-arm to return home.

Knoll was upon one of the flanks, and had said but little, when we observed a tall figure wrapped up in a cloak, one corner of which was thrown over his shoulder, advancing towards us. "That's the fellow," exclaimed Knoll, "mark how I'll astonish him." It was no sooner said than done. Before we could move hand or foot to detain him he sprang into the middle of the road, and clapping the muzzle of the candlestick against the stranger's breast, he brought up the socket with a crash, and ordered him to stand and deliver.

The dullest of living men could not have retained his gravity at what followed. Trembling from head to foot, the Spanish officer pulled out his purse and offered it to Knoll, while at the same time, he begged for his life, in a tone of such alarm, as to convulse us with laughter. Yet we were not blind to the probable consequences of so injudicious a joke. We gathered round the parties, and reminding Knoll of the risk which he ran of involving net only himself, but us in trouble, we begged the Spaniard to put up his purse, and told him the whole affair was a frolic. If the gentleman was frightened when he believed us to be robbers, he became mad with rage as soon as the truth had been told. He would have revenge. A captain of Spanish Infantry was not the sort of person to be insulted with impunity—he would call the guard—get us arrested on the spot, and report the circumstance as soon as it was light to the commander-in-chief. Nor, indeed, was it without the utmost difficulty that Hettendorff, who was our spokesman, succeeded in mollifying his ire. At last, however, he consented to return with us to the tavern, and to accept at our hands as much both of wine and other good things as he might fancy; promising that no report should be sent in by him, on condition that we would engage to keep a secret that might possibly tell against his character.

We were of course most happy to accede to these terms of accommodation, which on both sides were faithfully kept. For, except among ourselves, the affair of the candlestick was never alluded to till long after its occurrence; and Captain Alberto (such was his name) made no hostile report to the commandant.

It was late on the following day when we formed our parade on an open space of ground, near the extremity of Reuss. Every balcony and window was crowded to behold us, and amid the waving of handkerchiefs, and good wishes for success, the columns began to move. We proceeded no farther than to Villa-Franca, a neat, clean town, on the road from Tarragona to Barcelona, where billets were issued to as many troops as the place would hold, and other preparations made apparently to spend the whiter.

Meanwhile an advanced guard under Colonel Adam, consisting of one battalion of the 27th English Regiment, of the Calabrian Free Corps, some Spanish Infantry, and a few guns, were pushed forward some miles towards the Labrigat; which occupying the Pass of Ordal, was there supported by a detachment of cavalry—the 20th, the Brunswickers, and the Foreign Hussars, taking it by turns to supply the pickets.

The Foreign Hussars had been relieved over-night, and were

returned to their quarters in Villa-Franca, when at an early hour in the morning of the 12th, long before the day dawned, the sound of firing in the front roused us from our beds; and amid the blowing of trumpets and the roll of drums, we stood to our arms. The noise, which had at first been comparatively slight, became continually more tremendous; cannon and musketry intermingling, in one ceaseless roar, which drew every moment nearer. and nearer. Then came staff officers galloping into the town, with information that the enemy were advancing; and that unless Colonel Adam were promptly supported, he must be overpowered. The general, however, either because he distrusted the intelligence, or that he was unwilling in the dark to quit the shelter which the town afforded, persisted in holding his ground, till an abrupt cessation of the tumult told us too plainly that the contest was over. Then, indeed, we got the order to march; but the Pass of Ordal was already carried, and the brave men who maintained it for three hours, against ten times their numbers, were either cut to pieces, or scattered to the four winds. Lord William, however, seemed bent upon recovering the credit which the total destruction of his advanced post might seem to have cast upon him. He therefore pushed on, and formed his line in such a situation as has probably never before, at least in modern times, been occupied by an inferior army, in the immediate presence of the force which it was intended to check.

A few miles in front of Villa Franca runs the river Noya, a clear, rapid mountain stream, very rocky and uneven in its channel, and though fordable in many places, still extremely difficult to pass, by reason of the strength of the current. Across the Noya, on the high road, is a bridge of three arches, the centre arch of which the French had destroyed, but which we, in order to keep open our communications with the advanced guard and picket, had repaired in a temporary manner with fascines and boards. Over this bridge, so as to place the Noya in his rear, Lord William marched his army. Of the Spaniards, some, I believe, crossed at fords, both above and below; but the English and Germans, with the guns, tumbrils, and even the baggage, all traversed the bridge, as being the only means afforded them of passing. This done, the troops moved forward towards some eminences, along the faces of which they might form, and behind which, till the enemy should show themselves, they stood in column and concealed.

I cannot tell what corps held the right and centre of our line, nor how they conducted themselves, either now or afterwards; but the whole of the cavalry, with the Calabrians and some Germans formed on the left, just beneath the dip of a low hill, from the summit of which a commanding view could be obtained. Here, then, we remained for some time, the troopers standing by their horses, the light infantry thrown out as skirmishers, among certain vineyards and enclosures beyond, while guns were unlimbered, and placed in position, and all other preparations made that are the accustomed forerunners of a general action.

Our position was so near the crest of the hill, that a few paces to the front enabled me at any moment to see all that was passing on the side of the enemy. Their dark, dense columns had, indeed, been visible from the first, moving steadily towards us, covered, as their practice is, by crowds of tirailleurs; while long trains of cannon and tumbrils gave notice that in artillery, they surpassed us at least as much as in the numbers of their horse and foot. I observed, however, that they were not disposed to rush blindly into the strife. On the contrary, though their skirmishers pushed on, and soon began to exchange a dropping fire with our riflemen, the columns halted at the distance of about a mile and a half from the plateau on which we were drawn up; while several staff officers closely reconnoitred our line, and then retired again to make their own dispositions. No great while elapsed ere the nature of these began to develop itself. There was a village in our immediate front, towards which, in columns of *échelon,* some prodigious masses of men began to move, and then beyond it other masses showed them. selves, evidently bent upon turning our left, and doubling it up upon the centre. It was at this juncture that Lord Frederick Bentinck, who commanded the cavalry, and displayed his usual gallantry, rode up to our column. "Captain Jacks," said he, "I want your Sergeant-Major, with four men, to get as near to the French as he can; and to let me know whether they have occupied the village—in what force they are, and how they appear to be moving." I was ready, of course, to do my duty; and four volunteers, all excellently mounted, having expressed their desire to accompany me, I sprang into the saddle, and we moved off.

The orders given to me were, that I should on no account permit myself to be cut off—that I should approach the enemy as closely as could be done, with due regard to my own safety, and return as soon as possible with whatever intelligence I might be fortunate enough to pick up. In making our advance we were, after traversing some open country, particularly fortunate. We struck into a hollow road; the banks on both sides of which were just so high as to permit our seeing over them, at the same time that they completely hid all both of men and horses, except our heads and caps. To be sure, the lane wound a good deal; but there could be no doubt that it led down upon the village, and we were glad to take advantage of it, inasmuch as, on either hand, there were vineyards and copses; the first exceedingly inconvenient for horse to pass through, the last affording ample shelter to an enemy's *ambuscades*. On, then, we rode, obtaining a tolerably clear insight into the arrangements of the French, while we were ourselves concealed from observation, till we had approached within a few hundred yards of the village. Here a crowd of poor people met us. The peasants, flying from their houses, were carrying, some one thing, some another, on their back, and all, wringing their hands, and howling piteously, appeared in the greatest distress. I asked them whether the French were in the village, and in what numbers. The answer was precisely such as I expected to receive. The place was full of soldiers, and more were continually pouring in, and passing through it.

Satisfied with this information, and recollecting the orders which I had received, I determined to return; we accordingly wheeled about, and so long as we retained the shelter of the lane nothing presented itself to startle as; but no sooner had we emerged into the open country than we ascertained that our retreat was cut off. Pushing rapidly forward, and concealed from us by the woods and coppices, the enemy had thrown themselves between us and the body towards which we were moving, while their right, closing in fast, seemed as if it would gain the rear of the English line, and make prisoners not of us only but of all that were then in the field. Moreover, the heavy firing of cannon and the continued roar of musketry to the right of our position, assured us that there the battle was begun in earnest There was not a moment to deliberate, the French had seen us at the same moment when we became aware of their proximity, and a cloud of their cavalry darted towards us. I therefore called aloud to my comrades to follow, and dashing the rowels into my horse's flanks, I struck off to the right hand at the top of my speed.

For a minute or two our route lay over some turf, after which we were carried into the vineyards, through the stumps of which our noble animals threaded their way with extraordinary sure-footedness. The enemy, too, followed close at our heels, and from time to time discharged their pistols and carbines, the balls from which passed harmlessly over us. And now, to our great horror, we saw before us a wall of loose stones strongly built, as all such fences are in this part of Spain, and extending along the whole face of the vineyard; to dash round which either to the one hand or the other was impossible, seeing that on both flanks the French had got the start of us. Its height might be about four feet, a very serious impediment to a dragoon-horse, loaded as it is with his master's accoutrements and baggage, and not always in hearty condition. Yet there was but one way of dealing with it. The fence must be charged, and he who could not or would not take it, must lose either his life or his liberty. I was the first to dash at the wall, and, as Providence would have it, my charger went clean over. Three out of the four men followed with a similar good fortune, but the horse of the fourth swerved and refused the leap. In an instant he was a prisoner, and as we galloped on we heard the shouts of the French troopers, who, themselves unable to clear the fence, rejoiced beyond measure at having overtaken even one of our party.

The vineyard wall being now between us and our pursuers, we felt comparatively secure, for the shot flew too wide at all to incommode us, and we had leisure to look round from the point whence we had set out, and by which it had been our design to direct our movements in returning. But there was nothing there calculated to cheer or draw us on. The French, on the contrary, were between us and the left of our army, and the increasing violence of the fire both there and elsewhere, showed that our comrades were terribly over-matched. Under such circumstances, I determined to make for a Spanish picket, which occupying a commanding hill right before us appeared to have been as yet overlooked; though it lay to the rear, indeed, but directly in the line of the flank movement, by which the enemy manoeuvred to turn Lord William's position. The Spanish officer, however, not being able to distinguish our accoutrements from those of the French, caused his people to fire upon us with great spirit; and did not desist till we had approached so close as to make ourselves heard. Then, however, he commanded the fire to cease, and receiving us very kindly, pointed out a route by which we might make our way to the left of the English line.

I had my Vimiero glass always about me, by the help of which I soon satisfied myself that the directions given by the Spaniard were good. Accordingly we struck across the country, and keeping a good way towards the rear, found ourselves by and by near the spot which it was our object to reach. But the view which I obtained of the progress of the battle, while crossing the high-road between the Spanish picket and our own, was the reverse of encouraging. Everywhere the English were giving way. Infantry broken and disordered were falling back in heaps; guns were either dismounted or limbering up for a retreat; while the French in overwhelming numbers were pressing on, cheering and firing with the greatest animation. It was at this stage of the combat that we succeeded in re-uniting ourselves with the squadron, which still stood where we had left it, under cover of the hill, but which was now prepared for a charge as soon as the head of the enemy's column should have advanced sufficiently near to insure its being given with effect Nor had I resumed my place three minutes ere the orders to attack arrived. I was in the act, indeed, of explaining what had happened, when Lord Frederick Bentinck, with a staff-officer, came round the elbow of the hill waving his hat, and we, the Brunswickers, and the 20th, getting our horses into a trot, were in the heart of the French columns in a moment.

It fell to our share to encounter some squadrons of *grenadiers à cheval*—of all species of cavalry the least efficient, because encumbered by the very nature of their appointments. In addition to their swords and pistols, these men carried long muskets and bayonets, which, like the lancer's spear, were stuck into a sort of boot attached to the saddle, and leaned against their shoulders. With our good sabres we disposed of them in five minutes, and then dashing at the infantry, we produced such concision and dismay, that the whole column rolled back from the hill, like a wave which has broken against a cliff. Many gallant exploits were performed in that charge, which Lord Frederick led with a recklessness of danger that could not but inspire his troops with the utmost confidence. Yet had Lord Frederick well-nigh fallen a victim to his own intrepidity. He was in the heart of the enemy's hussars, laying about him, when a Frenchman made a cut at his head, which, but that a sergeant, named Dickson, pushed between him and the blow, must have proved fatal. For though Sergeant Dickson caught it in part upon his sword, such was the strength with which it was delivered, that it cleft Lord Frederick's hat in two. Poor Dickson was almost immediately afterwards slain himself, so that Lord Frederick never had an opportunity of thanking him for his chivalrous devotion.

Our charge cost us some valuable lives, and among others that of Captain Hanson of the 20th; but it accomplished its object. The French were driven back, and our routed infantry were enabled by these means to make good their retreat, if a retreat that can be called, which from the first had been a confused flight. And then were we called off, that the 20th and Brunswickers might form again and make ready for a second charge, while the hussars protected a couple of field-pieces that were ordered to cover the retrogression. But what a retrogression it was—for, as I have already stated, all our baggage had followed us, and both it and the women and children belonging to the army were on the east side of the river. Of these no heed of course could be taken, and they fell into the enemy's hands; while guns abandoned by their drivers, or disabled by the death of their horses, or the destruction of the wheels, stood here and there to be picked up by the victors, and preserved as trophies of our defeat

The two guns to which we were attached, after keeping up their fire till the French were close upon them, limbered up and moved to the rear. Repeatedly the enemy formed as if to charge them; but the bold front which our squadron presented struck them with awe, and they held back. Away, therefore, we went, till we had come within a short distance of the bridge, which, to our horror and amazement, though covered with the rout of the army, was on fire. The fascines that filled up the space between the double layer of boards were blazing terribly, and the smoke gathering in a cloud overhead, so completely enveloped the flying men, that band after band, as it reached that point, became to us invisible. What then were we to do? With our tumbrils full of ammunition and our heavy pieces, could we venture to pass between two volumes of flame, or were we to halt on this side and die with arms in our hands, or be taken?

Captain Jacks, fortunately for us, was a man of decision, and the officer commanding the artillery proved equally intrepid. "Dash at it, men," was the cry; and we did dash at it. With the very flames curling up on both sides, and the smoke meeting in an arch over our heads, we galloped across, bearing off our guns, tumbrils, and all our people safely. Yet scarcely were we across when a loud crash gave notice that the planks had failed. The bridge was broken, and multitudes of those who were crossing at the moment perished in its ruins.

Such was the issue of this disastrous day, of which, as far as I am aware, no faithful account has been published, either in the *Gazette* or elsewhere. The rout was on our side complete, for we lost all our baggage, several of our guns, all our women and children, and a prodigious number of men, either slain on the field, or drowned in crossing the river.

Neither did Suchet permit us to continue our march after the river was crossed in peace: he took the fords, and drove us back through Villa Franca in a state of disorder that beggars all description; and had he judged it expedient to pursue, would have destroyed us, without doubt, entirely.

Happily for us, the nature of his political position was not such as to permit his improving the victory, and we were enabled in consequence to re-assemble about Tarragona, and to present once more something like the appearance of an organised army.

Chapter 25

Adventures at the Outposts

I have alluded, in the previous chapter, to the loss of one of my followers, whose horse refusing to leap the vineyard wall, placed him at the mercy of the French cavalry that were in pursuit of us.

About noon of the day in which we began to muster once more near Tarragona, we were very much surprised to see our brother-soldier arrive in the bivouac, thoroughly stripped, to be sure, seeing that the enemy had taken from him his very boots, but sound in wind and limb, and both willing and able to resume his place in the ranks of the squadron.

He described himself as having been exceedingly well treated on the whole by his captors. They plundered him, no doubt, and considered, with great justice, that they had found in his horse a very valuable prize; but after carrying him to the rear, and putting him along with the other prisoners under charge of a guard, they had attended with perfect humanity to all his wants, and supplied him with food and wine regularly. A soldier of the Foreign Hussars, however, was not the sort of man to fold up his arms and rest satisfied with the condition of a prisoner of war. Our friend watched his opportunity, and in the dead of a dark night gave his guard the slip, and joined us, as I have stated, almost in a state of nudity, on the following day. Nor was this the only arrival in our camp from the same quarter.

It is not for me to assign a reason why not only the heavy baggage of the army, but the very women and children, were permitted to cross the Noya, and move up to our line, while we expected every moment to be engaged with the enemy. Even in situations where the retreat is far more open and more secure, a general usually removes such impediments as far as possible to the rear; and, on the present occasion, any one would have imagined that so much regard at least would have been had to the safety of non-combatants; but it was not so. Having first of all committed the grave error of carrying a comparatively weak force across a difficult river, and exposing it to be attacked there by an army surpassing it as much in numbers as it excelled it in the composition of the troops, Lord William Bentinck summed up his imprudence by sanctioning the advance of mules, wagons, sutlers' establishments, women, and children, as if the battle had been already won, and his corps were in the full career of victory. Only one consequence could arise out of such a preparation, and it did arise. All the baggage, supplies of various kinds, the women, the children, the sutlers, and I know not how much more, fell into the enemy's hands, who had in consequence the best ground for asserting that the English authority in Catalonia and Valencia was overthrown. It is but an act of justice, however, to record with what perfect generosity they conducted themselves towards the poor creatures who came thus into their power. The women were treated not only with delicacy, but with kindness. Tents were pitched for them in rear of the French lines. A guard was mounted day and night, who had it in charge to protect them from insult; and rations of bread and meat, and wine, were served out as regularly to them and their little ones as to the troops. Finally, after keeping them there a space of three days, they sent them back under an escort, each woman being loaded with provisions for herself and children, and all vying with one another in the praises which they bestowed upon their captors.

It is pleasant to record such things of an enemy; it is not less pleasant to be in a condition to describe the fidelity with which the Spaniards bore themselves, on all occasions, towards their English allies. I say nothing of their conduct in the field, because whenever I happened to see them engaged, they invariably did their duty; but during the progress of the rout, of which I have just given an account, an event befell, which showed how far the Spanish people were willing to commit themselves in order to save an Englishman from injury. When our army moved out of Villa Franca we left behind, of course, the paymasters and paymasters' clerks of the different regiments. One of these latter, a sergeant in an infantry regiment, got so drunk, that, when his countrymen were driven through the place, and the French rushed in and took possession, he was fast asleep, and totally incapable of providing for his own safety.

His landlord saw his plight, and hastened to screen him from its consequences. He stripped the drunken man of his uniform; concealed it as well as his arms somewhere about the house, and arraying the soldier in the attire of a Spanish peasant, watched beside his bed till he awoke, and then told him all that had happened. The consequence was, that the sergeant being mistaken for a waiter at the hotel, attended on the French officers during their sojourn in the place, and was ready in his proper garb to bid us welcome when we returned to it. I may as well add, that being tried by a court-martial, and found guilty, he was sentenced to be reduced, which sentence was carried into effect, though they permitted him still to act as clerk to the paymaster.

The sojourn of the French in Villa Franca was not of long continuance. Having levied a contribution on the inhabitants, they suddenly broke up from their quarters, and retiring across the Labrigat to their old position, left only a chain of pickets on the south side of the river to watch our movements. These consisted merely in a re-occupation of the ground which the enemy had evacuated, and the establishment of posts so far in front of it, as to guard against all hazard of being taken by surprise. At the outposts, I, as Sergeant-Major, had no business; but our cavalry, being scattered through the villages and farm-houses near the town, I found myself with about fifteen men quartered in a detached mansion, which bore about it an air, not of magnificence certainly, but of great comfort, such as seemed to class the proprietor among the more substantial land occupiers of his province.

When we first moved into the *estantia*, we were received with a good deal of reserve, mixed, however, with some appearance of kindness and good-will. The latter feeling Hettendorff, who was on all occasions my associate, took the utmost pains to improve; and his thorough knowledge of the language gave him facilities which he was careful neither to neglect nor to abuse. He soon discovered that to our host the French were objects of especial hatred—that he was well-disposed to open his heart to the English, as far as might be consistent with the dictates of prudence—but that, having heard a great deal of our marauding propensities, he was fearful of giving us his confidence, lest we should regard one kind act as nothing more than a ground from which to aim at an-other. Hettendorff, thanking him for his candour, made haste to assure him that such was by no means our disposition, and that he might safely open out to us both his heart and his stores, inasmuch as we should never dream of abusing them. Finally, it was settled between them, that, provided I, as commanding the detachment, would undertake that no depredations should be committed, the *Padrone* would confer on us many serious advantages, not the least prominent of which consisted in this, that he would every day supply us for two-pence with as much wine of the country as we could purchase at a sutler's store for twice the amount. As in duty bound, I came in at once to the arrangement, and for several weeks we spent our time under his roof with great satisfaction to ourselves and very little to the inconvenience of our entertainer.

Our host was a man of considerable wealth, a large portion of which consisted in flocks of sheep and cattle—which, feeding on the level pasturage round his house, were, on the first alarm of an advance of the French army, driven to the mountains. By these means he assured me he had contrived to avert the ruin under which most of his neighbours had sunk; while, at the same time, he was accumulating to himself a store of valuables, taken from the persons of the invaders; for it came out that he not only hated the French, but acted as a *partisan* against them. He was, in short, a guerilla, and the leader of a band of guerillas, who, since the province was first invaded, had put to death some hundreds of their invaders. Their mode of proceeding was this:

As soon as the French sent troops into the neighbourhood, these pugnacious agriculturists, having first driven away their flocks and herds to the mountains, laid themselves out for more active operations. They would abide in their own homes during the day, but at night they sallied forth, and having communicated one to another such information as they might have been able to collect, they arranged their plans accordingly. There was a stream near my host's dwelling, the name of which I have forgotten, which, intersecting the line of the highroad from Villa Franca to Felichi, was crossed by a bridge of a single arch. On both sides of that arch the banks were so closely planted with underwood, that by an ordinary observer its existence might well escape notice—for the rivulet was quite inconsiderable, and there was no such rise in the centre as to make the common traveller aware when he stood upon a bridge at all. There our *Padrone*, with some six or eight of his neighbours, were in the constant practice of laying themselves up in ambush. They would never attack a body of the enemy which were in numbers superior to themselves; neither, indeed, were they much given to wage war upon equal terms. But the stragglers from a column, or the weak, or the wounded, that lagged after a retreat, they were sure to pounce upon, and they invariably put them to death without mercy. I inquired how many had fallen on their side since the contest began—and I was assured that they had lost only seven lives, which lives were foolishly thrown away at the outset ere they learned to reserve their attacks for such as they were sure to overpower. But of the French some hundreds had fallen beneath their blows, and their bodies now enriched the soil of his farm, as their arms and even their clothing were piled up in his secret store-room. The better to convince me of all this, the good man led me to several places where, from beneath a slight covering of earth, legs and arms were protruding; while in a closet in his house he showed me helmets, carbines, pistols, swords, muskets, and even great-coats, hung up to the amount, I should conceive, of little less than five or six score.

If he hated the French cordially, our host gave the most substantial proofs that he entertained a widely different feeling towards the English; for he supplied our horses with forage and ourselves with wine and bread, and other luxuries, at a cost so moderate as hardly to amount to a remuneration. Yet though they were fully alive to his kindness, and repaid it by abstaining rigidly from plunder, even in trifles, the method which he chose to adopt in dispensing it excited in no common degree the curiosity of the soldiers. We were instructed to leave our empty canteens every night in a certain part of the house, and in the morning we found them again filled with wine; nobody being able or willing to tell whence the supply came, inasmuch as there were neither casks nor pig-skins to be seen about the premises.

This, together with the production from time to time of a choice morsel of bacon, so wrought upon the anxieties of my people, that they determined, let it cost what it might, to discover the situation of the host's magazine. Now, it so happened that the *Padrone* was a remarkably good Catholic; regularly as Sunday came round he repaired to a neighbouring church, being content to leave his domicile in charge sometimes of his wife, sometimes of a little girl of eleven or twelve years old, and sometimes of both.

It was on a Sunday that my fellows determined to push their researches to the uttermost; and they were too skilful in the art of marauding not to push them successfully.

While some kept the landlady in conversation, and some amused the child, others, after having ransacked the interior of the *casa*, mounted the roof, and, observing that the thatch lay awkwardly on a particular part of it near one of the gables, they pulled it about till it began to move. Thus encouraged, they pushed on, and gradually rolled back a sort of trap-door, which unclosed to them the mouth of a wide aperture, against one of the sides of which the top of a ladder was resting. To descend that ladder was an act as it were of intuition, and they became forthwith masters of the secret which had so long been kept back from them. The house had on this side a double wall: there was the gable or outside wall, between which and the partition that closed in the apartments on that wing lay an aperture, measuring some twelve or fourteen feet in width; and there, arranged in order, stood barrels of bacon, skins of wine, casks of flour, with brandy, oil, wearing apparel, linen—indeed every thing, not even excepting plate, of which a wealthy housekeeper was likely to be in want I must do my people the justice to say, that they returned as they had entered, empty-handed; and that, chuckling over their own skill, they replaced the trap-door with so much care, that I have no reason to believe the visit was ever suspected.

I have stated that while we continued to occupy these quarters a chain of posts was established a good way in front—one of which, consisting of a subaltern of cavalry, two sergeants, two corporals, and fifty troopers, was posted in a guard-house upon the high-road, not far from the Ordal. It was the business of the officer commanding this party to detach, just before darkness set in every night, about a thousand yards to his front a corporal with eight men, who in their turn pushed forward a couple of videttes to a short distance further along the high-road. Then by patrolling continually from the rear to the front, and occasionally diverging right and left, such a lookout was kept, or was supposed to be kept, that no surprise could possibly occur. And to sum up all, the officer's instructions required him, so soon as daylight: should return, to ride with his whole picket as close to the enemy's posts as a regard to his own safety would allow; concerning which, after he had reconnoitred them both to the right and left, he was expected to send in such a report as circumstances might appear to warrant.

These orders, laid down with such precision, that there was no possibility of misunderstanding them, had been obeyed from day to day with perfect accuracy, and still the report sent in gave notice that all continued quiet in front. There seemed, moreover, to be little inclination on either side to engage in skirmishes, for the patrols never met, or if they did, both sides invariably drew off without coming to blows. It came to pass, however, one morning that the face of affairs underwent a change, and that our picket, consisting then of a troop of Brunswick Hussars, were the sufferers. The case was this:

There was one Lieutenant Schultz, a brave officer enough, in charge of the post on that occasion. He had his men as usual under cover during the day, and patrolled well and carefully all night; and as the dawn gathered strength, he kept them mounted and ready to execute the accustomed reconnaissance along the enemy's line. It may be well to state that the picket-house having formerly been a tavern, was of considerable extent. Ruinous, it doubtless was; that is to, say, the roof was in a great measure pulled to pieces, and the doors and windows were all knocked in; yet it afforded tolerable shelter both to men and horses; the stables being, like the *casa* itself a degree better than sheds. From this post then, Mr. Schultz, after receiving the last of his patrols, made ready to advance, and so soon as the dawn had increased into broad day, he carried his design into execution. He made, as usual, first for the corporal's party, which he picked up and added to his own, and then, with the whole troop in his train, he rode leisurely along the front of the French videttes and made his observations. There was nothing either to the right or left of the road which could in the smallest degree disturb his equanimity; so he gave the word, "Face to your right, and return home."

The troop reached the picket-house unmolested, and began forthwith to unbridle and feed. Where there are no stalls, as in the situation which I am now describing, this latter operation is facilitated by means of nose-bags, while the men shake out the haversacks for such fragments as may adhere to the crevices, and rap their canteens in order to ascertain whether or not they are empty.

Such then was the employment of the party in general, when one of their number, who had strayed accidentally into the garden, returned in all haste to assure them that there was a Frenchman in the story overhead. "I saw the fellow's helmet," said he, "as I cast my eyes accidentally towards the upper windows; and now let's hunt him out as we would a rat, and make him our prisoner." In a moment there was a loud yell, and the men drawing their swords, began, without order or regularity, to rush upstairs. But they little knew what awaited them there. At the top of the landing-place stood a body of French troops who saluted them with a volley, beneath the weight of which they came rolling down; some killed, some wounded, and others utterly confounded.

Nor did the matter end there. About a hundred and twenty French grenadiers came pouring down with fixed bayonets, stabbing and firing upon all whom they met.

Our people, completely taken by surprise, offered no resistance. The result was, that with the exception of one man, who being abroad at the moment, escaped on foot, the whole picket, including Mr. Schultz, were made prisoners, and with their horses and arms were marched without delay across the neutral ground into the French lines.

When the sad news reached us, there was of course a great deal of lamentation, with something of blame heaped at headquarters on the lieutenant; yet the fault was not his. He only obeyed his orders, and followed the example which his predecessors set him, when he left his picket-house unguarded, and patrolling with all his force to a distance from the high road, exposed himself to the disaster that actually overtook him; for this act of negligence on our part was not unnoticed by the enemy, and they turned it to account. Watching the opportunity, they threw forward a body of grenadiers, who mounting to the upper story, there lay hid till the moment for action arrived, and though prematurely disturbed, did their work effectually.

From that time forth care was taken that the picket-house should not again be deserted by the whole of the guard, a sergeant and twelve men being appointed to watch there, while the officer, with the rest, pursued his course of reconnoitring.

CHAPTER 26

Hostilities Come to an End

There was great grief at headquarters for the loss of this picket, as well as an earnest desire to take revenge, and no great while elapsed ere orders were issued for a general movement to the front What the object of that movement might have been, or how it was conducted in parts which came not under my own observation, it is impossible for me to state. But the results, as far as I can speak of them, proved eminently disastrous.

The French occupied, at this time, a position on the farther side of the Labrigat They could be assailed to the right and left of the high road, through fords, whereas the column that should move by the road itself must carry a bridge, covered not only by fortified houses somewhat in advance, but by batteries mounted with very heavy cannon. There were, for example, three pieces on the same level with the bridge itself, which swept the road to the front. There were four—two on each flank, which looked up and down the stream: there were a couple of twenty. six pounders on a mound just above the lower battery; and higher still a thirty-six on a-travelling carriage.

Moreover, these formidable works were to be approached over the summit of an acclivity, which, dipping down abruptly into the vale through which the Labrigat runs, most necessarily expose the columns as they approached to the whole weight of fire that could be brought upon them. Such was the point against which our column was directed; the leading regiment of which were Spaniards: while two others, in like manner headed by Spaniards, took to the right and left, and moved with great gallantry upon the fords.

In such operations the cavalry have, for the most part, little to do. We cannot storm houses nor clamber up the parapets of redoubts; we are therefore kept in hand, as the military expression is, that we may be used either to improve a victory or protect a retreat. Accordingly, our business this day consisted for some hours in simply moving forward at a slow rate, and listening to the ceaseless discharges of cannon and musketry, which told of the work of death in which our dismounted comrades were engaged. Thus it was till we arrived near the southern base of the height, beyond which lay the Labrigat and the bridge of which we were to win the command, when other evidences of the serious nature of the affray began to show themselves. Several spring wagons loaded with mangled men met us, the cries from which, not less than the sight of the blood, as it oozed through the boarding and stained the ground, affected us very deeply. For my own part, I do not hesitate to admit that there came into my head at that moment ideas more gloomy than I recollect to have had conjured up by any other spectacle that has crossed my path through life. "This will probably be my own fate in a few minutes," said I to myself; and, as if my words had been prophetic, we received, almost immediately, an order to advance. A staff-officer came riding to the rear, hat in hand, and called out, "Cavalry to the front," when we put our horses to the trot, and hurried forward.

We gained the brow of the hill in a few minutes, where, surrounded by his staff the general had taken up a position. His glass was out, and he was examining the bridge apparently with great care, as well as the loop-holed houses from which the French were retreating, and of which a body of Spaniards had just got possession. "Now," said he, "push forward a couple of six-pounders, and silence the enemy's fire; and look you, let the cavalry advance also, and cover the guns." The orders were no sooner issued than they were obeyed. Two six-pounders, escorted by our squadron, galloped down the descent, to engage six pieces of the, largest calibre, and securely posted!—an act of Quixotism second only to that of the renowned *Don* himself, when he ran full tilt against the windmills. Neither was there a man or officer, either among us or the bombardiers, that did not feel how absurd was the proceeding.

"What are we to do here?" said one to the other as we pushed forward. Yet we took our ground with the utmost steadiness; the guns were unlimbered, and the artillery-men began to fire.

It was quite evident that the French held us in sovereign contempt, for they took no notice whatever of our approach. They waited, indeed, till at two hundred yards distance they saw our gunners grasp their matches, when they gave us a single round which knocked over both our pieces, killed and wounded all the horses and men that stood near them, and placed us in the agreeable condition of persons who have altogether erred in their calculations. It is indeed impossible to conceive a piece of work more cleverly or move effectually done than this.

The wretched six-pounders lay shattered in the dust. Beside them were the mangled remains of the artillery. men, while we looked on as yet unscathed, but in every sense of the word powerless. It was well for us that Lord William caused the bugle to sound a retreat, and that we obeyed it instantly. In three minutes more there would have been an end of the, Foreign Hussars, for while the shouts of the enemy rung in our ears, their round shot ploughed up the ground among our horses' feet, and the grape went whistling between our files into the side of the hill beyond. It has ever since been a matter of unspeakable surprise to me that we did not lose a man in that wild affair. A troop-horse was killed, but the rider escaped unhurt, and regained his comrades after they had secured themselves on the opposite side of the hill.

Whatever the general's plan might have been, it failed in all its details. Our column, unable to force even the bridge, retreated, while the Spaniards, after carrying the fords, were attacked in force, and driven back again with great loss. Not, therefore, over and above delighted either with ourselves or our chief, we retraced our steps to Villa Franca, where arrangements were made to spend the winter.

Villa Franca, though a clean and airy town, was not sufficiently large to contain the whole of our army. Most of us were therefore scattered among the hamlets and villages near; and among others, the foreign, troop returned to the cantonments from which they had been moved in consequence of the surprise of Mr. Schultz's picket at Ordal. Our landlord received us very kindly, and perceiving that we were not disposed to abuse his kindness, be took care to render our situation as agreeable as possible.

The consequence was, that having little or nothing to do—no enemy threatening, nor accidents of any sort occurring, week after week and month after month rolled on, almost without our being enabled to perceive that the winter was rapidly wearing itself out.

I do not recollect during all this period any adventure that deserves to be recorded, unless it be the circumstances which attended an excursion to Villa Franca, in which, on New Year's Day, 1814, I took part As the quarters of our squadron were only a mile and a half from the town, and we wished to spend the day jovially together, my four brother-sergeants and myself obtained permission of the commanding officer to be absent from roll-call in the evening. This done, we proceeded about noon into Villa Franca, and after ordering dinner to be ready at five o'clock, we amused ourselves as soldiers are apt to do, by wandering from street to street, and seeing as many sights as these happened to afford.

We then adjourned to our hotel just sufficiently fatigued to relish the excellent fare that was placed before us, and to do justice to the healths which on that great day in the year it is the custom in my country to quaff. We had not, however, sat long at table when there entered our room a monk of the order of La Rosalia, very dirty in his person, very meanly dressed, and carrying in his hand the great emblem of his calling, a begging box. Probably I need not observe that Santa Rosalia is the great patroness of the eyes; that persons afflicted with ophthalmia or any other malady that affects the vision, have only to make interest with her in order to be cured, and that there is no method of ingratiating oneself into the good graces of the Saint so effectual as the act of bestowing alms upon her votaries.

The monk who visited us today carried on his breast a wooden box, with a slit in one of the sides, through which donations might be thrown in. Above the box was a marble plate having a pair of glass or painted eyes laid on it, and higher still was a small image of the Saint, likewise in marble. The whole were suspended about his neck by a riband, and his air and manner indicated at once excessive poverty and great humility.

His first prayer was, "Give me a trifle for the honour of Santa Rosalia." We looked at the man, and pulling out a few coppers each, we presented them to him. Encouraged by this he ventured to insinuate that if food were offered to him he could eat. We immediately ordered the waiter to lay a plate for the holy man on a little table that stood near, and to fill it. The monk ate greedily, and looking up, threw out a hint that a glass of wine would be acceptable. He got it, and looking down upon his empty platter, observed that Providence had blessed him with an excellent appetite. Now, though all this was done with perfect gravity, there twinkled in his eye a sort of humour which we were neither slow to perceive nor backward to encourage.

More food was sent to him and more wine, till he finished his bottle; after which, observing that we had dessert before us, he proposed to join our party.

"He's an impudent scoundrel," said one.—

"Oh! never mind," replied another—"let him come—we'll make him drunk enough, and then see what's in him." Accordingly we made room for him at our table, and Hettendorff taking him in hand, he was plied with wine till not only self-respect, but a regard to common decency abandoned him.

It was then proposed that he should sing a song: he refused for a while, and then struck up such a tissue of ribaldry that we were ashamed of him. Nor were we the only persons in the house whom his conduct scandalized. The landlord and the waiter overhearing his ditty, rushed in from an adjoining apartment, and loading him with abuse, insisted that he should quit the house on the instant. But he was too far gone by this time to have any control over himself. When he rose it was only to stagger about and to break box, plate, image, and any thing else, and then to be knocked downstairs with as little ceremony as if he had not belonged to one of the privileged classes.

Having thus got rid of our intrusive guest, and discussed as much wine and tobacco as we felt disposed to consume, we adjourned to the coffee-room, where among other persons present was our old acquaintance, Captain Alberto, or as we familiarly styled him, the Knight of the Candlestick. There was nothing in this re-encounter at all calculated to excite in us uneasy feelings, for Captain Alberto had already taken care to convince us that by him no angry recollection of the past was retained. He came up to us when we were on parade, the morning of our advance against the bridge, and assured us that all was forgotten; and now he met us with an outstretched hand, and professions of hearty goodwill. Nay, it was not without difficulty that we resisted his pressing demand to be regarded as our host while we sat in the coffee-room; so anxious was he to relieve our minds from every feeling in the most remote degree allied to distrust. Nor was this all; he introduced us to several of his brother officers; told the whole story himself; and bore with the best humour the quizzing of his friends, which, to confess the truth, was somewhat unmerciful. Captain Alberto was indeed an excellent specimen of a Spanish gentleman and man of honour, who will indeed avenge an insult if he can, but who never makes a promise, at least in private life, without keeping it.

From this date up to the return of spring, there was on both sides a complete suspension of military operations. Rumours of peace indeed began to spread among us ere we again took the field, and finding that the enemy had retreated from their strong position, about Molinas del Rey towards Hospitalite and other places in the rear, we could no longer doubt as to their growing weakness. Still their movements were all made with becoming circumspection.

Our patrols cleared the way for us, out pickets continued to cover our front; and so we moved on, crossing the Labrigat by the bridge which the enemy had blown up, and pressing them back from Hospitalite into Barcelona. That this retrogression was caused not by any superior strength on our part, but by political considerations, of which it would be unwise in me to speak, nobody who has seen the position of Hospitalite can doubt. A range of inaccessible hills traversed only by the main road was then in the enemy's keeping, from which it would have proved impossible for us to dislodge them had we surpassed them in numbers, as much as, in point of fact, we fell short of them.

I had well-nigh forgotten to mention that when we opened the campaign of 1814 a new chief was at our head, and Lord William Bentinck, recalled to the management of Sicily, had given up the command to Sir William Clinton, of whose skill as a leader no opportunity was given of judging, inasmuch, as he had scarcely appeared as such ere hostilities ceased. Whether this took place under the sanction of a formal treaty, or whether it was brought about fortuitously, I do not know. But it is certain that though we encamped about Barcelona and held the garrison in some sort blockaded, nothing was done on either side that can be spoken of as a deed of violence.

We were thus situated, rumour after rumour coming in, now of the great victory won by Lord Wellington, now of the advance of the northern powers upon Paris, when, one day in March, I think about the 29th, an order was issued for the whole army, Spaniards as well as English, to form in a long double line along the main road. The troops stood by brigades—here a brigade of Spanish infantry—there a brigade of British infantry—here a body of horse—there a detachment of artillery—all the troops of all the allied nations being interlaced, and all extending to a great distance, both rearward and to the front For ourselves, our position was a remarkable one, just under the guns of Monjouic, so close, indeed, to the works, that we could distinguish the very features of the garrison, as they crowded the rampart to witness the spectacle. Yet no acts of hostility passed between us. On the contrary, the French appeared, like ourselves, to be equipped for an occasion of gala; and the result showed that, in coming to this conclusion, we had not committed an error.

The lines had been formed perhaps an hour and a half and each man asked his neighbour what was going to happen, when some staff-officers came at full speed from the front, and passed the word to mount and draw swords. We did so, of course, and presently the thunder of artillery, as brigade after brigade fired its salute, warned us that some great personage was approaching. All eyes were accordingly turned in the proper direction, and in due time two horsemen made their appearance, followed at an interval of perhaps ten or twelve paces by a very numerous staff. One of these persons we instantly recognised as Sir William Clinton—the other was pointed out to us as Ferdinand VII., the King of Spain. They rode very slowly, thereby affording us an excellent opportunity of examining the King's appearance—and it struck me at the moment to be by no means forbidding. He was not a tall man, but be was stoutly made—his leg and thigh, in particular, being muscular, and his broad face had about it an expression of good humour, to which, in all probability, the florid nature of his complexion contributed. I perfectly recollect that he was dressed in a blue coat, with white leather breeches, and high boots— and that he smiled upon us as he passed, like a man who rejoices in some striking and unlooked-for change of fortune.

We stood upon our ground till the *cortège* passed, and then filed off; the French garrison not only offering no interruption to the ceremony, but firing, as our artillery did, a salute in honour of the King.

Chapter 27

My Changes of Fortune

The war in Spain was now virtually ended; for Ferdinand was restored to his throne, and the French had bound themselves by treaty to evacuate such strongholds as they still held in the south provinces. Under such circumstances it was considered by those in power that a portion of the English army might be withdrawn, and employed to greater advantage on another theatre of strife which had recently been opened. In short, we were taken to Italy; but only to be transported back again to Gibraltar on our return voyage; and as nothing occurred of particular interest the reader need not be detained from the conclusion of this narrative.

While we lay at Gibraltar, the extraordinary intelligence of Napoleon's escape from Elba was received. It excited, as may be imagined, a remarkable stir in the place, and caused such vessels as were homeward bound to gather together and put themselves under the protection of a larger convoy; for the American privateers which had harassed us off the coast of Sardinia were brought in as prizes; and but for the renewal of war with France, we might have acted as if the seas had been delivered from an enemy. But Buonaparte's marvellous success threw us back again to the state in which we had been twelve months previously. The admiral accordingly retained us till he had made his arrangements for protecting the homeward trade; and when we raised our anchor, it was in company with a considerable squadron.

We had rough weather all the way home; and as we entered the Channel the gale increased so much that the fleet was scattered. The ship in which I took my passage, however, reached Portsmouth at last; and after a short quarantine we landed. We were ordered to Portsea Barracks, where quarters were allotted to us, and all our accounts made out and settled to the last farthing. This done I received, with my three men, a route for the Tower of London, where, during some weeks, we continued to draw our pay, the authorities appearing, as it seemed to me, somewhat irresolute how it behoved them to deal with us. At last, however, came the news of the Battle of Waterloo, and London exhibited the aspect of a city of madmen. From the Prince Regent to the match-girl, there was the most extravagant rejoicing; and the coffee-houses, and-other places of public entertainment were filled with visitors. But upon us the overthrow of the French Emperor had the single effect of bringing our doubts, respecting our future fate, to an issue. We were ordered to attend at Chelsea Hospital, for the purpose of being discharged, and removed in consequence to certain lodging-houses in the vicinity.

While I resided at what is now a gin-shop, bearing the sign of the compasses, a little circumstance occurred, of which I may, perhaps, be permitted to make mention. A gentleman met me one morning, and, being struck with my uniform, which was very rich, he began to question me relative to my past services and future prospects. I told him all: upon which, observing that I had served only twenty-two years and nine months, he exclaimed, "You must not think of claiming your discharge now. They will not give you any thing like the pension you ought to have; for a year and a quarter are yet wanting to complete your time, and they will be sure to deal with you as rigidly as possible."

"What can I do, Sir?" was my answer.

"Go with me," replied the gentleman: "I am Colonel Hamilton, of the Royal Wagon Train; take service in my corps; and though I cannot enlist you, except as a private, I will make you both corporal and sergeant immediately. I promise you, too, that we will do all we can to make yon comfortable."

I liked the colonel, but told him that after haying acted as sergeant-major to the Foreign Hussars, I could not think of becoming even a sergeant in the Wagon Train; partly because I should feel that I was descending from a superior to an inferior rank, and partly because I was quite ignorant of the duties of a wagoner, and had no wish to learn them. The colonel was very kind, and pressed me hard; but I would not accede to his proposition—so we parted.

On the 20th of June I presented myself, along with many more, at the Board Room. Colonel Hamilton was there, and resumed his entreaties, but I had made up my mind, and was not to be shaken. "I will rather take the pension, whatever it may be, that is awarded me," said I, "and spend the rest of my days in some peaceful occupation." Even Sir David Dundas at the Board advised me to go with Colonel Hamilton, but I would not. The consequence was that I was discharged upon a pension of one shilling per day.

My career from that date has in most respects varied so little from that of the generality of persons in my situation of life, that it is scarcely worth while to give an account of it. Of my relatives in Germany I had received no accounts for years; and the last information conveyed to me was not such as to create any desire to return to them. My mother was dead. My uncles likewise were gathered to their fathers, and the business of the distillery had gone on so badly, that there were not effects enough to cover the debts that had been incurred.

In Germany, therefore, I could not hope to reclaim the position to which my birth and early education entitled me; and I concluded that since I must live in obscurity, it would be better to take an humble station in a land of foreigners than at home. I therefore cast about in my own mind as to the sort of employment to which I might turn, and I had, at one time, serious thoughts of opening a shop. But besides that I had no connection, my knowledge of trade was too superficial to render it prudent to embark in it I therefore concluded that the best thing for me would be to pass into some gentleman's service as a groom; and I began immediately to look round for a situation.

Archdeacon England of Dorchester, advertised for a man to take care of his stable, and I answered the advertisement He took me without a character, and I lived with him for twelve months very creditably; but the work was too hard, and I quitted him. In his service, however, I had acquired some knowledge of the duties of an indoor servant; and, as he gave me a strong letter of recommendation, I was received as butler into the family of Dr. Cowper, a physician in ———.

With him I was exceedingly comfortable, and would have probably remained with him till this day, but for the calling out in 1819 of the pensioners; and I had no other alternative than to obey the summons or lose my pension. I did obey it nothing loath, for I flattered myself that I had now a prospect of completing the period of military service that would entitle me to one shilling and ten-pence a day; but fortune failed to smile upon me. Being forwarded to Plymouth with as many invalids as could be collected in one neighbourhood, I there reported myself to the adjutant of the ——— Veteran Battalion, and, with his sanction, took upon myself the responsibility of pay-sergeant to my company. I made up the books, got them into good order, and adjusted everything, when the captain arrived. I learned from him that my services would not be required. In fact, they did not, on that occasion, receive into the corps of invalids any individuals who had served as troop sergeant-majors in the cavalry, and I was in consequence cast adrift upon the world with only a shilling a day.

I was a good deal chagrined at this, for with one shilling and ten-pence I felt that I could have done well; yet mine is not a desponding temper, so I lost no time in looking out for another situation. Mr. ——— ———, a banker in ———, advertised for a groom, and I answered the advertisement. I lived with him twelve months, at the end of which his father took me, and I was in his family well treated, and happy for six years. But we never know when we are sufficiently well off, and I began to grow impatient. I learned that in London there would be a wider field for my exertions, and I gave up my place. London, however, was not now the theatre for such an actor as myself. I was too old for gentlemen's service; in the police I had no interest, and my finances began to get low.

Under these circumstances, I made up my mind to apply for admission into Chelsea Hospital. I did so—my request was acceded to, and since the ——— of ——— I have been a contented, and, I trust, not an unworthy inmate of the soldier's last home in the land of the living.

ALSO FROM LEONAUR
AVAILABLE IN SOFTCOVER OR HARDCOVER WITH DUST JACKET

CAPTAIN OF THE 95th (Rifles) *by Jonathan Leach*—An officer of Wellington's Sharpshooters during the Peninsular, South of France and Waterloo Campaigns of the Napoleonic Wars.

BUGLER AND OFFICER OF THE RIFLES *by William Green & Harry Smith* With the 95th (Rifles) during the Peninsular & Waterloo Campaigns of the Napoleonic Wars

BAYONETS, BUGLES AND BONNETS *by James 'Thomas' Todd*—Experiences of hard soldiering with the 71st Foot - the Highland Light Infantry - through many battles of the Napoleonic wars including the Peninsular & Waterloo Campaigns

THE ADVENTURES OF A LIGHT DRAGOON *by George Farmer & G.R. Gleig*—A cavalryman during the Peninsular & Waterloo Campaigns, in captivity & at the siege of Bhurtpore, India

THE COMPLEAT RIFLEMAN HARRIS *by Benjamin Harris as told to & transcribed by Captain Henry Curling*—The adventures of a soldier of the 95th (Rifles) during the Peninsular Campaign of the Napoleonic Wars

WITH WELLINGTON'S LIGHT CAVALRY *by William Tomkinson*—The Experiences of an officer of the 16th Light Dragoons in the Peninsular and Waterloo campaigns of the Napoleonic Wars.

SURTEES OF THE RIFLES *by William Surtees*—A Soldier of the 95th (Rifles) in the Peninsular campaign of the Napoleonic Wars.

ENSIGN BELL IN THE PENINSULAR WAR *by George Bell*—The Experiences of a young British Soldier of the 34th Regiment 'The Cumberland Gentlemen' in the Napoleonic wars.

WITH THE LIGHT DIVISION *by John H. Cooke*—The Experiences of an Officer of the 43rd Light Infantry in the Peninsula and South of France During the Napoleonic Wars

NAPOLEON'S IMPERIAL GUARD: FROM MARENGO TO WATERLOO *by J. T. Headley*—This is the story of Napoleon's Imperial Guard from the bearskin caps of the grenadiers to the flamboyance of their mounted chasseurs, their principal characters and the men who commanded them.

BATTLES & SIEGES OF THE PENINSULAR WAR *by W. H. Fitchett*—Corunna, Busaco, Albuera, Ciudad Rodrigo, Badajos, Salamanca, San Sebastian & Others

ALSO FROM LEONAUR
AVAILABLE IN SOFTCOVER OR HARDCOVER WITH DUST JACKET

WELLINGTON AND THE PYRENEES CAMPAIGN VOLUME I: FROM VITORIA TO THE BIDASSOA by *F. C. Beatson*—The final phase of the campaign in the Iberian Peninsula.

WELLINGTON AND THE INVASION OF FRANCE VOLUME II: THE BIDASSOA TO THE BATTLE OF THE NIVELLE by *F. C. Beatson*—The second of Beatson's series on the fall of Revolutionary France published by Leonaur, the reader is once again taken into the centre of Wellington's strategic and tactical genius.

WELLINGTON AND THE FALL OF FRANCE VOLUME III: THE GAVES AND THE BATTLE OF ORTHEZ by *F. C. Beatson*—This final chapter of F. C. Beatson's brilliant trilogy shows the 'captain of the age' at his most inspired and makes all three books essential additions to any Peninsular War library.

NAVAL BATTLES OF THE NAPOLEONIC WARS by *W. H. Fitchett*—Cape St. Vincent, the Nile, Cadiz, Copenhagen, Trafalgar & Others

SERGEANT GUILLEMARD: THE MAN WHO SHOT NELSON? by *Robert Guillemard*—A Soldier of the Infantry of the French Army of Napoleon on Campaign Throughout Europe

WITH THE GUARDS ACROSS THE PYRENEES by *Robert Batty*—The Experiences of a British Officer of Wellington's Army During the Battles for the Fall of Napoleonic France, 1813.

A STAFF OFFICER IN THE PENINSULA by *E. W. Buckham*—An Officer of the British Staff Corps Cavalry During the Peninsula Campaign of the Napoleonic Wars

THE LEIPZIG CAMPAIGN: 1813—NAPOLEON AND THE "BATTLE OF THE NATIONS" by *F. N. Maude*—Colonel Maude's analysis of Napoleon's campaign of 1813.

BUGEAUD: A PACK WITH A BATON by *Thomas Robert Bugeaud*—The Early Campaigns of a Soldier of Napoleon's Army Who Would Become a Marshal of France.

TWO LEONAUR ORIGINALS

SERGEANT NICOL by *Daniel Nicol*—The Experiences of a Gordon Highlander During the Napoleonic Wars in Egypt, the Peninsula and France.

WATERLOO RECOLLECTIONS by *Frederick Llewellyn*—Rare First Hand Accounts, Letters, Reports and Retellings from the Campaign of 1815.

AVAILABLE ONLINE AT
www.leonaur.com
AND OTHER GOOD BOOK STORES

ALSO FROM LEONAUR
AVAILABLE IN SOFTCOVER OR HARDCOVER WITH DUST JACKET

THE JENA CAMPAIGN: 1806 *by F. N. Maude*—The Twin Battles of Jena & Auerstadt Between Napoleon's French and the Prussian Army.

PRIVATE O'NEIL *by Charles O'Neil*—The recollections of an Irish Rogue of H. M. 28th Regt.—The Slashers— during the Peninsula & Waterloo campaigns of the Napoleonic wars.

ROYAL HIGHLANDER *by James Anton*—A soldier of H.M 42nd (Royal) Highlanders during the Peninsular, South of France & Waterloo Campaigns of the Napoleonic Wars.

CAPTAIN BLAZE *by Elzéar Blaze*—Elzéar Blaze recounts his life and experiences in Napoleon's army in a well written, articulate and companionable style.

LEJEUNE VOLUME 1 *by Louis-François Lejeune*—The Napoleonic Wars through the Experiences of an Officer on Berthier's Staff.

LEJEUNE VOLUME 2 *by Louis-François Lejeune*—The Napoleonic Wars through the Experiences of an Officer on Berthier's Staff.

FUSILIER COOPER *by John S. Cooper*—Experiences in the 7th (Royal) Fusiliers During the Peninsular Campaign of the Napoleonic Wars and the American Campaign to New Orleans.

CAPTAIN COIGNET *by Jean-Roch Coignet*—A Soldier of Napoleon's Imperial Guard from the Italian Campaign to Russia and Waterloo.

FIGHTING NAPOLEON'S EMPIRE *by Joseph Anderson*—The Campaigns of a British Infantryman in Italy, Egypt, the Peninsular & the West Indies During the Napoleonic Wars.

CHASSEUR BARRES *by Jean-Baptiste Barres*—The experiences of a French Infantryman of the Imperial Guard at Austerlitz, Jena, Eylau, Friedland, in the Peninsular, Lutzen, Bautzen, Zinnwald and Hanau during the Napoleonic Wars.

MARINES TO 95TH (RIFLES) *by Thomas Fernyhough*—The military experiences of Robert Fernyhough during the Napoleonic Wars.

HUSSAR ROCCA *by Albert Jean Michel de Rocca*—A French cavalry officer's experiences of the Napoleonic Wars and his views on the Peninsular Campaigns against the Spanish, British And Guerilla Armies.

SERGEANT BOURGOGNE *by Adrien Bourgogne*—With Napoleon's Imperial Guard in the Russian Campaign and on the Retreat from Moscow 1812 - 13.

ALSO FROM LEONAUR
AVAILABLE IN SOFTCOVER OR HARDCOVER WITH DUST JACKET

A JOURNAL OF THE SECOND SIKH WAR by *Daniel A. Sandford*—The Experiences of an Ensign of the 2nd Bengal European Regiment During the Campaign in the Punjab, India, 1848-49.

LAKE'S CAMPAIGNS IN INDIA by *Hugh Pearse*—The Second Anglo Maratha War, 1803-1807. Often neglected by historians and students alike, Lake's Indian campaign was fought against a resourceful and ruthless enemy-almost always superior in numbers to his own forces.

BRITAIN IN AFGHANISTAN 1: THE FIRST AFGHAN WAR 1839-42 by *Archibald Forbes*—Following over a century of the gradual assumption of sovereignty of the Indian Sub-Continent, the British Empire, in the form of the Honourable East India Company, supported by troops of the new Queen Victoria's army, found itself inevitably at the natural boundaries that surround Afghanistan. There it set in motion a series of disastrous events-the first of which was to march into the country at all.

BRITAIN IN AFGHANISTAN 2: THE SECOND AFGHAN WAR 1878-80 by *Archibald Forbes*—This the history of the Second Afghan War-another episode of British military history typified by savagery, massacre, siege and battles.

UP AMONG THE PANDIES by *Vivian Dering Majendie*—An outstanding account of the campaign for the fall of Lucknow. This is a vital book of war as fought by the British Army of the mid-nineteenth century, but in truth it is also an essential book of war that will enthral.

BLOW THE BUGLE, DRAW THE SWORD by *W. H. G. Kingston*—The Wars, Campaigns, Regiments and Soldiers of the British & Indian Armies During the Victorian Era, 1839-1898.

INDIAN MUTINY 150th ANNIVERSARY: A LEONAUR ORIGINAL

MUTINY: 1857 by *James Humphries*—It is now 150 years since the 'Indian Mutiny' burst like an engulfing flame on the British soldiers, their families and the civilians of the Empire in North East India. The Bengal Native army arose in violent rebellion, and the once peaceful countryside became a battleground as Native sepoys and elements of the Indian population massacred their British masters and defeated them in open battle. As the tide turned, a vengeful army of British and loyal Indian troops repressed the insurgency with a savagery that knew no mercy. It was a time of fear and slaughter. James Humphries has drawn together the voices of those dreadful days for this commemorative book.

AVAILABLE ONLINE AT
www.leonaur.com
AND OTHER GOOD BOOK STORES

www.ingramcontent.com/pod-product-compliance
Lightning Source LLC
Chambersburg PA
CBHW031623160426
43196CB00006B/249